THE DAY RE

'Small Talk in Wiltshire is a delightful collection of anecdotes, curiosities and adventures skilfully assembled... a wonderful storehouse of unconsidered trifles about some of the extraordinary events and characters of the Wiltshire countryside. Chandler's presentation of his material is elegant, witty and engaging...' **Blackmore Vale Magazine**

'Small Talk in Wiltshire is a book to dip into and enjoy during spare moments. ...if you are ever called upon to entertain friends with a reading, this book is an ideal source.' **Wiltshire Times**

'... a treasure trove of delights.' **Wiltshire Gazette and Herald**

Cover: Colour photograph courtesy of Jim Lowe,
J & S Professional Photography, Melksham;
Bus picture reproduced from Wilts & Dorset, 1915-1985,
Millstream Books, 1995, courtesy of the author Steve Chislett.

The Day Returns

Excursions In Wiltshire's History

a collection, including

- Life in the Bus Lane
- Time Capsules
- Small Talk in Wiltshire
- and more

John Chandler

Foreword by Miles Kington

EX LIBRIS PRESS

Published in 1998 by
Ex Libris Press
1 The Shambles
Bradford on Avon
Wiltshire

Design and typesetting by Ex Libris Press

Cover printed by Shires Press, Trowbridge, Wiltshire
Printed and bound in Britain by
Cromwell Press, Trowbrdge, Wiltshire

ISBN 0 948578 95 5

Source of Illustrations

The author and publisher are grateful to Michael Marshman, Trowbridge Reference and County Local Studies Librarian, for his co-operation in providing illustrations. The sources of illustrations accompanying 'Time Capsules' items are given in the text (except pp.80, 94: see below).

frontispiece, p.15, 220 - Edward Duke, *The Halle of John Halle*, extra-illustrated copy, Trowbridge Reference Library. p.22, 28, 35, 44, 237 - Edward Hutton, *Highways and Byways in Wiltshire*. p.39 - *The Melksham Guide*, 1816. p.52 - *Trowbridge in Pictures 1812-1914*, ed. Michael Lansdown & others. p.56, 135, 173 - John Britton, *The Beauties of Wiltshire*, vol.2. p.80 - *Victoria History of Wiltshire*, vol.4. p.94 - *Stemmata Botevilliana*, 1858. p.108, 150, 213 - W.H. Hudson, *A Shepherd's Life* (1910 ed.). p.112 - Harnham WI, *A History of Harnham* (1981 ed.). p.118, 128 - Roger Pearce. p.122 - John Aubrey, *Wiltshire Collections* (ed. Jackson). p.156 - *Church Rambler*, 1878. p.167 - Thomas Rowlandson. p.175 - John Hissey, *Through ten English counties*, 1894. p.179 - C. Greenwood, *Map of Wiltshire*, 1820. p.181 - C.G. Harper, *The Bath Road*, 2nd ed., 1923. p.184 - J. Waylen, *The Highwaymen of Wiltshire*, c.1845. p.186 - W.Fletcher, *Steam on Common Roads*, 1891. p.189 - *Life and Poetical Works of George Crabbe by his Son*, 1901. p.192 - John Britton, *Autobiography*, vol.1, 1850. p.197, 199 - WAM, vol.1. p.207 - *Chambers' Encyclopaedia*. p.234 - J.H. Swinstead, *A Parish on Wheels*, 1897.

CONTENTS

FOREWORD
by Miles Kington

SOMEWHERE IN THIS BOOK John Chandler says he has a magpie mind, or if he doesn't, he should have done, because that is his great unashamed quality: a wonderful magpie mind, and a wonderful eye for the odd and quirky. He should have been born in another age, one of those gentlemen of leisure who collected eggs, and fossils, and bits of statuary, and forgotten books, and created their own collections. Perhaps that is what he has done, come to think of it, and perhaps that's what this book is – the Chandler collection of Wiltshire wonders, a cabinet of curios. Even the way the book has come together reflects a purposely haphazard way of doing things, being a mixture of his previous book (*Small Talk in Wiltshire*, now unobtainable), his bus journeys written for *Wiltshire Life*, his pieces called 'Time Capsules' and other odds and ends...

What a way to make a book. Magnificent, if you ask me. So many people slave away to make well-rounded books, with beginnings, middles and ends, whereas the most rewarding books are often those in which the ingredients have not been homogenised, like Mediterranean fish stews in which most of the fish are still recognisable. If you want to have Wiltshire neatly explained to you, then don't read this book. It is not a programmed history with megaphoned guide. However, if you want a wonderful trip round the unexpected, with not even the guide sure what's round the next corner, then jump on the Chandler coach for the Wiltshire Mystery Tour...

My first wife, in fact, used to say that what was special about Wiltshire was its air of mystery. As we sped through Wiltshire from London en route to somewhere else, she would shiver slightly at the sight of Silbury Hilll or Salisbury Plain and say: "Funny place. Too ancient for my liking". She still lives in London, whereas I live in Wiltshire with my second wife, which suggests that my first wife and I felt differently about the place, and other things too.

But then I think the way you see Wiltshire depends very much on who you are. Geoffrey Grigson, in his *The Wiltshire Book*, is struck above all by the county's openness. "Wiltshire has a delightful emptiness, a landscape windy and suggestive, stimulating and soothing..." Anyone who has seen any of the open, even bleak, country in the Marlborough/Calne/Devizes axis will know exactly what Grigson means. But if you came to Wiltshire first via John Chandler's writing you would be amazed that the county had ever been accused of emptiness. The last thing Chandler's Wiltshire is is empty. Chandler's historical Wiltshire is cluttered, stacked with little ornaments, studded with mysteries and cul-de-sacs… Everywhere, to Chandler, was out of the way.

Perhaps it still is. One of the most typical bits in the book is an account reprinted from an old paper of a man called John Hampden who haunted Swindon in the last century passionately trying to convert people to his belief in a flat earth. His passing, said his obituary drily, will mean a drop in postal revenue, as he was wont to write to leading astronomers to convince them of their error in supposing that the earth went round the sun, though none of them ever replied.

And it still happens. In my home village in West Wiltshire, I was in the post office the other day when the postmaster said, half out loud: "He's at it again".

"Who is?"

"Man in the village. He's always writing to world leaders. Pope, Gorbachev, Gaddafy, Clinton..He writes to them all. He's just handed in a letter to go to Fidel Castro."

"Nothing wrong with that…."

"No, except that I can't find the air mail rates to Cuba …"

What Wiltshire also needs is someone who is collecting today's oddities, I suppose. But our great good luck is to have John Chandler with this succulent bric-a-brac stall of the past. If books were required by law to list their ingredients, as food and drink are, then the list of ingredients for this book would be one of the longest on record, because it has the same richness and variety as a carpet sample book, or one of those big boxes of chocolates where every chocolate seems different and unfamiliar, or perhaps one of those cakes made extravagantly out of fruit and nut where you think have identified everything until you come across a green bit you can't put a name to….

I think this is a lovely book. I hope you do too. I'm just glad it isn't as fattening as it is delicious.

Miles Kington
Limpley Stoke

PREFACE

I KNEW THAT IT WAS ABOUT LONGLEAT, but I had never actually looked inside *The Year Returns*, by Elizabeth Hamilton. Then in 1991 I was collecting material for an anthology about Christmas, and found in her book a beautifully crafted, impressionistic piece about snow in Longleat Park. She had been a teacher there when it was a girls' school during the war, and wrote a nature diary through the seasons, which was published in 1952. We corresponded (she was by then in a nursing home), and she was happy to be included in my book.

About the same time I was formulating plans for another anthology, an assortment of the faintly absurd or extraordinary snippets of historical writing which I kept chancing upon in libraries and archives. This became *Small Talk in Wiltshire*, which was published in 1992, and has been out of print since 1995. My publisher's wish to reprint it has led to this collection, which includes not only *Small Talk* more or less as it first appeared, but also various other pieces of light-hearted Wiltshire history which I have written from time to time.

Between 1995 and 1997 I contributed almost monthly to the magazine *Wiltshire Life*. There were two commissioned series, entitled 'Life in the Bus Lane' and 'Time Capsules', and a number of occasional pieces. Versions of much of this work are included here, with the kind permission of the Editor and Publisher of *Wiltshire Life*. 'Life in the Bus Lane', a series of explorations of the Wiltshire countryside as seen through the windows of various buses, originally ran to six articles, but I have expanded it to nine.

There are two other pieces. 'The rise and fall of the Wiltshire carrier' began as a lecture, and was first published in *Wiltshire Folklife* (no.17) in 1989. 'Gastard Sunday morning' was included next to Elizabeth Hamilton's work, from *The Year Returns*, in my anthology, *A Wiltshire Christmas* (Sutton, 1991). I am grateful to the Wiltshire Life Society and Sutton Publishing respectively for permission to include them.

This collection was to be called 'A Wiltshire Omnibus', but mindful of Miss Hamilton's eloquent title we have settled instead on *The Day Returns*. Whatever else of historical significance that may conjure up, day returns are what you need in order to explore Wiltshire by bus.

John Chandler
July 1998

Life in the Bus Lane

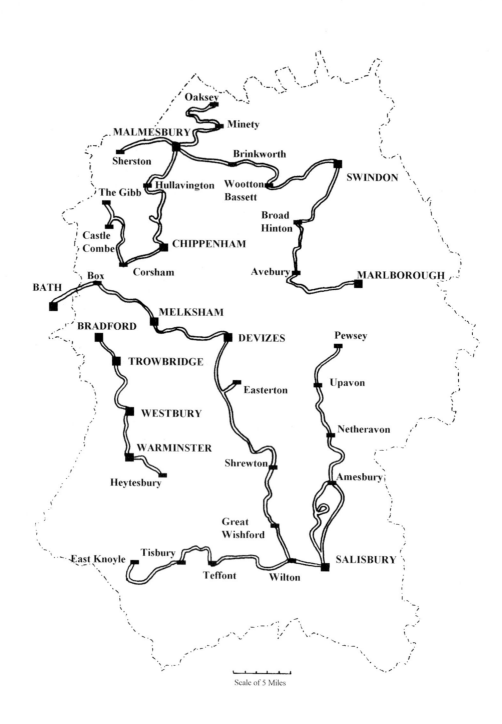

Scale of 5 Miles

The Source of the Kennet

THERE ARE THREE OF US. Upstairs, that is. I arrived first, so I've taken the front seat, over the driver. This, I believe, is traditional. The two teenage girls, pockets bulging with crisps and fizzy drinks, are sitting at the back. This too is traditional. Later, I surmise, a hint of surreptitious tobacco smoke will waft forwards from that back seat.

It is a crisp March Monday, and we are sitting on a bus in Marlborough High Street, facing the college, and waiting for 9.35. It is that time of morning which is common to all small towns, when those who have to be there have arrived and are at work; those who don't aren't, or if they are, can still drift along the capacious street and find a parking space.

While we are waiting I should tell you one thing that any intending bus passenger must understand. Buses (and I mean the ordinary country buses which we all used to catch before we bought cars) — buses like this do not take you from A to B. They take you from A to Z, via B, C, and D, not to mention W, X and Y. This bus may say that it is going to Swindon. And indeed it will take us to Swindon, if we persevere with it and have plenty of time. But Swindon is merely a by-product of the journey.

Let's face it. If anyone is desperate to go from Marlborough to Swindon, and they have a car, they will be there in fifteen minutes. This bus takes over an hour. And one reason for the discrepancy becomes apparent as soon as we set off. We are going the wrong way! Swindon is due north, and we are heading west. We are, in fact, embarking on a trip to the source of the Kennet, and on the way we shall call on most of the sixteen villages which grew up alongside the meagre waters of its upper reaches.

First above Marlborough is Preshute, its church hiding beyond the trees of the college. But Preshute is really part of Marlborough. The first real upper Kennet village is Manton, and here we leave the main road to make acquaintance with the river itself. It is lively here, eager to resume its old job of splashing over the millwheel, a teeming artery of winter rain surging bankful among its meadows.

In front of us are some six miles of Kennet valley and seven more villages before we reach Avebury. We cross and re-cross the river to visit them all. This is the land of the sarsens, the alien stones, the Saracens. At Piggledene and Lockeridge Dene they masquerade as drab sheep and lie asleep in flocks. From West Kennet to Avebury they march along upright like soldiers. In the villages they have been tamed and squared to serve as walls — incomparable walls of mottled silver, pink, and greenish-grey. And in Fyfield churchyard lie the men of the Free family, who tamed them and squared them, and who died prematurely from their dust.

The bus climbs from Lockeridge to West Overton, and at the crest of the hill a fine view is revealed. In the foreground Overton church, dressed in sarsen, looks down on a field of village earthworks. To our left the view is to Tan Hill, the highest place in Wiltshire; to our right the barrows on Overton Hill mark the line of the Great Ridgeway. And between them, in the far distance, we glimpse the Lansdowne monument above Cherhill. The bus winds down into Overton, slowing for an old border collie who is sauntering deafly along the road.

Now to East Kennet, where I have often admired the sarsen garden walls. But only from upstairs on a bus is their secret revealed, that behind them is hidden a swimming pool. On sultry summer afternoons, I daydream, sunbronzed bodies laze by the water, and reach discreetly for their towels when the double-decker trundles by. But no time now for daydreaming. The Kennet's proudest moment is about to be revealed. We are back on the main road and approaching Silbury Hill. After a wet February the river has collected every drop it can muster from its downland springs and streams, to form a silver moat around the hill. It is a spectacle purely for the locals, which the Kennet never repeats for the summer tourist trade.

At Beckhampton roundabout we must give up this self-indulgence, and do our duty at last and go to Swindon. The northward turn up to Avebury Trusloe is surprisingly hard work for a bus. I glance across to Adam and Eve, the two solitary sarsens in the field behind the stables. But I am thinking of breakfast. I heard a man interviewed on the radio, a manufacturer I think, about marmalade. He was talking about customers' preferences. 'Thick-cut marmalade', he said, as if he had just thought of it, 'is essentially a male preserve.'

Avebury's present appearance owes a good deal to marmalade — far more than it does to the National Trust. It was Scottish marmalade that enabled Alexander Keiller, heir to the family business, to indulge a passion for archaeological excavation, first in the twenties at Windmill Hill nearby, and then during the thirties in Avebury itself. He drew on his wealth to buy much of the village, and as buildings within the circle became vacant he demolished them, displacing the villagers to new houses at Avebury Trusloe. He excavated the ditch, re-erected the fallen stones, and established a museum which still exists. He died in 1955.

Eighteenth century Avebury

Beyond Avebury we settle into a different landscape. The bus is heading north now, so the Marlborough Downs are to our right. They have formed themselves into a steep escarpment, which rises green to the sky. Here and there ribbons of white climb the hill, remnants in sunless holloways of last week's snow. Against the snow the grubby chalk horse on Hackpen is a miserable creature. To our left now there is no corresponding hillside, just undulating farmland which teeters to the edge of a second escarpment, unseen from here, then suddenly down to the clay. Above Silbury the Kennet loses its vigour, and has not the strength to form a valley. It has become seasonal, gratefully receiving whatever normally dry tributaries can offer, and flowing only after winter rain — a true winterbourne.

We pass the villages which have grown up every mile or so along this unreliable stream. Winterbourne Monkton has survived, and Berwick Bassett, just. The next two have given up the struggle; the villages have been gone for centuries, and only single farms remain. A signpost tells us that they were called Rabson and Richardson. Even the road has turned away from them, and strikes its course slightly higher along the hillside.

Winterbourne Bassett comes next. The bus will not leave the main road to take us there, but it is only a field or two away to our left, and church, pub and cottages are visible among trees. I have a soft spot for Winterbourne Bassett, or more particularly for one of its former residents. Her real name was May Alexander, and she was the rector's wife — although that is not how I think of her. She came from Hampstead, but in 1897 she married a divinity tutor and fellow of Magdalen College, Oxford, the Rev Dr Robert Ottley, who was then in his forties. In the same year he left his academic duties and became rector of Winterbourne Bassett. A daughter joined them at the rectory in 1899, but the family did not stay long. They left in 1903 when Dr Ottley was appointed professor of pastoral theology at Oxford and a canon of Christ Church.

So much for Mrs Ottley (née Miss Alexander). But she had an *alter ego*. She was also Deborah Primrose, contributor to women's magazines, and author of *Beauty of Figure*. This was a guide for Edwardian ladies to physical exercises which they could do at home, to guard against such problems as 'abdominal stoutness'. It was published in 1905, and featured photographs of young lovelies in tunics and sensible shoes clinging to pieces of furniture, while demonstrating — for example — variations on abdominal vibration exercise XXXII. Not quite what one would expect from the wife of a middle-aged Oxford divine; and so the pseudonym.

Beauty of Figure was not the only book by 'Deborah Primrose'. In 1904, as soon as she had left Winterbourne Bassett, she published *A Modern Boeotia*. Beneath some pious and sentimental embroidery she concealed a witty portrayal of the village, emphasizing its isolation, the backwardness of its inhabitants, and above all the overwhelming tedium which she had endured there. Boeotia (pronounced *Bee-o-sher*), I should explain, was a region of ancient Greece renowned for its uncouthness. Winter on the Marlborough Downs, when the roads were a quagmire of mud, and for months together she never left the village, was a form of purgatory, and even her poetic descriptions of the chalk hills on a sunny July day — 'strangely, wonderfully like the sea' — sound a little forced.

I thought of poor Deborah Primrose the other day. Traffic lights had brought me to a stop on the High Bridge in Reading. Over the parapet I could see the River Kennet, wide and stately, flowing between office blocks on its way to join the Thames just around the corner. And I remembered her description of that same river at Winterbourne Bassett:

'There are no woods, and no water except a "brook", which holds the drainage of a farm-yard, to say nothing of pots and pans innumerable, and which the villagers boast is "part o' the river Temses". And indeed it evidently has a high opinion of its importance, since its presence permeates the place with an odour all its own.'

The food, it seems, was no more to her liking than the water. 'All our tradesmen live nine miles away, with the exception of a worthy butcher who comes over every day from a village four miles distant, and presents us — at extortionate prices — with arms and legs of old sheep who have apparently died of some subtle form of consumption, or at least of senile decay; which arms and legs, duly cooked, are perilous to delicate teeth and the habitual precursor of a nightmare.'

Our bus last encountered the Kennet by Avebury car park. As we near Broad Hinton the main road crosses it again. Deborah Primrose was right. It is no longer a river, more a watery ditch along the edge of a vast arable field. We are close to the source. But first one more detour.

Broad Hinton is larger than its neighbours, and warrants a visit, every now and then, from a Thamesdown bus. We turn obligingly along the narrowest of the three lanes which lead from the road to the village. Two-thirds along we get stuck. Quite seriously stuck. A car and trailer are blocking the lane, and seem to be connected with a miniature digger and some half-finished roadworks. Their owner is elsewhere, out of earshot. We stop, and the driver, assisted by various onlookers, begins house-to-house enquiries. Most of the passengers stroll out to look at the trailer, and a baby is pacified with some fresh air. A body of opinion is for manhandling the trailer out of the way, or even pushing the car (its window is open). But the bus driver, wary of possible insurance implications, vetoes these ideas. Eventually we stage a tactical retreat, the driver reversing his bus several hundred yards to a turn. A hint of surreptitious tobacco smoke wafts forwards from the back seat. Our second attempt on Broad Hinton, via a different lane, is successful, and we arrive at the village bus stop. There is no-one waiting.

Back to the main road, and across it to Uffcott. A workaday hamlet, of tractors, cows and slurry, Uffcott appears to be a survivor among the class of downland settlements which have clung to existence since prehistory. And like other such upland places, Ashmore and Buttermere, its life has revolved around a pond. But this is more than just a pond — it feeds a ditch which turns into a stream which swells to become the River Kennet. We have arrived, so far as this bus can bring us, at the source.

The farewell to Kennet country and to the Marlborough Downs comes a mile or so further, suddenly and dramatically, by the hangars of Wroughton airfield. A different world is spread below us, low hills set in the clay vale, the Thames beyond, a distant prospect to the Cotswolds and Berkshire Downs, and (in Larkin's phrase) the surprise of a large town.

Swindon at last. And curiously, despite wasting ten minutes at Broad Hinton, we are not late. The timetable must be designed to take account of horses and tractors and road blocks. After the descent through Wroughton we stop in Old Town, and I look across to the plaque over a shop by the bus stop. 'Here lived Richard Jefferies 1875-77'. And how he hated it. If, when he lived there, a bus bound for the Marlborough Downs had come along regularly, there would have been only one thing stopping his escape to the hills.

Mystic, naturalist, florid chronicler of the Wiltshire countryside, Jefferies produced a kind of autobiography, *The Story of my Heart*, which, had he written it in the middle ages, would have led to him being made a saint — or else burnt as a heretic. Because there was nothing christian about his mysticism. He worshipped the chalk downland, the timeless rolling hills, (to paraphrase his words) the sun of the summer morning on the dome of sward, the grasses sighing in the breeze, the bees humming in the heathbells.

So what would have stoppped his escape by bus? In a famous passage he tells us:

> 'It is eternity now. I am in the midst of it. It is about me in the sunshine; I am in it, as the butterfly floats in the light-laden air. Nothing has to come; it is now. Now is eternity; now is the immortal life... For artificial purposes time is mutually agreed on, but there is really no such thing. The shadow goes on upon the dial, the index moves round upon the clock, and what is the difference? None whatever. If the clock had been never set going, what would have been the difference? There may be time for the clock, the clock may make time for itself: there is none for me.'

Such a man would never have understood a bus timetable.

❧

Beyond the Elusive Forest

AFTER A FEW YEARS bowling along motorways, or touring Scotland, or day-tripping to the seaside, many luxury coaches take on second careers, as country buses. A little noisy around the exhaust, perhaps, and a few ashtrays awry, they ferry children to school, and bring bagfuls from Somerfield (with their owners) back to the remotest hamlet. They are the vehicular equivalent of a comfortable old armchair in a country saloon bar.

Such is the ageing yellow coach in Swindon bus station bound for Malmesbury. It is one of four which ply to and fro across north Wiltshire, along a route which travellers were using in the middle ages, and perhaps before that from prehistory. Seven of us today, and the job of breaking the ice (for bus travel is a sociable matter) falls to a cheerful Swindon lady with made-up face, sunglasses and striking auburn hair. 'I'm over 65 as well,' she tells the driver loudly, smiling to us down the bus, and although we had never really doubted it, we all applaud her state of preservation with incredulous grins.

There is nothing very subtle about Swindon. Once you have discarded the cherished myth, that everything begins with God's Wonderful Railway, then it all fits into place. In fact, modern Swindon owes its street plan to a canal, which was built across the pastures below the old hilltop town, a year or two before a certain I.K. Brunel was born. The canal ran beside an older valley road, the Fleetway, which led from the west towards Faringdon, and which has become Fleet Street and Faringdon Road. When the railway came it was built parallel to the canal and the road, but on the other side (as viewed from Old Swindon hill), and so the canal became a barrier. The several canal bridges, and the roads leading down the hill to cross them, developed as the main foci of the new town.

Land next to these roads, and between the canal and the railway, was avidly purchased to be built over piecemeal by speculators and building societies. The bus station partly overlies one such development, four terraced streets called Carfax, Oriel, Merton and Turl, which in the 1870s were crammed by the Oxford Building Society into a field next to the canal, Briery Close. As Victorian Swindon grew there were dozens of similar schemes nearby. Some survive as cottages, others became shops, many were demolished when the town centre was replanned in the 1950s and '60s, or more recently to make way for tall office blocks.

All this history reveals itself as our coach picks its way along Fleet Street. First the high-rise offices near the station; then shops old and new in Fleet Street itself; the original 'railway village' and the sad, decaying Mechanics' Instutute; next the colony built for an influx of Welsh ironworkers during the 1860s, opposite the GWR Park in front of the railway church. The Company had a marvellous knack of taking the credit for things that other people had paid for — including, curiously, the station itself. More redbrick terraces, then under the railway bridge and goodbye Swindon.

At least goodbye Old Swindon and New Swindon. But now for Neo-Swindon, first cousin to Milton Keynes. Here is a promised land of roundabouts and retail parks, tree-screened executive homes, smoky-glass business centres and the motorway. Yes, the windmill is real, sort of. But, like most of the people who work in the offices round it, it has come in from a nearby village (Chiseldon, in fact).

The motorway junction seems to herald genuine countryside beyond, and Sally Pussey's Inn is real enough. Sally (her surname was actually Purse) had a reputation as a wise woman, and died in 1885. From her signboard she fixes us with her beady eye as we drive past. But there is more Milton Keynes to come. Unexpectedly we turn off the main road and appear to be heading for a place called Interface — there it is, on the roadsign. At the last moment our coach veers right at a roundabout, and we make instead for the reassuring small-town urbanity of Wootton Bassett.

I haven't told you yet where we are going. To Malmesbury, yes, but I have a ticket for Sherston, some five miles further on. From a historian's viewpoint Wootton Bassett and Sherston have a good deal in common. They are both examples of Saxon villages, flourishing apparently when the Normans invaded, which were turned into small towns during the 13th century. This was done, in both cases, by laying out a wide new High Street, with regular house plots along each side, and these ran back to a service lane at the rear. Look at either of them on a map, or explore them on foot, and you will see how much of the medieval planner's vision survives.

Bassett was the entrepreneur at Wootton, and he has been rewarded with immortality of a sort — real locals used to (and may still) refer to their town as Bassett rather than Wootton. Sherston's progenitor is not so favoured. He was probably called Besil, but no-one is sure, and the locals call Sherston Sherston.

Town Hall, Wootton Bassett

In other ways, too, the towns have become very different. Two centuries ago they were much the same size, each boasting a population of around 1,000. Sherston is not much bigger now, but Wootton Bassett has grown tenfold, and much of this expansion has taken place since 1970, in the wake of the motorway and hi-tech Swindon. The consequence is that Mr Bassett's High Street, today on a warm April lunchtime, is teeming with people, and our coach dodges between market stalls and double-parked delivery vans. Whereas I fully expect that when I am dropped in Mr Besil's High Street I shall have it all to myself.

On the road from Wootton Bassett to Malmesbury there is only one village, Brinkworth. The road, for much of its course, has the character of a ridgeway, as it runs along the watershed between the Thames and the Bristol Avon. Seen from a coach window this makes for long and interesting views. Looking left the valley below Wootton Bassett begins as the former Vasterne Park, the Bassett family's hunting preserve, which is now crossed by main railway lines and the motorway. Beyond is the limestone ridge on which the town sits, running away to Bradenstoke, where as Lyneham Banks it peters out. The clayland valley broadens as the brooks watering it approach the River Avon, and the area is known as Dauntsey Vale. The river itself can be pinpointed by scanning the vale for the railway viaduct which was built in 1903 to carry the main South Wales line across it near Little Somerford.

The view to the right is of an almost empty countryside — empty that is of people, for this is Bradon. Bradon in Saxon and medieval times was a vast tract of woodland, a valuable resource on otherwise thankless soil, in which all the nearby communities, from Cirencester to Malmesbury, from the Lydiards to Cricklade, had a share. But almost no-one lived there, and there are no real villages there now. When the crown sold its interests in the former royal forest, just before the Civil War, there was still thick woodland. John Aubrey reported being told that a squirrel might have jumped from tree to tree all the way from Wootton Bassett to Brinkworth churchyard.

But not now. Bradon Forest is elusive. There are, it is true, still large compartments of woodland in what used to be Bradon, but they have to take their place within the crooked chessboard of hedges which the 17th-century inclosers spread across this landscape. The surly smallholders of Brinkworth moaned about the loss of common rights, as did all their neighbours. They were pacified with a share of the patchwork, and continued milking their cows beholden to no-one. Least of all to the rector, for their hostility to the established church was renowned.

In Brinkworth, near the Methodist chapel, a respectable elderly lady makes her way to leave the coach. She was recognized as a slight acquaintance, while we were still in Swindon, by the auburn-haired woman, and they have been gossiping all the way. She thanks the driver politely, and retires to her discreet bungalow. I recall the words of Samuel Heath, who founded the Primitive Methodist cause in Brinkworth in 1824, from where it spread across Southern England. His description of the village as, 'proverbial for its wickedness, deplorable ignorance, glaring vice, and barbarous practices,' seems on this pleasant afternoon seriously incongruous. But I suppose that things might liven up in the evenings.

After Brinkworth the view to our right — northwards — begins to change. We have traversed the elusive forest and are approaching the Cotswolds. In the distance is a mansion, Charlton Park, the seat of one of the Tudor dynasties who cleaned up after Malmesbury Abbey's demise. But the striking feature about Wiltshire's Cotswold edge is not its grand houses; it is something far more utilitarian. For a reason — hydrological I assume — which I have never discovered, this landscape is thick with water towers. Malmesbury has one of the best, and you can see it from the coach long before you see Malmesbury itself.

In fact, Malmesbury can wait until our next journey. It will be sufficient here to tell you that in the Cross Hayes I am transferred into one of those hybrid vehicles (often seen hurtling around city centres) which share many of the characteristics of a bread van, a minibus, and a dodgem car. It is bound for Yate, via Sherston, but first we have the important job of redistributing an entire luncheon club of post-prandial senior citizens around the sprawling housing estates west of Malmesbury; estates whose extent and complexity come as such a surprise to those only accustomed to visiting the town's historic bits. A useful tip to remember on such occasions is that all passengers are expected to join in the chorus of good wishes to anyone leaving the bus, and then to wave goodbye.

The last few miles to Sherston are spent enjoyably by the few of us left in passing round a jumping bean, one of three which a small child is taking home from his visit to Malmesbury. The proceedings are enlivened, too, by a muffled electronic noise. This is tracked down eventually to a digital alarm clock in the shopping bag of a large lady with a pink hat. But, apart from a few general remarks about spies and time-bombs, its significance is never explained.

Between Malmesbury and Sherston the countryside becomes true Cotswold, and where we cross the line of the Fosse Way near Easton Grey we are only a few hundred yards from the Gloucestershire border. A miniature Cotswold valley, belonging to a headwater of the Avon, appears on our left, and when we reach Sherston we feel that we have arrived in a true Cotswold town. Or rather, village, because as I predicted, its High Street is deserted. There are just the two of us, the pink-hatted undercover agent (who we helped off the bus with some difficulty), and myself.

I never tire of bringing people to Sherston. It has everything that a historically-minded tourist might wish for, including a complete lack of tourists. Like Malmesbury it is perched on a steep hill, like Marlborough it has a stately wide street, with a town hall of sorts at one end, like Castle Combe it has picturesque houses and a fine church. Its presiding genius is a character called Rattlebone, a little stone figure whom you will find facing east on the church porch. A great warrior, he supposedly fought on for Sherston despite terrible injuries, clasping a tile to his wounded stomach to keep his innards in place.

I brought a group of elderly American students here once. I walked them round, showed them Rattlebone and the church, explained about the planned medieval town; I mentioned other things, which I have not told you — the disastrous fire in 1511; and the way in which the old Oxford to Bristol road was diverted to bring traffic along the High Street. I talked about religion and nonconformity, and demonstrated old conflicts by showing them the two datestones: one on the chapel school, dated 1844; the other on the church school, dated 1845. I took them in the pub.

They loved it. Here at last was a place unspoiled by the 20th century, a haven undiscovered by the tourist industry, a technological backwater, genuine old world England. The illusion was sustained right up to the moment when one of them wandered down an alleyway, and discovered the Sherston Software Company.

ॐ

Joining up the Dots

• •

'DOOR STICKS. TURN HANDLE AND PUSH HARD.' I pushed hard. I pushed harder. I pushed as hard as I could. Then I spotted another notice, along the familiar lines: 'We are sorry that this door is now kept locked. The key may be obtained...'. Which is a pity, because my bus is due in a minute, and there is no time for key-finding.

I am at Oaksey, in north, north Wiltshire. Gloucestershire is just a short stroll up the lane opposite, and I am awaiting the bus from Cirencester to take me to Chippenham. Remote it may be from the mainstream of Wiltshire life, and quiet this Monday lunchtime, but Oaksey is no backwater. Its village street, in fact, is a veritable slalom of up-to-the-minute traffic calming measures.

The church is more traditional. I should have liked to have put my head round the door, because I know that St Christopher is inside. He is a larger-than-life figure on the wall opposite, and one of the best-preserved mural paintings from medieval Wiltshire. True to his legend he strides across a river which teems with fish (between his legs, in fact, is a mermaid with a looking glass), as he carries the infant Christ to safety.

There was a medieval superstition, later transferred to key fobs, that anyone who looked on the image of St Christopher would be preserved from all danger for the rest of the day. So naturally (with no reflection on the bus company) I am anxious to lay eyes on him. I peer through the keyhole, and as many windows as I can reach, but it is dark inside and the saint is elusive.

I shall have to make do instead with the little sculptured figurine set in the outside wall of the church near the entrance. She is a celtic fertility goddess, known technically as a *sheela-na-gig*, and described coyly by embarrassed antiquarians as, er, 'a female exhibitionist'. Quite what magic a glance at her will bring to my bus journey I am not sure.

Oaksey and its neighbours hereabouts — all the way to Chippenham, in fact — lie along that tract of countryside where the Wiltshire claylands to the east meet the limestone Cotswolds to the west. You really cannot see the join. There are no great hills, no abrupt escarpments, no dramatic views. Just a carpet of thick-pile grass, shimmering in the May sunshine, and sprinkled with buttercups and dandelion clocks. Alone in the fields, or gathered loosely into hamlets, are the dairy farms and cowmen's cottages, all built of the local rubble limestones, known as cornbrash and forest marble, which lie never far below their clay pastures. In the distance blocks of woodland, darker than the fields, mask the horizon.

Malmesbury is the capital of this unassuming landscape, and that is where we are heading. But not directly. Clayland villages, unlike their counterparts in the chalk valleys, are not strung out in an orderly line. They are dotted here and there across the countryside, and it is no straightforward matter to devise a route which will visit them all. The bus turns down lanes, joins the main road and leaves it again, heads south-east, south-west, east, south, west. Crudwell comes and goes, Hankerton, Charlton, Garsdon and Milbourne.

The bus — a middle-aged coach, in fact — is warm and comfortable, and I begin to doze in the spring sunshine. I half notice the magnificent trees outside Crudwell church; I glimpse the mansion in Charlton Park; was I imagining that vignette of Hankerton church which someone had painted in their satellite dish? And did that sign really say 'UPPER MINETY, TWINNED WITH LOWER MINETY'? Just imagine the twinning ceremony, the cultural exchanges, the messages of goodwill, the schoolchildren sampling each other's lifestyles.

The dots are all joined, and we come to Malmesbury at last. The bus pulls up Holloway, past the Moravian chapel and the stargazing tower, and into its appointed stop in Cross Hayes. Malmesbury is a miniature Durham, a peninsula of rock nearly surrounded by the two branches of the Bristol Avon. And like Durham its religious links stretch back almost to the days of the first Christian missionaries. Life here for some nine centuries, from their founder Maildulf onwards, revolved about the monks. The abbey accumulated land and villages to create its own little palatinate in north-west Wiltshire; and it built a spire to cap its church so high as to rival Old St Paul's in London. The spire fell a few years before the abbot, and in 1539 his abbey became workshops, and his church was reduced and adapted for the town.

Market Cross, Malmesbury

The town has remained small. Its heart is the market cross, and its spine is the High Street. Cross Hayes, a medieval open space created as a second market place from the back gardens behind the street, is I suppose its lung. This is where life is breathed into the old place, where folk come and go, slam car doors and generally bustle. Because Malmesbury is small people seem to know each other's business. The bus driver passes on as a general announcement to his passengers happy news about the latest Malmesburian, 9lb. 7oz. There is talk of needing a wheelbarrow.

Time to go, and we set off down the High Street to St John's Bridge and Avon Mills. By car or by bus you cannot do justice to Malmesbury. Too much flashes past to take it all in. You are given a taste, but you must resolve next time to come back and devote a whole afternoon to pottering along its streets and alleyways. A last look back from the main road before Corston, and there is the classic view of the town on its hill, with the great hulk of its abbey dominating the horizon. In your mind place Salisbury spire on those naked shoulders, and add a bit — there you have the fairytale prospect of Malmesbury as the medieval traveller saw it.

The bus sticks to the modern A429 for a few miles now. But the road does not feel very modern. The man-made landscape respects it, and it does not cut across any older field boundaries. Its bends are sinuous and gentle, not the awkward inventions of some land-surveyor in the eighteenth century. Only at Corston, where it drops to cross a minor tributary of the Avon, does its general south-westerly progress falter. The clue to its antiquity is suggested when we reach the railway bridge, for here is Kingway Nursery; and Kingway, as it turns out, is the name by which this road has been known since at least 1100. Further south, when it becomes a dual carriageway, it is still following an ancient line. A document over a thousand years old seems to be referring to it when it mentions a boundary crossing 'Erge's Path'.

Hullavington airfield is our signal to leave the main road and join up a few more dots. Mention Hullavington to almost anyone, and the same image is called to mind. It is of the grass-covered aircraft hangars, which stand in pairs around the runway like modern long barrows commemorating some race of giant warriors. Everyone has driven past them, and wondered how the grass is mown in stripes with such military precision. Were the Germans ever fooled by so many convex cricket pitches?

To visit Hullavington village, and its neighbour Stanton St Quintin, our bus dives down a series of country lanes which together take us right around the airfield perimeter. Hullavington itself is quite a considerable place, of stonebuilt houses spread along a meandering street for half a mile or more. The buildings of the airbase, too, are more impressive than most. Unlike the majority of former airforce sites in Wiltshire, Hullavington was not built in wartime panic, but a few years earlier, as a flying training station in 1936; the quality of its architecture seems to reflect this. At the end of its long avenue we pick up our first passengers — military wives and their children — since we left Malmesbury, and return to the main road.

The motorway, already during its first quarter-century, has established itself here as a kind of cultural barrier. Northwards is Malmesbury country; Chippenham to the south, and linked by its dual carriageway road, seems very close. In a car this leg of the journey takes no more than five minutes. The bus has a more leisurely approach, and there is time to pick out familiar landmarks, such as the Cherhill white horse, away in the distance to our left. We are also treated to a double helping of Kington St Michael, another long ribbon of a limestone village away from the main road, where the bus picks its way between parked cars to an empty shelter, backs around and returns the same way.

We tend to take for granted the countryside of these few frantic miles to and from Junction 17, but in their modest way they have inspired profound art and timeless literature. This is Wiltshire's Kilvert country, less dramatic and less memorable perhaps in the diarist's pages than the wild and remote mid-Wales landscape around Clyro; but here, at Hardenhuish, Francis Kilvert was born, and then at Langley Burrell he served as his father's curate, walking the lanes to Kington and Allington, Draycot and Yatton, and immortalizing with his pen the village characters he had known from childhood.

Kilvert's diaries were rediscovered in 1937, and most of what has survived was first published between 1938 and 1940, seventy years after their author had died in obscurity. I have a first edition, old library copies bought for a few pence, battlescarred and worthless after years of borrowing, but now honoured in retirement. Another set belonged to Robin and Heather Tanner, of Kington Langley, who knew every inch of this country, and who in 1939 published their own celebration of their surroundings, *Wiltshire Village*. It was a bittersweet experience for them, two pacifists thrilling to Kilvert's idyll of the land they had always known, as they watched it being overturned to support the war effort. Robin and

Heather are both dead now, but from the bus window I can look across to the trees which surround their house at Old Chapel Field.

Robin Tanner was an etcher, and an artist of incomparable perception. His subjects were the plants and buildings of his native countryside, and he was an acute observer of details — the latch on a gate, the felloe of a cartwheel, the tangle of leaves in a hedgerow. In 1984, when he was eighty, he gave an address to the Devizes Festival, and he later recalled the occasion in his autobiography: 'I explained that all I have ever wanted to say on copper is contained in a small corner of north-west Wiltshire — a land of Cotswold stone, but a countryside that is Cotswold with a Wiltshire difference: warmer and more lush than Gloucestershire: pastoral dairy country, with small meadows and high hedges, and an ancient church every three miles or so in all directions.'

Tanner country, as perhaps it will come to be regarded, ends abruptly at Chippenham Golf Course. The last mile of our journey, if we choose to notice it, gives us a crash-course on urban history. Chippenham is the perfect mirror to reflect the growth of small towns. The images flicker past the bus window like lantern slides. Beginning with the new roundabout to the out-of-town supermarket, we move on to the 1930s ribbon housing, the municipal park, and the Victorian suburb built around the railway station. After the viaduct there is a typical mix of ruthless 1960s redevelopment and older survivors, followed by a High Street of banks, civic buildings and the former inns of an erstwhile coaching town, and culminating in a market place infilled by the medieval Yelde Hall and later shops. An opulent clothiers' church, St Andrews, oversees the town, and behind it, hidden from the traffic, is Chippenham's peaceful Georgian showpiece, St Mary's Street.

So into the bus station, where our journey ends. This also is part of the town's unfolding history. Its site is the former canal wharf, built at the opening of the nineteenth century to make a strong market stronger, a vigorous town more vigorous still. We seem to have arrived safely, with or without St Christopher. And no, er, female exhibitionists — so far.

☙

The Curse of Dolittle

TO THE LONDONER, complaining of a five-minute wait in Oxford Street for a number 23, it may seem odd that some bus services run only once a week. In Devon years ago I saw in a timetable a bus which ran on the last Friday of each month except December – eleven journeys a year. These are market day buses, of all public transport the most intimate. They are not to be missed. If you do miss one, you will have a very long wait.

So here I am, in very good time, sitting in Chippenham bus station aboard the twice-weekly bus for The Gibb. More of The Gibb later, but meanwhile I am feeling let down. By now, I would have thought, the shopping-trolley batallion should be arriving, eager to be home for lunch in their remote hamlets of north-west Wiltshire. But they are nowhere to be seen. I am the only passenger — and today, Tuesday, is not even market day in Chippenham. I must have miscalculated.

It is some consolation, as we sweep past the Angel and the White Hart (now Iceland) in Chippenham market place, to imagine the young Charles Dickens and his fellow travellers setting off from here in their stagecoach for Bath, 160 years ago. And to know that, a few miles down the road, he would encounter for the first time an ordinary roadside village whose name ever after has become linked inseparably with him, and with the whole stagecoach ethos. We too shall visit Pickwick, after we have called in at Corsham.

For the thousands of Bath-bound coach passengers, during the decades before Mr Brunel built Chippenham railway viaduct, this stretch of the journey must have come as a relief. After the rigours of the wild Marlborough Downs they found themselves trundling between the tamed landscapes of gentlemen's parks, and there on the left a glimpse of Corsham Court, a foretaste of the genteel society awaiting them.

Unlike Dickens and his friends we turn off the high road, and make for Corsham. Corsham has one of the most attractive high streets of any

Wiltshire town, but you do not see it in a car or from a bus. The abiding impression is of muddled and disconnected car parks. And it is next to one of these that we stop.

Now everything becomes clear. Tuesday is definitely market day in Corsham, and our arrival has been noticed. From various quarters the ladies (mostly) and gentlemen (a few) for whom this bus is intended amble their way across to the bus stop. There is no great hurry — another ten minutes before noon, when we leave — but plenty of bustle. And plenty of shopping trolleys. By noon the bus will be nearly full, and everyone who might be expected will be accounted for.

While we are waiting I should explain a little more about market-day buses. They are the successors of village carriers, who sprang up all over the Victorian countryside. There had been carriers before, back to Elizabethan times at least, but these tended to travel long distances at a ponderous pace, with a train of packhorses or a lumbering covered waggon reminiscent of the wild west.

The Victorian horse-and-cart carriers, many of them part-time, drove in from their villages to the local town on market day, taking produce and passengers, running errands while they were there, collecting parcels from the station, and returning with all the merchandise which the village itself could not produce. This carried on, week in, week out, until between the wars, when the motorbus proliferated. Some of the carriers gave up, some were taken over, and some bought their own bus and have carried on ever since. Their story is told in more detail in **The Rise and Fall of the Wiltshire Carrier**, later in this volume.

I am sitting near the back, and all the surrounding seats have been filled by a contingent of ladies from Upper Castle Combe. Our driver, who joins them for a few minutes' chat, expresses mock concern for my moral welfare, and opens all the windows. If I should suffer any personal injury, he explains, I shall have to fill in a form.

One more diversion before we leave. A card is being passed round for signatures, to congratulate the bus proprietor on his retirement, 'From the Old Faithfuls on the Corsham Bus'. I don't really count, but am encouraged to add my signature, along with the only other strangers, two girls up at the front. (One of them, on closer inspection, turns out to be a boy, and everyone is embarrassed.)

On the stroke of noon we set off, to weave between hedgerows along north Wiltshire lanes, shedding passengers as we go. After Pickwick, and the estate village of Hartham at the gates of the great house, we come to one of my favourites, the duck pond and just-so gardens of Biddestone. We make an unscheduled stop, for the driver to rescue one of his charges from the attentions of a troublesome bee, and then pull up at Yatton Keynell, whose elegant church tower is a permanent reminder of the late-medieval villagers' good taste. Roads and paths converge on Yatton from all directions, and we choose the old B-road to Badminton. The Gibb is not far away now, but first we have a little detour to make.

Nothing along the way has prepared us for Castle Combe. We have traversed a land of handsome, well-kempt villages set in undulating Cotswold countryside. They are normal enough places, where people carry out home improvements, bring up families, and try to pay off their mortgages. Then, quite unexpectedly, we find ourselves entering the abyss. Our bus noses down a hollowed-out lane, deeper and darker, steeper and narrower, into the underworld until, at last — we arrive. But is it heaven or hell?

There are plenty of cars, and hundreds of people swarming round, like wasps at a bottle-bank. There are buildings too, and they fit together to make a village, of a sort. But the people don't appear to live here, and the buildings seem too perfect to live in anyway. Why are all the children walking around with ice cream and clipboards? No, this is not reality, and it isn't even history. Real villages have television aerials, and real history is littered with tumbledown houses as well as smart ones. What we have at Castle Combe is Heritage, the confection of history, the lacquer of antiquity.

My problem with Heritage is that it elevates the exceptional and ignores everything else. I suppose that I am a 'holistic' sightseer, searching for context and seeking to explain what I see. Castle Combe is an aberration from the norm; its undeniable beauty stems from its being at the bottom of a wooded valley beside the stream, whereas all its neighbours are on top. Why?

Sir John Fastolf, a 15th-century soldier and businessman who lurks somewhere behind the Shakespearian character, acquired Castle Combe in 1409, and turned it into the medieval equivalent of a manufacturing town. He installed all the latest water-driven technology for making cloth and built more than fifty workers' houses. The place prospered for a while, and was then overtaken by competitors. In its decline it became picturesque.

'Castle Combe is a famous beauty spot romantically placed...', my 1911 guidebook to Wiltshire tells me; so it was discovered by visitors long before 1962. But in 1962 a village beauty competition, staged to encourage Americans in England 'to get off the beaten track', voted Castle Combe number one. Instantly the track was beaten to it, and traffic chaos ensued. Worse was to follow. In 1966 it was chosen to be 'Puddleby-on-the-Marsh', the setting for the film version of Hugh Lofting's children's novel about a talking vet, *The Story of Dr Dolittle*. And so it has become The Prettiest Village in England, and from that day on has never looked forward.

The Market Cross, Castle Combe

Perhaps (I muse as I watch from the bus window) I am being too hard on Heritage. Aesthetically Castle Combe is wonderful, of course, and it has an interesting history. But for me (insufferable tourist that I am) it is no more interesting than Yatton Keynell up the road, or anywhere else? To me the centuries-old tradition of travelling back from Corsham or Chippenham market, which our bus re-enacts every week, seems to be the real history, not the film-set outside.

After performing the clever trick of reversing past the market cross without knocking anyone over, Pat (our driver) makes the mistake of giving someone a toffee. The other passengers become restive, and so (not having enough to go round) he pacifies us by asking a riddle, which we have to solve before the top of the hill. His riddle, and the traveller's pastime of riddling, is as old as the hill itself.

At Upper Castle Combe, where real people live, most of the passengers, and the last of the shopping trolleys, disembark. Waves, kisses even, are exchanged (although I shall not be needing to fill in the form); and then the last mile is uneventful, to our destination, The Gibb. The name itself is a riddle. You might guess (correctly) that it denotes a younger village than most of its neighbours. It seems, in fact, to be one of several roadside hamlets which developed around here as road traffic increased during the 17th and 18th centuries. The Shoe and Giddeahall have similar histories, and so, in a way, does Pickwick.

The Gibb stands alongside the road from Chippenham to Chipping Sodbury. This became part of an important route from London to South Wales via the ferry at Aust, and was improved by a turnpike trust in 1751. They put a tollgate here, where it crosses the great Roman road, the Fosse Way. Slowly over the next century or so a hamlet grew up next to its most important building, its pub, the Salutation Inn.

Well, it's Tuesday lunchtime, and this bus doesn't run again till Saturday. So there should be time for a drink... I beg your pardon? — Oh, the riddle. Yes, the Salutation used to be the Gibraltar Inn — The Gibb. Cheers!

ॐ

Even Melksham

Crossing the road one day outside Comet in Bath, I was struck by a large green and yellow bus. Metaphorically, that is. I was struck by its destination — *X71 EASTERTON*. Could this be the Easterton I knew, hidden in a secluded greensand valley on the edge of Salisbury Plain more than twenty miles away, a quiet street of timber-framed cottages beside a stream, and an all-pervading aroma of cooked strawberries (from the nearby jam factory)? My curiosity aroused I made enquiries, and discovered not only that it was the very same Easterton, but furthermore that the X meant an express service (relatively speaking), and that it ran every hour through much of the day. Why was Easterton so privileged, I puzzled?

Easterton is the furthest of a little complex of settlements surrounding Market Lavington, and I suspected a historical reason for its special bus service. A scan of a few old trade directories and reference books uncovered Edwin Potter's horse-bus, which began running from Market Lavington to Devizes in about 1875. Potter's successor was the Lavington and Devizes Motor Services, who started up with motorbuses in 1912. This seems to have been an enterprising concern, and it developed a network of routes, including a service from Market Lavington to Bath, through Devizes and Melksham. In 1932 it was taken over by Bath Tramways Motors, one of the forerunners of today's Badgerline. And that, I imagine, is the pedigree of X71 Easterton to Bath.

All right, I hear your muttering. No, it doesn't matter a jot... except that, like most idle questions of a local history nature, it leads to weightier matters. A service was provided, and so a demand was created and satisfied. There came a moment, in Victorian Lavington, when people woke up to a wider world. They hopped on a horse-bus to sample the excitements and temptations on offer in Devizes. Their grandchildren in the 1920s were more adventurous still. Off to Bath for the day by motorbus

— what sophistication!

And this new-found wanderlust did not just affect Lavington and Easterton. Of course not. It struck everywhere, with profound effects on Wiltshire rural society, and indeed on the status of Bath, as west Wiltshire's emporium. These things *are* important, you see, after all.

As we sat in our strawberry haze outside Easterton jam factory, my driver confirmed what I had suspected. People these days seldom ride on the bus all the way from here to Bath. Most jump on and off at Devizes or Melksham, anonymous strangers who travel together a few miles to go their separate ways again. And so it was today. My ride to Devizes was pleasant but uneventful, and of Devizes itself I shall speak on another occasion.

From Devizes to Melksham I must have driven a hundred times. On a bus it is different. There is an opportunity, as you descend Caen Hill, to savour the view across to Salisbury Plain out of one window, and the Marlborough Downs from the other. I always assumed that there must be long views, because at night the orange streetlights of Caen Hill are visible from most of Wiltshire; but usually, like everyone else, I am too busy pretending it is Silverstone to take much notice. Later, after we have crossed the canal at Martinslade Bridge, there are closer horizons, Seend on the left, Sandridge on the right.

Then, when Melksham looms, we are treated to an excursion around unfamiliar housing estates, places we have never been, names we have never encountered. This is an endearing habit of local buses. But as we shake off Bowerhill on our course towards Queensway and Forest, my vigilance is rewarded by something special, a row of stately Regency profiles staring out from behind a hedge.

Here, forlornly beyond a roundabout, are the remains of an ill-fated bid for gentility. In 1814 plans were laid to promote two recently discovered chalybeate wells, and surround them with all the trappings of a spa — a pump room, baths, a hotel, and a group of tall, foursquare lodging-houses. Forget Leamington, forget Cheltenham, Bath even — and come to Melksham.

But they didn't. After the scheme had failed the main building became a school. For a while the water, 'the greatest purifier of the blood ever yet discovered,' continued to be bottled and sold by a Melksham chemist, Mr Nosworthy. It was a wonderful remedy, his 1850s advertisement tells us, for scorbutic eruptions, scurvy, giddiness in the head, costiveness and piles. A man from Cheverell wrote in to say that his late wife had been cured of leprosy by it (but not, presumably, of something even worse), and a grateful Somerset clerk announced that it had cured his diseased leg of 22 years' standing. Scrofula, jaundice, nervousness, rheumatism — all were defeated by the miraculous liquid.

Melksham Spa, c. 1816

In Melksham market place I break my journey. What are we going to do about Melksham? The poor town has an image problem. People think that it is unattractive, and they denigrate it. Just a few pages back, you may recall, I wrote that Castle Combe was interesting, but no more so than anywhere else. I nearly added, '... even Melksham'. But that would have been unfair.

'A clean, unpretentionus old market town', my 1911 handbook described it. The Shell guide in 1935 said that it was well laid out and had, 'a certain subdued dignity in spite of its business character'. But then came Pevsner's verdict, in 1963, that, of the small towns of Wiltshire it had the least character and least enjoyable buildings. I take that as a compliment to the other towns. Pevsner could be far more forthright in his criticism. When describing Somerset towns he wrote: 'Radstock is really desperately ugly.'

Here, then, are a few suggestions for the visitor wishing to enjoy Melksham. First (and this is true of nearly everywhere — except, possibly, Radstock), look above the shop windows and the signboards to the upstairs architecture. Imagine those handsome casements and honeyed stone as once they were, at ground floor level too. And, while you are about it, remove in your imagination the yellow lines, the tarmac pavements and the cars in front of them. Second, try to ignore (or forgive) the shopping precinct and the other tacky 1960s buildings near the Lowbourne roundabout.

Third, take a turn down Church Street. Beyond the car park and the post office the world takes on a rosier hue. On either side of the war memorial in Canon Square, like a group of old comrades on remembrance day, stand two rows of distinguished houses, reminders of Melksham's clothmaking prosperity. Although they are dressed up as Georgian, most are much older. Two are medieval cruck buildings mentioned in a document of 1543.

Canon Square leads us down a lane and through sturdy ironwork gates to the church, which is as large and fine and perpendicular as any in a west Wiltshire town. The other turning off Canon Square is Melksham's secret, not to be wasted on those who deride the town. This is Church Walk, and here, tucked away from the High Street traffic and the passers-through, is a backwater of miscellaneous old houses, from medieval to 19th-century, which any of Melksham's more illustrious neighbours would be proud to possess.

My hour between buses is nearly spent, but there are a few minutes to sit on a wall in the sunshine near the town hall. Opposite is the King's Arms, an echo of Melksham's coaching days before the railways, when stagecoaches crossed west Wiltshire from Devizes to Bath, along the same route as my bus. Time, too, to glance through the Melksham town trails which I bought in the tourist office. I discover that the late Barbara Woodhouse, canine celebrity, lived in Spa Road during the war, and kept a Jersey cow in her garage.

Industrial Melksham — what remains of it — lies beyond the river, but soon we are past it and on the open road again. At Shaw the Corsham and Bath roads divide, beside an extraordinary and rarely celebrated church. Spiky and pinnacled in Arts and Crafts Movement style, it dates from 1905, and was the extravaganza of a Wiltshire architect, Charles Ponting, after years spent studying and restoring medieval churches in 'correct' Victorian styles.

Shaw and Atworth have grown towards each other along the main road, so that for a couple of miles we pass between bungalows, farms, and solid limestone houses. After Atworth's tribute to Queen Victoria, its distinctive clock tower, we leave suburbia and begin a gentle climb. Wormwood Farm is at the summit, and I notice from my map that we have regained exactly the altitude of Devizes. From here it is downhill all the way to Bath.

Bowling down to Box from Fiveways, sore and buffeted stagecoach passengers must have felt that they were nearing journey's end. The stream which rises in the grounds of Hazelbury Manor, on the hill to our right, has formed a steep and darkly wooded valley. When we emerge Box is revealed.

Box for me is a place of fine views, good company, and excellent dogwalking. As Wiltshire villages go it is large, and there is plenty going on; but it retains its sense of community and a friendliness which I have often enjoyed. On this July afternoon all the handsome Box-stone houses on their hillside seem to be sunbathing.

Box is the last Wiltshire parish in this direction, so after Box Bridge on the A4 my editor will disallow anything I write. Idly, therefore, as we run into Bath, I ponder another local history conundrum. Why is there so much electricity in Melksham? Has anyone else noticed how the processions of pylons from all over Wiltshire converge on the place? They meet in a great temple of bakelite, a forest of giant bedsprings, at a lonely spot between Whitley and Beanacre, just north of the town.

No, I suppose you're right — it doesn't really matter. But there again, one day local historians will study electricity supply, and it will become an important part of the history of towns... even — *especially* — Melksham.

A Road Well Travelled

I HAVE NEVER CARED GREATLY for William Cobbett – quotable, yes, but so self-opinionated, always fomenting long-forgotten battles, full of hyperbole, indignation, bluster. Not my type. *Rural Rides* seldom passes my lips, for two personal reasons. One problem is that it has trouble getting out. My mouth, you see, is the wrong shape — 'Wuwal wides', Rhhhruwrwal rhhwides', 'Wrhrwhruwal hrrwrides' — hopeless.

The other reason goes back to 1978, when I first encountered Cobbett's unspeakable book. I was collecting information about Amesbury, and eagerly scoured his famous chapter, 'Down the Valley of the Avon', to see what he said about the place. He spent a Tuesday morning, 29th August 1826, riding to Amesbury from Fyfield near Pewsey, and arrived soaking wet at lunchtime. While his clothes were drying, he wrote, 'I sit down to make some notes of what I have seen since I left Enford...... but, here comes my dinner: and I must put off my notes till I have dined'. And that is the last we ever hear of Amesbury, infuriating fellow.

Still, plenty of later travellers have been sufficiently affected by Cobbett to emulate his journey, on horseback (George Winder), on foot (Brian Vesey-Fitzgerald), and even by bus. Yes, the Avon valley bus figures in literature twice. Sir Henry Bashford, King George VI's physician, published in 1953 a meandering account of his life in retirement at Easton Royal, deep in Pewsey Vale. *Wiltshire Harvest* includes a splendid description of a village fete, starting with the line, 'All village fetes are the same fete.' There is also a chapter, 'Bus to Salisbury', in which he travels on the upper deck from Pewsey down the valley, daydreaming about catching trout, a farmer's eight comely daughters, and a particularly good luncheon which he had once enjoyed, with a good Burgundy, somewhere near Rushall. More penetrating stuff is V.S. Naipaul's observation, in *The Engima of Arrival*, of tension and conflict enacted on the school bus back from Salisbury to Wilsford. Even in Arcady...!

A bus ride from Salisbury to Pewsey, therefore, can be a literary as well as a geographical experience; and I was not at all surprised when, on our way back, the ghost of Sir Henry (for so I assumed him to be) climbed aboard at Lower Woodford. A dapper man, of slight build, he was beautifully turned out, despite a hot summer's day, in tweed jacket, check trousers and buttoned shirt (no tie), hair immaculate beneath a tweed hat. A kindly face with a jovial smile, he seemed at peace with his world — for few worlds are more peace-enducing than the Woodford valley between Amesbury and Salisbury.

But the Woodfords must wait (and you really ought to read Naipaul's book before you explore them). Our outward journey was to take us by the main road, past Old Sarum and along the watershed between the Avon and the Bourne. In Castle Street, however, we coasted to a halt with a broken throttle, precisely opposite the bus garage. Two mechanics and a second bus, much longer than the first, were summoned, and the ten passengers filed off the one and on to the other. Human nature dictated, of course, that we all contrived to sit in precisely the same positions relative to each other, though we now had twice as many seats to choose from.

Northward from Salisbury the modern road follows an ancient ridgeway, the Old Marlborough Road, as far as High Post. Here they slowly diverge, the old route eventually crossing the airfield. You can see one of its milestones in the field near the golf course, and there is another, which I spotted from the bus, behind the security fence between buildings at Boscombe Down. The first of the series, outside St Francis's church in Castle Road, is inscribed with the date 1748, and this corresponds with a note on a 1751 map of Salisbury, 'milestones are new erected all the way to Marlborough...' But by whom? — the road was not a turnpike until much later.

When I collaborated on a book about Amesbury, in 1979, I insisted on calling the place a town, whereas my co-author generally referred to it as a village. Sweeping down Boscombe Road some twenty years later in a large bus, between the ever-broadening suburbs of housing estates, Amesbury appears very townish. And pulling into its spanking new bus station, that impression is confirmed. How many small towns have a bus station these days, let alone a new one? The reason, of course, is that Amesbury has expanded to serve the everyday shopping needs of (often carless) army families quartered in the nearby garrisons. It is busy by day, and can be lively at night.

Diana House and Grey Bridge, Amesbury

Leaving Amesbury, our bus took the main road, 'the front way' as Sir Henry called it, as far as Upavon, apart from excursions into Durrington and Netheravon. I spent the journey looking out for buildings and views which Cobbett would have recognized. There is a little group near the river at Amesbury, of Diana House, Grey Bridge, Countess Farm and the little brick tollhouse, all of which he must have seen; but their seclusion has been spoiled now by the Granada Services, Travelodge and A303 roundabout. At Netheravon Cobbett mused on the gradual decay and depopulation of the valley. He had stayed in Netheravon House eighteen years earlier, but now found it out of repair, the gates rather rotten, and the dog-kennel roof falling in. Its subsequent career would have surprised him. The Hicks Beach family (with whom he had stayed), sold it eventually to the War Office, and the house became the centre of a cavalry school, and later surrounded in its grounds by a hutted and then a permanent camp for machine gun and artillery training. Try as I might, I failed to glimpse the great house behind its screen of trees and security fence.

North of Fittleton the valley still belongs to the army, but wears civilian clothes. Around Chisenbury, in fact, I saw a landscape which Cobbett would have appreciated, of green riverside meadows used as summer cow pasture, and barley being harvested on the hillsides. Brian Vesey-Fitzgerald, writing his *Hampshire Avon* (1950), stopped here on his walk to admire the view, and to consider the career of Cobbett's friend, the political agitator Henry Hunt, who was born nearby at Widdington. Another view of valley life was soon revealed to him, for at Enford he fell in with a smartly dressed and Oxford-educated purveyor of quack medicines (a 'crocus', in their travellers slang), who proceeded to describe his many and various amorous conquests among the lonely housewives of the Avon villages. But no salacious eavesdropping for me; by now there was only one other passenger.

Upavon Square always seemed an important staging-point for buses. Whenever you drove through it there was a bus or two making important connections. But today no-one was waiting and we did not even slow down. After the throttle problem we were still ten minutes late, and we pressed on for Pewsey, our destination. At Pewsey, according to my timetable, I had a choice. I could poke around for an hour and investigate the community tea shop (which had been warmly recommended), or, if I hurried, I might just catch a bus straight back. I chose the latter, although I need not have hurried. The return bus was ten minutes late, for the very simple reason that, although a different driver, it was the same bus. I settled back into my still warm seat and replayed my journey. The escarpment south of Pewsey, from where Cobbett surveyed the beautiful vale, was looking magnificent. It is a great abstract sculpture, a community effort of trackways and lynchets imposed on the natural erosion of the chalk hillside, to which a white horse has been pinned like a badge. I dozed off.

I broke my return journey at Amesbury, and sat for a while in the sunshine of the King's Arms courtyard with a lunchtime pint. Twenty years ago, when I worked in the library here, I knew most people, but today, such is the transience of a service population, I recognized no-one. I started to write up some notes about the day's events..... but, here comes my dinner: and I must put off my notes until I have dined (clever trick, that, Mr Cobbett).

From the pub back to the bus station, where I had determined to catch the Woodford valley bus to Salisbury. This runs four or five times a day, and is Wilts and Dorset number 1. It was in fact the service with which the fledgling company began, in August 1914, when its only competition was Harold Eyres, a horse-and-cart carrier. Harold eventually yielded to progress and bought his own bus, but, unlike Wilts and Dorset, he kept the carrier's mentality. A 1920s advertisement for his service describes him as 'The Old-Time Carrier', and his bus was available on alternate days for picnics. Meanwhile the Wilts and Dorset was building an empire of interconnecting routes, stretching from Basingstoke to Weymouth.

But Harold appreciated his surroundings. His advertisement points out that from his bus, 'a good opportunity is afforded to visitors of viewing Old Sarum and rural life in this charming valley'. This remains true, although I do not see its attractions marketed now by Wilts and Dorset. In fact the driver, when I told him I was going through to Salisbury, at first recommended the faster, main road bus in the next bay. I sat tight. The Woodford valley, you see (as the lazy, wandering reaches of the Avon between Amesbury and Salisbury are known), is unsurpassed in Wiltshire for the beauty of its scenery. The sunshine dappled the crystal river through luxuriant foliage, distant harvesters droned on ripened hillsides, and cottages of thatch and banded flint lined the lanes in twos and threes.

Of rural life there was less to see. Our driver scoured those lanes for any sign of passengers, even venturing across the bridge at Upper Woodford, and doubling back beside the tranquil river to Great Durnford. Here one night in 1654 John Evelyn watched spear-fishing for trout from boats by lamplight. Today the only rural life was going on in the pub garden and car park outside the Bridge Inn. And since (as commonly at country pubs) there seemed far more cars than people, no-one wanted our bus. Two when we left Amesbury, our tally only ever rose to five.

Cobbett rode down the Woodford valley, too busy by this stage with calculations and injustices to comment much about the scenery. But beyond Little Durnford the majestic profile of Old Sarum comes into view, and Cobbett certainly noticed that. For him it was 'the Accursed Hill', the epitome of electoral injustice, the rottenest of Parliamentary boroughs. Seen from a distance, he remarked, it somewhat resembled three cheeses of diminishing size, laid one upon another. He rode right up to its summit, the Stilton on top of the Gloucester, and swelled (as he put it), 'with indignation against the base and plundering and murderous sons of corruption'. Had he stayed in the valley, as we did in our bus, he would have discovered a most blatant example.

Much earlier in his political career Cobbett had been a fierce critic of the administration of the then prime minister, William Pitt the younger. The Pitt dynasty had represented Old Sarum in Parliament off and on since 1688, and had become the major landowners (so that they could control their meagre electorate). In 1711 one of them had rebuilt the church tower at Stratford sub Castle, not so much to the glory of God, as to advertise his own importance. His self-satisfaction has endured. There, as we pottered past in our bus, the sun shone on his tower, and on its inscription in massive square capitals, THO. PITT ESQ. BENEFACTOR. I don't think that Cobbett would have been very pleased.

᠅

BA12 to BA15

· ·

IT IS MID-MORNING, Monday 15th August 1921, and in Heytesbury village street the first ever Wilts and Dorset bus is about to appear. The war is over and the wounds have begun to heal, Britain still has an empire, and the great economic slump which will slide into the unemployment and depression of the mid-20s is still a few months away. People want to travel, and it is a time of opportunity for bus companies. Wilts and Dorset have been running a regular service from Salisbury to Bournemouth for several months, and have bought for it a new 35-seat Leyland, the star of the fleet, which is clocking up 896 miles per week at about 7 miles per gallon. They are just taking over their main rival company in Salisbury, the 'Yellow Victory', and they are advertising daily charabanc outings to the seaside, Stonehenge, and the New Forest. The muddled railways are about to be reorganized. Now is the moment to conquer the west.

And so began the bus service (later the 241, then the X41, and now the X4) which I am waiting for outside the Angel in Heytesbury. It was advertised in the *Salisbury and Winchester Journal* during August 1921 to run three times daily (including Sundays) between Salisbury, Heytesbury, Warminster, Westbury, and Trowbridge, with connections there to Bath, Frome, Chippenham, Melksham, and Beckington. These days it runs via Bradford through to Bath, and Bradford is my destination. My entire journey will remain within West Wiltshire District, and I shall visit all but one of its five towns (I explored the other, Melksham, a few pages ago).

In postcode terms (which is the vogue among geographers) my bus will proceed from BA12 through BA13 and BA14 to BA15. Postcodes, in fact, offer quite a useful insight into the way the world works, since from their own perspective they define the sphere of influence of particular centres. In the claylands of west Wiltshire, from Warminster up as far as Chippenham and Calne, the towns are quite evenly distributed, and each has a recognizable territory around it. The limits of BA13 (Westbury) or BA15 (Bradford) are quite similar to the Saxon land divisions known as hundreds, and the large ancient parishes dependent on these centres — not to mention the Victorian administrative paraphernalia of poor law unions, sanitary districts, urban and rural districts. Sensitive travellers may spot the stream, or hilltop, or bend in the road, which tells them that they are now passing from one territory to another.

Strange those trains of thought which clutter one's head at a bus stop. (The composer Sir Arnold Bax once wrote a tone poem, *November Woods*, while waiting for a bus in Buckinghamshire). When the bus actually arrives our sightseeing can begin. First Heytesbury itself, which was once a small town and Parliamentary borough in its own right. In the space of 80 years it suffered two major setbacks, a fire in 1765 which destroyed 65 houses in two hours, and the Reform Act of 1832 which extinguished its franchise as a rotten borough. The rival inns remain: the (Blue) Angel was the Tory headquarters (but is now painted green); the Whigs used the Red Lion as their base (which is now painted blue). The High Street (now by-passed) is probably as quiet as it was in 1921, and its appearance has not changed a great deal.

The same cannot be said for our approach to Warminster. By Boreham Bridge we divert to serve the Woodcock housing estate and Kingdown School. In 1921 and throughout the inter-war period much of the present Woodcock Road was a footpath across fields. Then the army came, and Warminster began to expand. The Woodcock estate, currently one of the most depressing in Wiltshire with its empty, boarded-up houses, was built during the 1950s, and moulders on as a post-war period piece. The only excitements along Woodcock Road are the speed humps which, from the back seat of a bus, seem particularly spiteful.

Actually I like Warminster. It is a true thoroughfare town, where the old coach roads from Southampton to Bristol and London to Barnstaple met and crossed. The elongated High Street retains its Georgian feel and old-fashioned demeanour. The architecture is good quality but tatty (in places), which is better than being imitation and twee. We stop outside the Old Bell, and exchange three elderly ladies for three other, identical, elderly ladies. Then it is down to the Athenaeum, around the roundabout, and we strike north up Portway. Older Warminster ends with the railway line of 1851 and Louisa Warren's almshouses of 1873. 'Be ye kind one to another', she inscribed on the gable.

After Warminster long views unfold, and we realize, not only that we are about to shuffle from one postcode to another, but that the very stuff of Wiltshire, the geology, is changing. Any journey north-westwards across Wiltshire takes the traveller back through geological time, and this bus ride exhibits all the main formations. The chalk of Salisbury Plain is edging away to our right, and the view westward beyond Cley Hill is to the wooded greensand slopes of the Longleat estate. The claylands are about to begin. After Upton Scudamore we cross Biss Bottom, and thereby enter BA13, the land of Westbury.

The true character of Westbury is not well seen from a bus, nor for that matter from a car. Its attractions lie around the square and the church, and they must be enjoyed on foot. From a bus all we see are ribbon development, bungalows, the dismal Haynes Road with its adjacent shopping mall and car park, and the ever-lurking threat of disruptive roadworks. We leave the main road to visit the railway station, a full mile away from the town centre. The railway came to Westbury in 1848 from the north, and forked here for Salisbury and Weymouth. Later, in 1900, the main line from London to Exeter was added, and Westbury remains the principal railway depot for west Wiltshire, with substantial stone traffic from the quarries around Frome. When railway cuttings were built here during the 1840s iron ore was discovered, and a small but flourishing open-cast iron works operated next to the station from 1858 until about 1921. Eden Vale lake beside the station approach is the water-filled remains of the mine workings. Other industrial concerns, including a processed cheese factory, congregated near the station, and since the 1920s the whole area between the town and the railway has gradually filled with housing.

Westbury Station sits on clay, but beyond the line runs a ridge of higher ground, known as The Ham. This is an easily overlooked section of the Corallian ridge, a long, narrow belt of limestone which separates Wiltshire's two main clay deposits. Suddenly and surprisingly, we are treated to long views on both sides — westward across the flat lands of

Southwick and North Bradley to Somerset and the Mendips; eastward over Westbury town to the white horse on Bratton Hill, and the sinuous Salisbury Plain escarpment. A mile or two more over clay takes us past Hawkeridge to Yarnbrook, where we rejoin the main road.

Yarnbrook can be a bottleneck at rush hours, and before they built the roundabout it was a notorious hold-up for holiday traffic on Saturdays. When next you are stuck here, consider the pub, The Long's Arms. Its signboard proclaims that it is, 'famous for its Hungry Horse big plate menu', and it is perhaps transmogrifying itself (at least in popular usage) into The Hungry Horse — one of several ways in which pubs change their names. The older name commemorates a branch of one of Wiltshire's leading gentry families, whose seat was nearby at Rood Ashton from 1597 until 1924. Their house became a stately ruin, but one of its lodges can be seen beside the road to Melksham beyond West Ashton village. The last of the Longs, Walter Hume Long, was created a viscount in 1921 after a distinguished political career. He masterminded the reorganization of British local government (in 1888), and later served as President of the Board of Agriculture, Chief Secretary in Ireland, Secretary of State for the Colonies, and First Lord of the Admiralty.

But what catches my eye, as we swing round the corner, is the Long's arms themselves, emblazoned on the pub signboard, and especially the Latin motto, 'Longus Limbus'. I don't believe it. And later, in the library, I confirmed that my incredulity was justified. There is indeed a Latin word *limbus*, but it means a hem or girdle. 'A Long Girdle' seemed a strange motto, and indeed the Long family boasted something quite different, 'Pieux Quoique Preux' ('Pious though Valiant'), or sometimes 'Preux Quoique Pieux' ('Valiant though Pious') — depending presumably on the circumstances. Nevertheless I was impressed by 'Longus Limbus'. There is, you see, a long tradition of making up spoof Latin, which stretches back to the middle ages, and which has been known since the 16th century as 'macaronics' (because the hero of one poem so constructed was an Italian macaroni-maker). May I humbly submit that the pub's next motto should be 'Ravenus Equus'?

There is not much open country left between Yarnbrook, North Bradley and Trowbridge any more. Ribbon development along the main road

Trowbridge Town Hall

during the 1920s and 30s was followed by post-war housing estates, and in the '90s by out-of-town shops and a business park. The drive-in Macdonalds and the superstores are, of course, a by-product of the motor car, but it is important to remember that, between the wars, a similar symbiosis existed between suburban expansion and the motorbus. Burgeoning council estates during the 1920s presented the bus companies with a wonderful opportunity, and their regular services between home, town, and workplace became an essential element in carless suburban living. Only when we reach the stonebuilt terraces of Trowbridge's Newtown area, within easy walking distance of the shops and factories, have we arrived at the pre-motorbus era.

Trowbridge is always a busy town, with a more important feel and a greater range of shops than its west Wiltshire neighbours; and there is generally plenty going on outside the town hall, where the country buses stop. I watch a girl collecting for a flag day, whose roll of labels is suddenly unravelled by a gust of wind, scattering sticky paper badges into the air and along the pavement. There are, as usual, several ladies with clipboards conducting surveys. They rarely seem to want to interrogate the likes of me. Indeed, the last time I was approached was in Canterbury. I explained that I lived hundreds of miles away, so my opinion would be useless, but the man persisted. 'Did I receive Meridian TV?' 'Well yes, as it happens, but I rarely watch it.' 'Do you drink lager?' 'Not if I can help it.' 'I don't blame you,' he muttered sadly. And we parted the best of friends.

There are still green fields between Trowbridge and Bradford, although the two towns are only three miles apart. The high ground of Trowle Common, where we slip from BA14 to BA15, permits us more long views across the clay vale, before we step back once again in geological time. For Bradford sits in the limestone belt, Wiltshire's Cotswolds, and the contrast of scenery and townscape between Trowbridge and Bradford could hardly be greater. I am wary of labouring this comparison, which is so often made, because I know that Trowbridge too has fine architecture, and a rich industrial and social history; and that Bradford too has its depressing, nondescript corners. So I'll keep quiet. Except to say that, when the bus arrived in Trowbridge I stayed on board. Now that we're pulling into Bradford, excuse me, I'm going for a walk.

ﺩ

In Mr Bartlett's Day

I REMEMBER telling a lady from Tisbury that we were planning to move to East Knoyle. That would be in 1991. 'It's all right,' she said, 'provided that you have a car. But I expect that you do have a car.' She was right, of course, on both counts. It is very difficult to run your life without a car from a village such as ours, five miles from a railway station and any town, and away from the daily bus routes. And yes, I do have a car. But today, for the first time ever, I propose to leave my village by public transport. I am going to catch the Tuesday bus to Salisbury.

East Knoyle lies in the south-western corner of Wiltshire, close to the Dorset and Somerset borders. We used to be a traffic jam on the main road from Warminster to the coast, but in 1996 our by-pass was opened, and now we seldom see a lorry in our street. From the windmill above the village the view is south and west, across Blackmore Vale, and we identify with the small towns in and around the Vale — Shaftesbury, Gillingham, and Mere — rather than with the large town which is our postal address, Salisbury, nearly twenty miles away. Our upstart neighbour, Hindon, which was created in a corner of our parish during the 13th century, feels a little nearer, and has regular daily buses to Salisbury. But, except on market day, we are a stop too far.

It is 9 o'clock, and we are standing opposite the war memorial. A mother with three young children and a buggy, an elderly couple whom I have said hello to for years, and myself, all waiting for Lever's bus. We are discussing Haslam's Shop, the actual birthplace of Sir Christopher Wren, which was demolished in the 19th century, but stood a few yards from where we are waiting. Many people are aware that Wren was born in East Knoyle, the son of the rector, but you have to live here to know that he was born in a shop, while the rectory was being repaired. We still have a village shop, with a post office, and another small shop attached to the petrol garage, both friendly and excellent, but Haslam's is no more.

In fact our street used to be lined with shops, as my bus stop friends recalled, and you could buy almost everything you needed without leaving Knoyle.

If you did wish to leave there was a daily Wilts and Dorset bus which called on the way from Mere to Salisbury, and in the other direction you could go to Yeovil. Mr Bartlett was the village bus proprietor, and he ran into Shaftesbury every day. 'And wasn't the village bus called Sally', I interjected, having learnt this once at an old slide show?' No, that must have been before their time. But they could remember when the bus to Salisbury was full of Knoylians, 60 on a 39-seater, and how Mr Bartlett used to run three buses, overflowing with villagers, to Weymouth on Sundays in the summer.

Our bus arrives, I stow the buggy in the boot for the woman with the handful of children, we buy our tickets from Tim, the driver, and all set off down the village street. We shall not, of course, go straight to Salisbury. First there is Semley, our neighbour to the south, and then Tisbury, the miniature metropolis of Wardour Vale. Semley used to have its own railway station, set apart from the main part of the village, and around it grew a typical industrial hamlet which included a milk depot. The station and the depot have closed, though the line and various commercial premises remain. We picked our way along Station Road, where trains once stopped for Salisbury and London, Exeter and Plymouth, but no-one requires our service today. It is the same at Semley Green, and at Newtown. Only when we reach Tisbury does our bus begin to fill.

Semley stands at the head of the valley (often called the Vale of Wardour) which is formed by the River Nadder and its tributaries on their way down to Wilton. Wardour Castle is only one of many great houses overlooking this vale, which between them have divided up and controlled it. The feudalism has gone now, but we can still think of the Fonthill estate, the Wardour estate, the Compton estate, and — most influential of all — the Wilton estate. They have their distinctive architecture, the Fonthill estate cottages at the Ridge, the Wilton model farms at Burcombe and Bemerton. The first of these mansions, Pyt House, where the local landowner's unpopularity provoked a tragic confrontation between labourers and the yeomanry in 1830, to me still looks down menacingly from the hillside as we potter past the scene of the battle. And, gazing across the peaceful valley from Tuckingmill, there is still a twinge of the old religious prejudice, which set the Catholic Arundell family of Wardour (across the river) apart from its Protestant neighbours on this side.

If from a Knoyle viewpoint Hindon is an upstart, then from Hindon's viewpoint Tisbury is much more so. Until the 19th century Hindon was a Parliamentary borough, and the centre of local administration. Then in 1859 the railway came to Tisbury, and an old village became a new town. It was, curiously, a Hindon man, a speculator and entrepreneur, who began the transformation. Archibald Beckett leased and then developed an area known as Paradise, between the existing village, the church and the railway station. He opened a brickworks on the land to supply the raw materials, built and later rebuilt the imposing 'Wiltshire Brewery' on the site of an old workhouse, and laid out a new High Street and Square, with houses, shops, and a hotel. Meanwhile the vicar, the Rev. Hutchinson, set out to counter this outbreak of Mammon with a school, library, new vicarage, and a row of school houses overlooking the churchyard. By 1900 the face and pace of Tisbury had changed.

Teffont Manor House and Church, before rebuilding

The bus begins to fill, and after several stops and turnings we negotiate a lane which is the same width as the bus, past the Ridge, to Chilmark and Teffont. Teffont is the most attractive village in the Vale of Wardour, and anyone who wishes to prolong the pleasure of visiting it should follow the example of our bus, by leaving the main road and pursuing the stream (the Teff) down to the picture-book church and the lake beyond. It only takes a few seconds longer than the way everyone else goes, and you rejoin the main road at the top of the hill. Teffont is actually two villages, Teffont Magna at the northern end, and Teffont Evias down towards the lake. Teffont Evias church was almost completely rebuilt in 1824-6, but the delicate steeple is a few years later. It stands tastefully in the manor house grounds, waiting to be viewed across the lake.

At the junction with the main road is a signpost, 'Salisbury 10 miles', and I look at my watch. We have been travelling for nearly an hour, and I am now nine miles from home. Most of my fellow-passengers are elderly, and some are very elderly. Only elderly people seem to have the time to travel at this pace. And yet they have the least time left to waste. The thought strikes me that perhaps it is only those people content to take life slowly who are likely to become very elderly. And I notice something else. The bus passengers have graded themselves according to age. We are more than half-full now, and the front twenty or so seats are all occupied by (I should think) over-70s — Ivy and Phyllis and Leonard and their friends, who are now passing round holiday snapshots. Towards the back are the Kirstys and Matthews and Rebeccas with their mums. I am sitting in between, where the middle-aged gravitate, on my own.

At Dinton and Barford St Martin we take on more passengers, so that hardly any seats remain empty. This is not because we are the only bus these villages receive — in fact we have been leap-frogging from stop to stop with a Wilts and Dorset all the way from Chilmark. Our bus is slower, and older, and much more crowded, but we have the attraction that we are also much cheaper. For me one more attraction is that from Barford to Wilton we take the seldom-used back road, through Burcombe, and so from the bus window there is an excellent view of the little Saxon Burcombe church, perched above the main road across the valley. In complete contrast to Teffont Evias with its lofty spire, Burcombe has a tiny squat tower over its porch which does not even reach as high as the nave roof.

From Wilton the ride is uneventful to Salisbury, and we park in the traditional place for the multi-coloured village market-day buses, aslant in New Canal. I observe one last ritual. The regulars have all brought spare plastic bags, and these are now wedged into the vacated bus seats, 'bagging' their places for the journey home. But I shall not be joining them today. From Salisbury I have to catch a train.

Trains are not like buses, not at all like market-day buses. This has little to do with comfort, or efficiency, frequency, speed, or anything like that. On a train I am anonymous, a stranger among strangers, going nowhere in particular, for all anyone cares. Train passengers try to look sophisticated, up-to-date, and aloof, with our lap-top computers and mobile phones. By contrast the village bus seems a dinosaur, on the point of extinction. Travelling has changed, but perhaps that is a symptom that society has changed. In Mr Bartlett's day, it would seem, most of my village were happy to sit on each other's laps, and go off slowly and uncomfortably to the seaside together. In Mr Bartlett's day we were fellow-travellers; now, for the most part, we travel alone.

᪥

The Riddle of the Till

REMEMBER the 1995 heatwave? I had earmarked the day before the sweltering weather broke (so it turned out) in late August for the last of my bus rides. Like my first, which took me up the Kennet in winter, I was intent on an expedition to the source of a Wiltshire river. Like the first time, too, the bus company had laid on a double-decker for the trip. And I have never discovered a better way to explore the countryside without expending my own energy than from the front seat upstairs of a double-decker bus.

Homing pigeons circle around the sky before setting off, and in similar fashion our Devizes-bound bus, released from Salisbury bus station, made a complete circuit of the market place and New Canal before determining that westward, over Fisherton Bridge, was the correct direction. Salisbury at noon on market day is a busy place, and the traffic inched lethargically along Fisherton Street and Wilton Road. Only when the congestion thinned, after the railway bridges beyond Wilton, could we reach the modest speed expected of a country bus, and by then we were twenty minutes late. The heat was unrelenting.

The A36 north of Wilton is fast, crowded and dangerous. It torments South Newton and Stoford, and afflicts this whole stretch of the sublime Wylye valley. Two highlights remain, nonetheless. Great Wishford, on the further riverbank and unaffected by the traffic, cuts a fine figure. The delicate church tower has had its stonework top renewed, and wears it now as a duchess might a coronet. The second delight came as we climbed the hillside beyond Stoford and, rounding a corner, looked down on glinting meanders of the Wylye in the great sweep of its valley, which stretched away towards Heytesbury as far as the eye could see.

But the object of my attentions on this occasion was not the Wylye. It was the River Till — or rather the valley of the Till, because I hardly expected to find much water during August in this most seasonal and unreliable of chalk streams. The Till, you might imagine, should rise at Tilshead, in the heart of Salisbury Plain; and so it does, sometimes, when the winter rains make an informal lake which floods the main road below the village. Last winter it began higher in its coombe, towards Gore Cross, and once, after heavy snow in January 1841, it swept away 74 cottages in the villages along its banks. But it is seldom more than a muddy ditch above Orcheston or Shrewton, and after a dry summer it may only flow for the last three miles, before it joins the Wylye at Serrington.

By Serrington we left the main road, and our journey up the Till began. Stapleford, the first village, has a picture-postcard group of cottages around an interesting church. But I always look out for Rose Cottage, an unremarkable brick house next to the road, which is where, I believe, the composer Vaughan Williams worked on his fifth symphony. This must have been in 1938, when it was still possible, as he recollected doing after tea on just such a summer day as this, to saunter along what has become the A36, all the way to Salisbury. The object of his walk was to visit the cathedral organist, who as night fell took him into the cathedral and played Bach in the cavernous echoing darkness.

Rose Cottage is surrounded by memorable walking country, and I vividly recall the occasions when I climbed Ebsbury from Wishford, and Chain Drove from Stapleford, for the views across the valley. I suggest to fellow *aficionados* that the best way to explore these hills is with a personal stereo playing the third movement of Vaughan Williams's fifth symphony, music which he later revised to invoke the House Beautiful in *The Pilgrim's Progress*. Then you can imagine the 65-year-old composer, the Pilgrim himself, shuffling along behind you... 'I have been wonderful walks on the downs,' he wrote in 1938, 'they were perfect — sun, high wind and wonderful July flowers — the kind I like best.'

The countryside, as our bus took us beyond Stapleford to Berwick St James and Winterbourne Stoke, was somewhat past its summer best. The grass was fading to a pale yellow, and everything seemed to be gasping for rain. The Till was making a pretty feeble show as it flowed under Berwick Bridge, and in a nearby garden a swimming pool was in heavy demand.

Berwick epitomizes the dozens of villages which have settled in the valleys of the chalk rivers converging on Salisbury. Church, pub, manor house and two lines of cottages are spread along a quiet village street, prudently arranged to sit just above the highest point that the river in spate might be expected to reach. Flint under thatch predominates, with stone blocks for the corners and window surrounds. Bands of brick were sometimes incorporated, or blocks of chalk rock or Portland stone to form a chequer pattern with the flint, referred to as 'pepper-and-salt' work. Winterbourne Stoke manor house displays this chequer pattern on the grand scale.

At Winterbourne Stoke we met, joined and left the A303. For the first time our road abandoned the valley and climbed the hillside, until — briefly — we had a downland view of Salisbury Plain, from Yarnbury to Beacon Hill, entirely devoid of houses. It was a rougher and bleaker landscape than we had encountered on our journey so far, and I could vaguely imagine the terrors that earlier generations of travellers felt on first encountering the great and savage Plain. No such qualms for us, cocooned within a Wilts and Dorset bus, and rapidly we descended into the relative suburbia of Shrewton. But no more Till — all that was running through Shrewton was a dry ditch.

Shrewton nowadays has the appearance of a large, unified village. But in reality it is an amalgamation of eight smaller places, which all clustered around this stretch of non-existent river. And they must have been well aware of how unreliable it was, because originally they were nearly all called Winterbourne. Indeed Winterbourne, the stream that only flows in winter, was the name of the River Till itself until about a hundred years ago. Its new name is a misunderstanding of Tilshead, which really derives from someone called Theodwulf, who had a hide of land there. To avoid another confusion all the Winterbourne villages took on second names, mostly after their owners. So we have Rolfe's farm (Rolleston), Elias's farm (Elston), Amesbury nunnery's, or maidens' farm (Maddington), the sheriff's farm (Shrewton), and so on. They have all grown together, and now we think of them as one.

Above Shrewton our bus plodded on to Orcheston, tucked obscurely in the valley, and then we climbed up to the main road once more. This road through Tilshead acts as a corridor across Salisbury Plain, and on each side are slopes of cultivated farmland, concealing the rugged wilderness of the military lands beyond. Tilshead itself is like an oasis in the heart of the Plain, almost as remote as the ill-fated village of Imber, and yet with a main road running through it.

Nobody yet has solved the riddle of Tilshead. Were it not for Domesday Book the riddle would not exist. But there it is, in 1086, listed as a royal and apparently ancient borough, a town with sixty-six burgesses, nearly a hundred other householders or individuals, and nine mills. Nine mills! Windmills had not been invented, so they must have been watermills. But where was the water to drive them? And what on earth were all those people doing in the middle of Salisbury Plain? Nobody really knows. But you can still see from the plan of the present village how it might once have been a town, with a main street widening by the church into a market place, side streets leading off, and back lanes almost encircling it. What seems certain is that Domesday Book recorded it coming to the end of its life as a town. After 1086 it was never so important again, and a few years later Henry I gave most of it away to an abbey in Normandy.

So let me recap. My bus has visited a non-existent town called Tilshead, which is not named after the river called Till, which is not there anyway most of the time, and which until quite recently was not called the Till, but the Winterbourne. And I have been driven through a group of eight

villages, which all used to be called Winterbourne (after the river) which isn't there, and then none of them was called Winterbourne, and now they are all one village, which is called Shrewton. Phew! It is getting hot on this bus. You'll tell me if I start to ramble, won't you...?

Time

Capsules

Match of the Day

SUNDAY FOOTBALL (remember the European and World Cup finals) is nothing new. During the Puritan 17th century, when the national game, along with other Sunday amusements (dancing, cock-fighting, happy hours in the pub) were forbidden, Wiltshire villagers often fell foul of the church authorities. In 1614 John Cheney of Everleigh was reprimanded for going out of his parish to 'footeball' on the sabbath. In mitigation he told the court that he was only there, on Collingbourne Down, as an onlooker for the space of an hour and a half (evidently the game did not go to extra time), and that he made it home in time for evening prayer. Richard Bowles of Tisbury, perhaps Wiltshire's first football hooligan, was in court the following year. He had become 'overtaken with drink' and was accused of 'unseemly fighting in the company at footeball'.

Puritan ministers were hard on sabbath-breakers, and so were some Victorians. Francis Kilvert recalled being told that the rector of Langley Burrell habitually lurked on the touchline at Langley Common on Sundays. 'He used to come round quietly under the trees and bide his time till the football came near him when he would catch up the ball and pierce the bladder with a pin.' So next time the footballers outwitted him; they took along a spare bladder.

History does not record who won these matches, although one cautious scholar has concluded that football was played more in the chalklands than in north Wiltshire. John Aubrey believed that Bishop's Cannings could have challenged all England at football. Mind you, we just don't know how good the England squad was in the 17th century.

[**Sources:** WRO D1/39/2/7, f.72; D2/4/1/12, f.197; Kilvert, *Diaries*, 4.2.1873; Aubrey, *Natural History*, p.109]

Light Relief

A SMALL WILTSHIRE CELEBRATION on August 3rd (1996) was perhaps in order. On or about that date in 1596, 400 years ago precisely, Sir John Harington announced to the public his invention of a 'devise'. A ladies' man at court, Sir John translated book 28 of Ariosto's *Orlando Furioso* (which is rather rude) to titillate the maids of honour. Queen Elizabeth was not amused, and as his punishment made him translate all the rest.

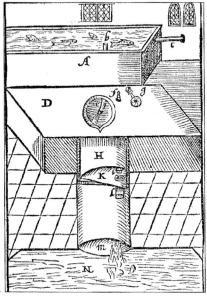

His invention stemmed from a conversation between four eminent house-guests, including himself and Sir Henry Danvers of Dauntsey, and their host, Sir Matthew Arundell, at Wardour Castle. What they had come up with was something which, unchanged in most important details, we all still use every day — the water closet! Not sure about the wisdom of keeping fish in the cistern, but otherwise, full marks — a Wiltshire brainwave.

[**Source:** Sir John Harington, *A new discourse...* (ed. Donno), 1962]

The Merchant's House

THE BLACKEST DAY in Marlborough's history was 28th April 1653, when fire took hold on a tannery at the west end of the High Street, and swept along the houses and shops, destroying much of the town. 'The most furious fire that ever mortall creature ever saw,' wrote Thomas Bayly, a wealthy silk merchant, in a letter two days later. 'We were all in the dust within three or foure houres.' Bayly's house was destroyed, and most of his stock was plundered, lost or burnt. His losses totalled £2,339, a small fortune. He set about rebuilding, nevertheless, and in 3 years 5 months he had reached roof level.

Such precision is possible because, scratched in the attic plastering of the house he rebuilt, now 132 High Street, is the date 10th October 1656. On my way to look at it I was shown too the sumptuous panelling and fireplace of the first-floor chamber, the remains of boldly striped wall paintings in the dining room, and the *trompe-l'oeil* painted balustrades up the staircases. The tasteful opulence of the 17th-century owners, though crumbling and fragile, is still everywhere apparent.

The Bayly family's home is now called the Merchant's House, but most Marlburians will remember it as W.H. Smith's former shop. When Smith's moved out Marlborough Town Council, recognizing its architectural worth, bought the house and leased it in 1992 to a newly-formed Merchant's House Trust, with the intention that it be opened as a Museum of Seventeenth Century Life, incorporating a study centre and museum for Marlborough's history.

❧

A Lonely Fragment

VISITING THE CRICKLADE AREA recently, I was reminded of an argument which was rumbling on a century ago, in 1896. It had begun in 1892, when the respected Wiltshire architect, C.E. Ponting, reported on Leigh (pronounced *lie*) parish church. It was in ramshackle condition, low-lying, damp, and often flooded; the parishioners wanted to abandon it and build anew. But by the late 1880s the ruthless tide of church restoration and rebuilding was ebbing, and campaigns to preserve 'unspoilt' churches were under way. Inglesham, nearby, was rescued through the efforts of William Morris and his friends in 1888-9.

Ponting, impressed by the architectural interest of Leigh Church, was sympathetic, and proposed repairs and improvements, including making a weatherproof access to it. His report was rejected, however, and an enquiry decided that a church on a new site was essential. The archdeacon suggested a compromise, that nave, tower and porch be carefully moved to the new site, while the chancel should remain behind.

Ponting agreed that this was feasible, and in March 1896 the necessary permission was obtained. Morris's Society for the Protection of Ancient Buildings objected, but work began nevertheless, and continued through 1897 under Ponting's supervision, every stone and timber being replaced in its original position. The reconstructed church was opened in February 1898. Meanwhile the vicar had discovered the bowl of the medieval font, missing since 1638, in a pub at Ashton Keynes, where it had graduated from a cattle trough to a cheese-press.

The old chancel at the Leigh is an atmospheric building, a lonely fragment in a churchyard overgrown with wild flowers. It is beautifully maintained, and inside the medieval shell are 18th-century painted texts and woodwork. To find it, park at Waterhay Bridge car park, walk up the lane towards the Leigh, and look for signpost to the right (SU058928). [**Sources:** WRO 1431/12-12a; *WAM*, vols. 27, pp.121-3; 29, pp.87-8; 30, pp.35-8]

❧

The End of the Road

MODERN PROBLEMS may have long histories. Road rage, for instance, often fuelled by alcoholic bravado, was common among 19th-century stagecoach drivers. Much earlier, around 1249, Adam son of Maud was run over at Bremhill, and his death was only one of nine waggon-related casualties preserved among court records in that year. Road accidents have been a perennial problem. The North Wiltshire coroner dealt with twelve fatalities during a 6-month period in 1777. Most involved falling (sometimes intoxicated) from a waggon or a horse; others occurred to

children playing in the road, or when horses ran out of control and vehicles crashed. Such was the fate of John Biggs and his companion at Horton, near Bishop's Cannings, in 1785, when their cheese waggon overturned and trapped them. The coroner recorded that they suffocated.
[**Sources:** Meekings (ed.), *Crown pleas...1249* (WRS, vol.16), no.219 etc; Hunnisett (ed.), *Wiltshire coroners' bills, 1752-1796* (WRS, vol.36), nos.1035-71, 1445-6]

ॐ

Sticky Little Fingers

● ●

YOU DON'T SEE so many people blackberrying these days. Stung knees and scratched thumbs are abiding memories of my childhood, followed by the all-important weighing of the contents of our plastic bags. So I am indebted to Ivor Slocombe for some extraordinary statistics from nearly eighty years ago, contained in a paper about education in Wiltshire during the first world war.

As part of the war effort in 1917 and 1918, schools were encouraged to pick blackberries, to make jam for the army and navy. In the former year 172 Wiltshire schools took part, and they collected 15,315 lbs, which I think is nearly 7 tons. At Ashton Keynes alone a grand total of 1,715 lbs was achieved, by devoting 7 half-holidays to the effort spread over about a month. Their record was 355 lbs on a single afternoon, 4th October. In 1918 the county total was much larger: 280 schools took part, and over 88 tons of blackberries were collected.

Acorns, horse chestnuts and fir cones were also gathered, not for jam, but to be distilled for acetone, which was used in making cordite. Castle Combe school collected 84 bushels of acorns in November 1917. One school which declined to take part in the scheme was Tidworth. The fields and hedgerows all around them were used as firing ranges, and by airmen for practising bombing missions.
[**Source**: *WAM* vol.90, pp.132-3]

ॐ

Go Forth upon thy Journey

• •

THE PREHISTORIC BARROWS of Wiltshire are identified by their G numbers (Amesbury G58, for instance), in recognition of the archaeologist who meticulously investigated and catalogued them during the 1950s. Leslie Grinsell was a remarkable man, who by the time of his death in 1995, aged 88, had compiled inventories of barrows in much of southern, eastern and midland England. He lived in Bristol, and did not drive; the course of his archaeological forays was governed by the location not only of the barrows, but also of bus stops and tea-shops. Shorts above long woolly socks were his preferred attire, and gave him the appearance of an old-fashioned scoutmaster.

Of one so knowledgeable about burial rites it might be expected that his own funeral plans would be carefully laid. From an obituary I discovered that Leslie announced his own 'departure for eternity' in *The Times*. Then, with his lederhosen, his walking stick, a fez brought back from war service in Egypt, and an apple turnover for his journey, he was cremated. The ashes were placed in a replica Bronze Age urn, taken to a barrow on the Mendips where they were scattered, and then the urn was ritually smashed.

[**Source:** *Proc. Dorset NHAS*, vol.117, pp.177-8]

ॐ

Happy Events at Wishford

• •

THE HATCHER SOCIETY, Salisbury's senior local history society, celebrated its fortieth birthday in 1996. The brainchild of the ebullient Hugh Shortt and Dora Robertson, both long departed, it once boasted a membership of 250 (and a waiting list). One founder member, Betty Hurdle, joined in the tea and birthday cake, at a talk and party for about thirty members at Wilton Carpet Factory. The splendid cake, ceremoniously cut by Lady Paskin (a former secretary and chairman) and the late Stella Pooley (then chairman), included a portrait of Henry Hatcher, the 19th-century historian of Salisbury, in whose honour the society was named.

Earlier in the evening the society met at Great Wishford, where Lady Paskin lectured about the church and village. With a passing allusion to modern fertility drugs, she described the medieval memorial to Thomas and Edith Bonham. Edith, according to tradition, gave birth to twins, an extravagance which so alarmed Thomas that he ran away for seven years. After he had returned Edith was confined again. This time, the legend tells us, she produced septuplets, who were all brought to church in a sieve to be baptized. Much later the churchwardens bought a fire engine, presumably to dampen the ardour of any like-minded parishioners.

[**See:** Lady Paskin's church guide, 1983 ed., pp.33ff.]

ॐ

Gone to Soldiers, Every One

● ●

A PROCESS which changed the face of south Wiltshire began a little more than a century ago. In January 1897 a widespread rumour was confirmed that, for the previous two months, land agents acting for the Government were purchasing estates on Salisbury Plain for military training, around Amesbury, Figheldean, and Tidworth. During 1897-9 over 41,000 acres were acquired, comprising most of the present central and eastern training areas.

Behind the decision lay several factors. The army was modernizing itself and developing new techniques; war-clouds were gathering in South Africa; and land on Salisbury Plain, following the agricultural depression of the 1880s, had become (according to one landlord) 'practically unsaleable on any terms'. Most people seem to have welcomed this new opportunity for a depressed region; landowners, in particular, were pleased by the generous terms being offered for their land.

Some, however, had mixed feelings. The squire of Netheravon, Sir Michael Hicks Beach, felt that military training should be directed elsewhere — to Cannock Chase or Aldershot — and he was one of eight owners whose land had to be compulsorily purchased. And that must have caused embarrassment, and not a few eyebrows raised. In line with his neighbours he received nearly £12 per acre for his vast estate, over £93,000 in all, and as he was Chancellor of the Exchequer at the time, he presumably had to sign the cheque himself.

[**Source:** N.D.G. James, *Plain Soldiering*, 1987, pp.9-19; *Devizes Gazette*, 10.8.1899, p.6]

⁊

Dauntsey Tales... 1

● ●

I HAD ALWAYS UNDERSTOOD that Bishop's Cannings was the place for off-beat occurrences, but maybe it has a rival in Dauntsey. Most Dauntsey stories involve Lady Meux, as Val Reece (a notorious hostess at the Casino de Venice, Holborn) became, when she married into the aristocracy in 1878. Remind me to tell you sometime about the elephant and the Beaufort Hunt, and the interconnecting bedrooms (that's two separate stories, you understand). Meanwhile here is something for eagle-eyed church visitors.

During his lifetime Sir Henry Meux lavished jewellery on his wife, and his death in 1900 made her one of the richest women in England. The glass in the east window of Dauntsey church is her tribute to his memory. Biblical scenes flank a saint or angel of striking beauty, modelled on her ladyship. 'It is,' wrote the historian of Dauntsey, 'one of the very few representations of an angelic figure wearing ear-rings.'

[**Source:** P.Phillips, *The Meux succession...*, 1986]

⁊

Dauntsey Tales... 2

● ●

WHEN I TOLD MY WIFE about the ear-rings she reminded me of another Dauntsey story, which has nothing to do with Lady Meux. In December 1877, the local newspaper carried a long and congratulatory account of the official opening of the Malmesbury branch railway, which had overcome all manner of difficulties in order to connect the town to the main line at Dauntsey. Buried later in the same issue is a much smaller news item, headed 'Accident on the Railway'. It is the stuff of those panic dreams which wake you up in a cold sweat.

Between Dauntsey and Great Somerford there was a level crossing controlled by a pair of massive wooden gates, and a gatekeeper's house, all brand new of course. As the first scheduled train on the day after the opening approached this crossing, it became clear that the gatekeeper, a man of 35 years' unblemished railway service, had omitted to open the gates. The train 'dashed through, shivering the gates to atoms'.

And the old man's explanation for his oversight? When he had gone to open the gates the door handle had come off in his hand, leaving him trapped inside his house, and a helpless spectator to the impending disaster. A spokesman for the railway company (in that timeless tradition) announced that an inquiry would be held.

[**Source:** *Wilts and Glos Standard*, 22.12.1877]

Small is Beautiful

RECENT DISAGREEMENTS at Aldbourne over its replacement church organ recall a debate which began in Wiltshire in the 1850s. John Baron, rector of Upton Scudamore, was raising money for church restoration, but could not afford the prices quoted for a new organ. Anyway, he mused, why should a small village church need a powerful and expensive instrument? Surely the organ was to assist, not to drown, the congregational singing?

So, with one of his parishioners, he designed a simple organ himself. It worked, and they set up in business supplying other churches. They built more than twenty organs, moved to premises in Warminster, and in 1858 persuaded a famous London organ-builder, Henry Willis, to go into mass production. Soon they could boast more than 200 orders.

Baron wrote a book advocating Scudamore organs, and demonstrated one at an architectural congress in Oxford. The 'organist' was a servant lad who had learnt a few tunes, and because there was no room on the platform for a seat, he had to execute the pieces standing on one leg, and working the bellows with the other.

[**Source:** J.Baron, *Scudamore organs...*, 1858, Bath Ref. Library]

After Yew

GIRTH MEASUREMENTS, writes Hilary Lees, can be used as a rule of thumb for dating yew trees, and she estimates the ages of the oldest yews recorded in Wiltshire churchyards. Alderbury, Alton Priors, Longbridge Deverill, and Lyneham, all appear to have trees of 1,500-1,700 years old, and Tisbury's is reckoned to be 4,000. Other oldies are at Dinton, Edington, and Kilmington.

Now just let those statistics sink in! In each case (and there are hundreds more across the country) these venerated trees are older than the church, indeed, as old as Christianity itself in Britain. The church must have replaced something earlier on an already sacred site. Roman remains beneath churchyards are not unusual, and at Ogbourne St Andrew there is a prehistoric barrow next to the church. The continuity and longevity of churchyards is staggering.

Hallowed Ground: the churchyards of Wiltshire, is Hilary's excellent book (Picton Publishing, £8.95). She covers every aspect of her subject, including history and folklore, lychgates, walls, tombstones and memorials of all kinds, epitaphs, lettering, and churchyards as nature reserves. She also deals in greater detail with twenty particularly interesting churchyards. Hallowed ground indeed.

ﻩ

Episcopal Indigestion

MY NAMESAKE was consecrated Bishop of Salisbury in December 1417, and his enthronement took place during the following April. He was already a well known figure around the diocese, having been Dean for more than a decade, and before that a residentiary canon. So Bishop Chandler would have had plenty of friends to invite to the banquet which he threw upon his installation. I recently came across the menu.

The first course included: Venison in boiled wheat; 'Cyprus food'; boiled capon; swan; pheasant; peacock; meatballs in jelly; sliced meat; and fruit tart. Between courses was an ambitious paste confection, known as a subtlety, depicting the Lamb of God. Then on to the second course: a choice of two soups ('Royal' and 'Golden'); piglet; kid; crane; roast venison; heron; stuffed pulses; partridge; spiced sliced meat; and currant and date pie. Then another subtlety, representing a leopard. And to follow: 'Royal' mince; bitterne; curlew; pigeon; rabbits; doterells; quails; larks; 'red-hot' food; sliced meat; date fritters; puff pastry; and jelly. Then, in case anyone had not had enough poultry, one final ornithological touch — the last subtlety was an eagle.

[**Source:** Early English Text Society, vol.91, 1888, pp.60-1]

ॐ

Still Waiting
● ●

LONG-AWAITED is the overworked cliche brought out whenever a new by-pass is proposed, announced, or completed. Until deleted from the roadbuilding programme, the Salisbury by-pass was certainly longer-awaited than most people realise. Here are the comments of a visitor to Salisbury after he had walked along the Town Path towards Harnham.

'One evening, during the late summer of this wettest season, when the rain was beginning to cease, I went out this way for my stroll, the pleasantest if not the only "walk" there is in Salisbury. It is true, there are two others: one to Wilton by its long, shady avenue; the other to Old Sarum; but these are now motor-roads, and until the loathed hooting and dusting engines are thrust away into roads of their own there is little pleasure in them for the man on foot.'

The passage is from *A Shepherd's Life*, by W.H. Hudson, which was published in 1910, nearly ninety years ago. His sentiment reflected Lloyd George's 1909 budget speech, which set up the Road Board. This was given powers (not immediately used) to build new roads primarily confined to motor traffic, to widen and straighten existing roads, and to make deviations round villages. By-pass construction began in earnest in about 1920 (Croydon and Eltham were among the first), and by 1928 some 226 miles of by-passes had been or were being built.

[**Source**: C.D. Buchanan, *Mixed Blessing*, 1958]

ĐE FONETIC NIIZ.

CONDUCTED BF ĐE PROPRIETUR, ALECSANDER J. ELIS, B.A.

NR 1.]

SATÉRDA, 6 JANUERI, 1849.

[PRIS 4½d. STAMPT.
Per Cwarter in advạns, 4s. 6d.

(FACTS FOR SPELLERS OF THE OLD SCHOOL.

READER! Do you ask why we propose to change the English orthography? We reply:—

1. IT IS A FACT, that no one can tell the sound of an English word from its spelling.

Proof.—To *read* the book he has *read*; to *present* a *present*, the *slough* of a snake found in a *slough*; *lead* me to the *lead* mine; *refuse* the *refuse*, &c., &c.; the words in italics are pronounced differently, that is, are different spoken words, according to their meaning alone; and there are 201 words of this kind in our language, which are pronounced in 405 different ways.—2. The same combination of letters has very different significations in different words: compare *hear, heart, heart; here, where; bow, shoe; row, cow, sow (o), doth; eyed, keyed, conveyed, journeyed;* and so on, in an infinite number of cases.—3. There is a very large number of words concerning the pronunciation of which even orthoepists are not agreed: as, *knowledge,* (nol-ledge, no-ledge); *leisure,* (lee-zhur, laih-ur); *intinical, inimical,* and so on.—4. No one can be sure of the pronunciation of any word he has not previously been taught; let the reader try the unusual words, *balmon, beaufin, rowlock, bour-geoise* (type); and the names of places and persons, *Beaulieu, Le-mincol, Hucklesgu,* and so on. Turn the page and read:—

ᴡǝᴜᴉɔ ɯɐʞ Ꮷᴉɯᴉ ᴉᴉᴉʞ ᴦᴉᴉᴉƆ ʍᴉᴉ ᴦᴉᴉᴦ ʍᴉᴉᴦᴉ ꓷꓷᴉᴦ ᴉᴉ

2. IT IS A FACT, that no one can tell the spelling of an English word from its sound.

Proof.—1. There are 405 spoken words, spelled in 537 ways; but the variations of the spelling never depend on the sound, and cannot be learned from it.—2. There are upwards of 1509 words, about the spelling of which authors are not agreed.—3. Thé style of spelling cannot even be predicted from a knowledge of etymology; compare *fancy phantom, concede succeed, island bay, husband house, rhyme, ghost, city, flys flies, burgess bourgeoise burgher,* &c., &c.—4. No sound in the language is uniformly represented by the same sign.—

The sign (ʹ) is prefixed to l, m, n, to show that they form syllables by themselves; thus, *litʹl, spazʹm, opʹn*=little, spasm, open. The parentheses () indicate that the inclosed words are not spelled phonetically.)

ĐE ENGLISH FONETIC ALFABET.

The letter			is always	The letter		is always
written,	praind	sounded as		written,	praind	sounded as
Ɛ Ɛ	Ɛ ɛ	*ee* .. in *eel*		*Р p*	Рp	p .. in *pole*
A a	A a	*a* .. *ate*		*B b*	B b	b .. *bowl*
A a	A a	*a* .. *alms*		*T t*	T t	t .. *toe*
Ɔ ɔ	Ɔ ɔ	*a* .. *all*		*D d*	D d	d .. *doe*
O o	O o	*o* .. *ope*		*Ɔ ɔ*	C c	ch .. *cheer*
U u	U u	*oo* .. *food*		*J j*	J j	j .. *jeer*
				C c	C c	c .. *came*
I i	I i	i .. *ill*		*G g*	G g	g .. *game*
E e	E e	e .. *ell*				
A a	A a	a .. *at*		*F f*	F f	f .. *fear*
O o	O o	o .. *olive*		*V v*	V v	v .. *veer*
U u	U u	u .. *up*		*T t*	T t	th .. *thigh*
U u	U u	oo .. *foot*		*Ð ð*	Ð ð	th .. *thy*
				S s	S s	s .. *seal*
I i	I i	i .. *isle*		*Z z*	Z z	z .. *zeal*
O o	O o	oi .. *oil*		*Ʃ ʃ*	Ʃ ʃ	c .. *vicious*
Ǝ ǝ	Ǝ ǝ	ow .. *owl*		*Ʒ ʒ*	Ʒ ʒ	s .. *vision*
U u	U u	u .. *mule*		*R r*	R r	r .. *rare*
Y y	Y y	y .. *yea*		*L l*	L l	l .. *lull*
W w	W w	w .. *way*		*M m*	M m	m .. *mum*
				N n	N n	n .. *nun*
H h	H h	h .. *hay*		*Ŋ ŋ*	Ŋ ŋ	ng .. *sing*

Adjunal leters for foren sundz: hwig du not ocúr in Inglif.

rit'n,	printd	Er leter rit'n,	printd	is alwaz sunded as
A a	A a	A á	freng	(é)
A a	A á	A á	freng	(á)
U u	U ú	U ú	freng	(ú)
E e	E é	E é	freng	(eú)
		E é	freng	(e)
A a	A ạ	A ạ	fr. fort	(aú)
O o	O ọ	O ọ	fr. fort	(ọ)
O o	O ọ	O ọ	fr. fort	(ụ)
A ñ	A ñ		ɑñ	freng	(uṇ)
O ñ	O ñ		oñ	reng	(ọṇ)
O ñ	O ñ		oiñ	freng	(uṇ)
U ñ	U ñ		uñ	freng	(oṇ)

rit'n,	printd	is alwaz sunded as
Ḥl ḥl	Ḥl ḥl	welf (ḷ)
Ḥr ḥr	Ḥr ḥr	welf (ꝛ)
L l	L ḷ	ital'yạn (ḷ)
N ŋ	N ŋ	ital'yạn (ŋ)
K k	K k	jerman (cḥ)
Q q	Q q	dug (ɣ)
Ɔ ɔ	Ɔ ɔ	árabic ʻǝin
IƷ ʒ	IƷ ʒ	polỵ (ɣ)

Er stroṇli prẹnạst dúbḷe leters cẹr indẹcẹted in rit'n, bị subscrịbịṇ, and in print bị prefịcsiṇ, a dot, đus, *Mu.hámməd Ádẹ ʼAcbm=net Áli*.

For furđer partịcụlars, and đặ samebls, fẹr intẹrmẹdiet sundz, se đe Eserçạịz on Fonetics, bị Alecsander Jon Elis, B.A.

Đẹ ịgnorạnt or foren longwejẹs ạr advịzd tụ prọnọns

á, ȧ, ẻ, e, ọ, ȯ, i, k, ḏ, ḡ, ẻ; ca ᴀ, ᴀ̇, ᴏ, ᴏ̇, ᴏ̈, ᴘ, ᴘ̇, ǝ, ȯ, ȯ̇.

respectivli, tụ omit ᴀ, ọnd tụ dịsrẹgạ́rd đẹ more or strọṇ leterẹ, ụntil đẹ cạn lẹrn đẹ trụ sundẹ. In freng ǝ, ᴀ mạ bẹ prọnạst as ar, ᴘ, ọnd ọ̇, ᴀ os ᴀ, ᴀ̇; in jerman ọ, ọ mạ be sṗọk'n lịẹ ạ, ᴀ, ọnd ọ̇ rịle oi, oiḥ̇; ọ̇ sịn (ᴘ̇ in plạst ovr đe vọl ᴀ ịs ọnsẹrtẹd slịtlị, ọr ọ̇t ọl os clọsẹ. Hwen ịt ịs nọt prịntẹd, đẹ wordẹ mụst be red as ịf ịt stụd

1) ọn đẹ lạst slịb'l lọst sẹns ọv ọl wụrdẹ ọr ọl wụrdẹ ẹndịṇ ịn ẻ or ịẹs, ọnd ọr ọl wụrdẹ hav'ṇ ᴀ, 𝑦 or ᴀ 𝑦 befọ̈r đạr lạst vọwẹl, ọr ọl wụrdẹ havịṇ os e, e, ẻ, ɔ, ᴀ, 𝐴, ẻ, or ᴀ ịn đạr lạst slịb'l bụt wẹn; ọnd

2) ọn đẹ lạst slịb'l ị bụt tụ ọv ọl ụđer wụrdẹ. Wụrdẹ bolḏ prịntẹd ịn cạpịtalẹ, ọnd frenẹ wụrdẹ, (hwig hạv nọ rẹgụlạrḷị ọcsentẹd slịb'l) hạvn đẹ ọnḷ ecsersịsn đẹ đẹ ọđ'r rulẹ.

REDUCED FACSIMILE OF THE TOP PORTION OF THE FIRST PAGE OF

"THE PHONETIC NEWS"

Fonetic Niuz

ISAAC PITMAN, who died in 1887, spent his life championing two causes. One, the use of phonetic spelling (as advocated in a short-lived journal, *Fonetic Niuz*, in 1849) fell largely on deff eerz. But phonography, his system of shorthand based on sounds rather than letters, won him worldwide fame.

The son of a Trowbridge millowner, he worked in a local cloth factory before training as a teacher. He invented phonography in 1837, when still in his twenties, and by 1887 (the invention's golden jubilee) and his knighthood in 1894, it was reckoned that 95% of reporters in the English-speaking world were using his system. There is a permanent display devoted to him in Trowbridge Museum.

In his lifetime, just as in ours, society underwent an information revolution, as newspapers, government reports and bureaucracy proliferated. Perhaps Isaac Pitman, and the printing press and Phonetic Institute which disseminated his ideas, should be seen as the Victorian equivalent of the software wizards of today.

[**Sources**: A. Baker, *Life of Isaac Pitman*, 1908; WAM, vol.29, pp.212-13]

⁂

Shut that Door!

I THOUGHT that we might begin collecting sobriquets — you know, 'Bradford gudgeons, Aldbourne dabchicks', that sort of thing. While I am out looking, here's a somewhat similar story about Purton.

For reasons long obscure it used to be said, when someone left a door open, 'Oh, you must come from Purton!' During World War One a young soldier, who did come from Purton but did not know the saying, was serving in France. To his astonishment, having left a door open, he was shouted at by an apparently clairvoyant fellow-soldier, from Cornwall, 'Oh, you come from Purton!'

'What do you know of Purton?' he exclaimed, to discover that the Cornishman had no idea where Purton was, only that it was the place where they never shut doors.

[**Source:** Ethel Richardson, *The Story of Purton*, 1919, pp.105-6]

૨ટ

The Bishop and his Flock

MEDIEVAL BISHOPS were very big businessmen, and none bigger than Winchester plc. Perusing his annual accounts for 1301-2, recently published in the Hampshire Record Series, I find that the Bishop of Winchester then owned nearly sixty manors and ten boroughs in seven counties, including a number in Wiltshire, such as Downton.

Accounts survive for most years from 1208, and present a wonderfully detailed glimpse of estate management and everyday medieval life. On and on, page after page, manor after manor, everything was accounted for, down to the last farthing. In Downton in 1302, for instance, 322 summer cheeses were made (from cow's and sheep's milk), two every day from 12 April to 24 August, and thereafter only one. It was a bad year for piglets (only 39), and 89 of the 547 lambs had died of the murrain before weaning. Two feeble old plough-horses were sold, for four and five shillings, and some running repairs were needed for the carts. There were thirteen peacocks, and a shilling was raised by selling their feathers. Mending the park gate cost sixpence, and 2,500 nails were bought for re-roofing the stable. Oh, and the bailiff bought a new tablecloth and a towel.

[**Source:** Mark Page, *The Pipe-Roll of the Bishop of Winchester, 1301-2*, 1996 (HRS, vol.14)]

૨ટ

The London Apprentice

NOT TO BE OUTDONE, the Wiltshire Record Society's 1997 volume is, at one level, a fascinating collection of hard luck stories. Wiltshire people swarmed to London during the 19th century to make their fortunes, but many fell on hard times. In 1817 the Wiltshire Society was formed by county noblemen and gentry with London connections as an apprenticing charity, to assist children from poor Wiltshire families living in the capital to train for a worthwhile career. Around 1,000 apprenticeships were funded by the Society up to 1922, mostly in London but some within Wiltshire, and Mr Bob Henly of Swindon has edited the Society's record books to present brief portraits of them all.

Albert Kilminster, apprenticed for six years in 1855 to a City Road cabinet carver, is typical. His parents came from Calne and Derry Hill, and moved to Spitalfields so that his father could work as a tailor. But father's employment was precarious, and his eyesight was failing, so that it was becoming a struggle to support his family. The apprenticeship gave young Albert his big break.

By 1871 over 27,000 Wiltshire natives lived in Greater London. *The Apprentice Registers of the Wiltshire Society 1817-1922*, describes what happened to a few of them. My sympathies are with George Walkerdine, who in 1892 was apprenticed for seven years in the Barbican to an account book ruler. Fine for the first morning, until he got the hang of it. But just imagine the tedium of the other 6 years 364 and a half days.

à

The Snuff Maker's Assistant

COMPOST ELSEWHERE, perhaps, but to a Wiltshireman 6X means only one thing. So I was intrigued to discover that Wadworth's used to brew 2X and 4X as well. My source is *Devizes Voices*, a smartly produced book of oral reminiscences.

Also in the chapter about working life is a graphic description of snuff milling. No-one in their right mind would have wanted to be the snuff maker's assistant, recalled Arthur Cleverly of his days at Anstie's factory in New Park Street. Snuff was made from waste, old, or damaged tobacco, including the factory sweepings, which was moistened in heaps until well rotted, then dried and milled. The milling rooms had low ceilings, no ventilation, and windows which remained shut on the hottest of days. 'When they started to grind it was just like a brown fog in the room. No masks were worn and the first time you did it you lasted only about an

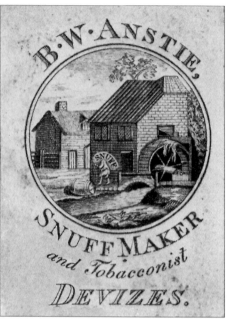

Snuff labels

hour before you had to rush from the room and be very sick. You could feel yourself filling up with snuff, your mouth was coated with it, it was in your ears and nose and clothes.'

[**Source:** David Buxton, *Devizes Voices*, 1996]

ટ⁀

Madam Arundell her Booke

● ●

COUGHING AND SPLUTTERING? Troubled with garden pests? Try this, from a book of remedies dated 1677, among the archives of the Arundell family of Wardour Castle, in the Wiltshire and Swindon Record Office.

'Sirrope of snailes my Lady Herons way: Take halfe a pecke of snailes in the shell, scatter half a handfull of salt upon them in a halfe tobb [*tub*] with good store of green fenell and lett them cleane themselves all night. In the morning wash them well and dry them with a cloth. Then putt them to fresh fenell and after they have clensed themselves take a bodkin [a large pin] and make a hole quite through it [i.e. *them*], then fill the hole with the best refined sugar, and putt them into a jely bagg, and they will drop the oyle that will cure any cough or commution but death. If you please to putt a quarter of a peint of clarret wine into the bagg amongst the snailes. Take a good spoonfull as soon as you wake, and another an houre before dinner, another att 4 of the clocke and att the goeing to bed. They must be so well cleansed that what they drop be cleare, not green. Try sugar insteed of salt. You may wash them with a little clarett before you putt sugar or putt them into the bagge.'

Alternatively, if you are 'troubled with a cold moyst braine', here is just the thing. It will make you 'voyde a great deale of rume'... Perhaps not.

[**Source:** WRO 2667/12/39, pp.35-6, 69-70]

Ϩ▲

A Stonehenge Symphony

'IT HUMS', exclaimed Tess, as she and Angel Clare listened to the wind playing on the edifice, like the note of some gigantic one-stringed harp. The closing pages of Hardy's tragedy, where Tess stumbles at night on Stonehenge, is arrested, and taken to Winchester for execution, have profoundly moved many, including the composer Ralph Vaughan Williams. The published score of his last symphony (his ninth, first performed in the year of his death, 1958) has no programmatic notes, but the composer himself hinted that there had once been a programme.

A few years ago Alain Frogley examined the sketches and manuscripts of the symphony, now in the British Library, and collected evidence for the lost programme. The second movement, the heart of the piece, has its opening theme inscribed on the manuscript 'Stonehenge', and the main idea of the central section is marked 'Tess'. The Stonehenge theme, played by a solo flugel horn, is juxtaposed against a menacing march, perhaps representing the stones' brutal pagan past. 'What monstrous place is this?' we seem to hear Angel saying. Later in the movement a bell tolls seven times, is interrupted by the sinister march, and is heard once more, signifying (as in the book) the 8 o'clock execution. Then the 'Tess' theme returns, and the music is transcended.

[**Source:** *Thomas Hardy Society Journal*, vol.2(3), Oct.1986, pp.50-5]

₰

A Quickie Divorce

STILL IN HARDYESQUE VEIN, devotees will recall that Michael Henchard, later to be the Mayor of Casterbridge, sold his wife at Weyhill Fair for five guineas (£5.25). Hardy set this episode shortly before 1830, and claimed that it was based on a genuine wife-selling incident at or near Dorchester. So Melksham readers may be interested to learn that in August 1833 one Isaac Spencer led his wife into their market place, with a halter round her neck, in the belief that selling her there would constitute a legal divorce. She was apparently quite willing to try a change of circumstances.

He sold her to William Watts, and both men were remanded in gaol. Watts was found not guilty of a misdemeanour, but Spencer was sentenced to three months' imprisonment and a £1 fine. Still, you might think, he would have plenty of change from his five guineas. But no, unlike the fictional Mrs Henchard, the real Mrs Spencer was not so highly valued. He had sold her for two-and-sixpence (12.5 pence).

[**Sources:** WRO A1/125/59; W.Dowding, *Statistics of Crime*]

₰

A Faithful and Enduring Record

RED CARNATIONS AND CHRYSANTHEMUMS decked a modest memorial in Salisbury Cathedral's north aisle over Christmas. They were placed there after evensong on 14th December 1996 by members of the Hatcher Society, to mark the 150th anniversary of the death of Henry

Hatcher.

When I am in the Cathedral, I usually pay his monument a visit. His epitaph, unlike many, rings true: 'A man of simple manners, deep and varied learning, silent and unobtrusive piety.' For a few years he was Salisbury's postmaster, and later ran a school, writing and researching all the while. The publication of his leviathan history of Salisbury in 1843 was surrounded by acrimony, as co-authorship was claimed on its title-page by the city's chief executive, Robert Benson, who had in fact contributed very little. Those in the know always refer to 'Benson and Hatcher' simply as 'Hatcher' (though I recently heard of it being called 'Benson and Hedges'), and it is after him alone that the history society and the local historical journal, *The Hatcher Review*, are named.

இ

On Closer Examination

● ●

LEAD BADGES were popular in the middle ages, and were worn either as souvenirs of pilgrimages, or to commemorate events, or as livery badges to denote allegiance to a master. Many have been found in Wiltshire, especially in the river-bed at Salisbury, and once conserved and identified, they have interesting stories to tell. But two of these apparently medieval trinkets gave archaeologists a shock. One, discovered at Westbury Leigh around 1993 (now in Devizes Museum), was cleaned up to reveal part of a hot air balloon. The other, found in the Avon at Salisbury in 1987, carried part of an inscription, now reconstructed to read 'Birmingham and Leverpool Rail Road'. The badge depicts an early locomotive.

[**Source:** *WAM*, vol.90, 1997, pp.145-7]

இ

A Piper at the Gates of Dawn

UNTIL the railway works closed in 1986 hooters were a regular feature of Swindon life. The steamship-style version in use in the 1860s had a range of 12-15 miles, and sounded every morning at 5.15, 5.45, and 6 o'clock. Lord Bolingbroke's bedroom at Lydiard Park was well within earshot, and during the two months each year when he was in residence on his country estate for the shooting, he was repeatedly woken by 'a loud piercing, roaring and distracted noise', which he claimed was detrimental to his health (the pheasants perhaps felt a similar grievance).

Not a man to take his unsolicited early morning call lying down, in 1873 he campaigned publicly for the withdrawal of its licence (yes, it needed a licence). Well, Lord Bolingbroke seems to have found himself in a minority of one. According to a petition 4,339 people in and around Swindon rather liked the hooter. Without it, they claimed, they would oversleep and be late for work.

At first his lordship's weak heart was regarded as sufficient cause for the licence to be revoked, but a massive groundswell of opposition reversed the decision. Lord Bolingbroke, as one protester pointed out, lived in London for ten months of the year, and 'the workmen might as well say when they had their trip to London that Big Ben should be stopped'.

After much acrimony the old steam whistle was abandoned, to be replaced by a new atmospheric one. Lord Bolingbroke may not have been very pleased, but his weak heart seems not to have minded. He died at Lydiard Park 25 years later, in 1899, aged 80.

[**Source:** Thamesdown Borough Council, *Lord Bolingbroke and the Swindon Hooter*, pamphlet, 1996]

&

A Legend in his Lunchtime

IF YOU DON'T possess a watch, and you're mowing in a field miles from a clock, how do you make sure that you've taken your full hour for lunch? R.H. Wilson, who farmed at Bishopstone east of Swindon, discovered the trick from Bob Dance, an old labourer (old, that is, in 1904) who had worked on the same farm all his life.

On the downland horizon above the village were two prominent clumps, which Bob referred to as 'One o'Clock Bushes' and 'Two o' Clock'. Wherever he was working his first task in the morning was to make himself a sundial. He would place two sticks in the ground, sighted on the two distant landmarks. When the sun reached a point over 'One o'Clock Bushes', gauged by the sticks, he would begin his siesta, and this would continue until the sun reached 'Two o'Clock', when he would pick up his scythe and resume work. Presumably the sun always shone in Bishopstone when Bob was haymaking.

[**Source:** R.H. Wilson, *The Sparrow Hunters*, 1975, p.5]

Windmill Business

'NINETIES SWINDON has adopted the reconstructed windmill, centrepiece of a business park near the M4, as a kind of emblem of its new-found prosperity. Until it was relocated and rebuilt in 1984, as most Swindonians are probably aware, it stood derelict at Chiseldon. Less well known, perhaps, is the story that in its former existence it once had a companion. 'There were formerly two windmills close together,' wrote the folklore collector Alfred Williams in 1913, 'but one was taken down at an early date, the reason of its removal being — as it is alleged — that there was not enough wind to turn the fans of both.'

Williams had heard another story about Chiseldon windmill. One customer brought a sack of corn to the mill on his donkey. He unloaded it, and because the mill was not working, tethered the donkey to one of the sails while he went to look for the miller. Just then the miller started up the machinery, hoisted the donkey high into the air, where it dangled for some time, until the halter broke and it was reunited with *terra firma*. Like me, I expect that you have heard the modern-day version of that tale, which involves a goat and an unmanned level crossing.

[**Source:** Alfred Williams, *Villages of the White Horse*, p.106]

Pork Scratchings

● ●

A FEW PAGES BACK I promised to begin collecting sobriquets, so let us turn to Alfred Williams again. Inhabitants of Liddington, he tells us, are called 'Pig-Diggers'. This is because one of their number was found on top of the hill excavating a flinty hole, and when asked what he was doing, said that he was digging for a pig. And so he was, in a way. Liddington Hill was part of Swindon's main road to London, especially after it was turnpiked in 1814. By spending their spare time collecting flints to sell as road metalling, some of the locals found that they could earn a few coppers, and so save up to buy a pig.

[**Source:** Alfred Williams, *Villages of the White Horse*, pp.128-9]

Mrs Wiltshire's Donkey

● ●

WHITE HORSES may be two-a-penny, but the white donkey of Tan Hill deserves to be better known. The late Kathleen Wiltshire of All Cannings apparently noticed its outline, in an overgrown condition, on the side of Tan Hill in about 1964. It was about 70 feet long, and the landowner knew nothing about it, although local shepherds referred to that part of the hill as 'Donkey Hill'. Mrs Wiltshire also knew a legend that the donkey, when it heard the bells of All Cannings Church, came down to drink at a dewpond near Cannings Cross.

[**Source:** Kathleen Wiltshire, *Wiltshire Folklore*, 1975, pp.59-60]

The Monster of Ham

● ●

WILTSHIRE'S RELATIONS with Berkshire may seem pretty friendly these days, but Anglo-Saxon attitudes towards our neighbour were perhaps more cautious. For one thing Wansdyke, that massive Late-Roman or Dark-Age defensive rampart which crosses the Marlborough Downs, at its eastern end forms the county boundary for a short distance. And it was along this stretch, according to a document describing the boundary in the year 931, that *grendles-mere*, 'the pond of Grendel', was to be found. The precise site of the pond is now forgotten, but it must have been near Lower Spray Farm, between Ham (Wilts.) and Inkpen (Berks.).

Who was Grendel, after whom this landmark had been nicknamed? Readers of the great Anglo-Saxon epic *Beowulf* will recall him. Grendel was the half-human evil monster who paid nightly visits to the royal palace and carried off the king's warriors. Beowulf fought him and, by delivering his fiendish opponent a mortal blow, improved his credibility at court hugely. Grendel's pond comes into the story too. When the monster's mother came to avenge her son's death, Beowulf chased her back to the pond, where he killed her too and found Grendel's corpse. He cut off its head and returned in triumph with his trophy.

[**Source:** *Archaeol.Jnl*, vol. 76, p. 228, etc.]

⁊

Clerical Error

SINCE I have introduced Berkshire, let us consider also a story about two of our other neighbours. Not far from Sherborne (in Dorset) is Yeovil (in Somerset), and a rivalry has existed between them similar to that between Bradford and Trowbridge, or Wootton Bassett and Swindon. The name Yeovil used to be spelled and pronounced in various ways, commonly 'Ivel' (like the river, and the imaginary saint of margarine). A story was current in Sherborne at the end of the last century, handed down from a most respectable source, about the arrival of a new vicar with a rather peculiar and high-falutin manner of speaking. When he led his Sherborne Abbey congregation in the Lord's Prayer, it is said, many of them endorsed the sentiment which they thought they had heard him enunciate: 'Lead us not into temptation, and deliver us from Yeovil'.

[**Source:** *Som. & Dor. N & Q*, vol. 15, p. 256]

More Haste, Less Speed

• •

CHRISTOPHER SAXTON, the pioneer Elizabethan cartographer, was the first person to make a county map of Wiltshire. It was published in 1576, and formed part of an atlas of all the English and Welsh counties which he completed in 1579. Saxton's work formed the basis for all subsequent Wiltshire maps for the next 150 years, and many of what purported to be new surveys were really only slavish copies, with a few additions and decorations. Am I being too harsh on famous names, such as Speed and Blaeu and Morden, in accusing them of plagiarism? Here is the evidence.

These early maps, as anyone who has looked at one closely will know, depict each village in the same way, usually a little symbol resembling a church behind a dotted circle. When Saxton was preparing his map of Wiltshire for the engraver from his surveying notes, he failed to notice that, a little west of Wilton, he had one more village than he had name. So his map was engraved with an anonymous village.

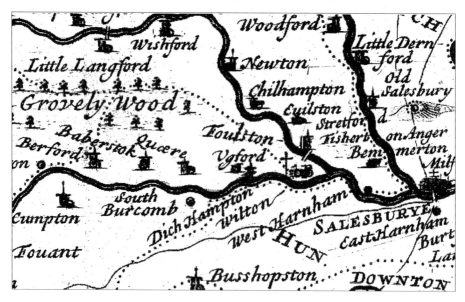

Quaere

Some thirty years later John Speed was using Saxton to prepare his own map of Wiltshire. He noticed the discrepancy, and scribbled the Latin word *Quaere* ('find out') against it. Unfortunately he forgot. His map went off to be engraved, and came back complete with the village of Quaere. It was published in 1610, and the hamlet of North Burcombe continued to be described as Quaere on map after map until 1720, when the eagle-eyed Emanuel Bowen spotted the error, and corrected it.

We all make mistakes. I wonder whether anyone else has noticed that the first-edition Ordnance Survey map of the Devizes area, published in 1817 and now widely used by historians, describes Stanton St Bernard (in Pewsey Vale) as Stanton Fitzwarren (which is near Swindon).

[**Source:** John Booth, *Looking at old maps*, 1979, p. 45]

ॐ

Marriage à la Mode
● ●

BESUITED, I was enjoying a village wedding in our parish church over Easter. The bride's family, near neighbours of ours, had been planning the smallest details for months, and it all went off splendidly — hats, outfits, bells, photographers, silver band, limousines.

Much nuptial paraphernalia has an air of tradition about it, but I am always reminded on these occasions of John Wilkinson. He was the rector of Broughton Gifford, near Melksham, from 1848 to 1876, and he wrote a sympathetic, but sometimes rather candid, description of his parish, which was published in 1859. 'The marriage ceremony', he wrote, 'is conducted about here in a manner which is not pleasing. It is a ceremony and no more... Nobody comes to church, but the bride and bridegroom, walking down the street arm in arm, followed by one or two couples more, who are "keeping company". Parents never think of gracing the union with their presence.' No bridal customs, no strewing of flowers, no favours, no nosegays. The only time things were done differently, Wilkinson recalled, was when a couple were married on Sunday, during the church service, and the groom gave his bride a kiss in front of the whole congregation. Such extravagance on the groom's part was explained in parenthesis — '(but he came from South Wilts)'.

After reviewing Broughton's customs and entertainments, Wilkinson summed things up in four words, 'We are rather dull'. He blamed this on the continued prevalence in North Wiltshire of a stern Puritan feeling, so echoing a conclusion about the differences between north and south which John Aubrey had reached nearly two centuries earlier. Well, life is less dull now, and I thoroughly enjoyed the wedding in our village (but then I come from South Wilts).

[**Source:** WAM, vol. 6, pp. 26-7]

ᏋᏋ

Ingeniose Conversation

●●●

IN 1997 we celebrated the tercentenary of John Aubrey's death [see **Our First Historian**, in this volume]. The more I discover about him, the higher he rises in my estimation. He was Wiltshire's first historian, and he had an incredibly agile magpie mind. Always perceptive, never dull, he is best known for his portrayal of his extraordinary collection of friends and acquaintances in *Brief Lives*. Many of them came from Wiltshire.

Take Francis Potter, for example. He was born at Mere in 1594, and served as rector of nearby Kilmington from 1628 until his death in 1678 (which must, incidentally, have required some nimble theological footwork). He was an expert chess player, invented an instrument for drawing in perspective (Christopher Wren later re-invented it), he had interesting theories about 666, the number of the Beast, and about bees' thighs, which he examined under a microscope.

He and Aubrey thought that they would try an experiment into blood transfusion, but their first attempt was not very successful. They were using a hen, Aubrey explained, but it was not big enough, and they did not have the right tools. Aubrey later sent him a lancet, and he published a paper about his experiments in 1652. 'Twas a pity,' mused Aubrey, 'that such a delicate inventive witt should be staked to a private preferment in an obscure corner where he wanted [lacked] ingeniose conversation.'

As a medical procedure blood transfusion did not become widespread until the first world war.

[**Sources:** DNB; Aubrey, *Brief Lives* (Penguin ed.), pp. 409-12]

A Day to Remember

• •

QUEEN VICTORIA and all her loyal subjects celebrated the diamond
jubilee of her reign in June 1897, and throughout Wiltshire public statues,
clocks, halls, streets, parks, etc, survive as a memento of that happy
occasion. Most of the festivities took place on Tuesday 22nd, and in towns
and villages across the land bells were rung, communal dinners were
eaten, and bonfires were lit. From Charlbury Hill on the Marlborough
Downs above Little Hinton 47 bonfires could be seen, as far away (it was
claimed) as South Wales, and from Windmill Hill above East Knoyle about
30 were visible.

Most celebrations followed a similar pattern, but there were variations.
Purton staged a wheelbarrow race, and Quidhampton raced donkeys; at
Downton teams played a cricket match dressed as clowns and cowboys
on horseback. Miss Maslin of Wootton Bassett decorated her bicycle as a
large jubilee bonnet with a crown surmounting the handlebars — she
received an immense amount of attention and won a prize. Marlborough
and Amesbury fired salutes by striking loaded anvils, and the over-60s
of Devizes were entertained at dinner by a ladies' orchestral band. Guests
of honour at Trowbridge jubilee procession were Mr and Mrs John Rogers,
who had married three weeks before the Queen's accession in 1837. At
Warminster bands of youths continued to parade the streets until close
upon 2 am (so what's new?), and then joined hands around the obelisk
to sing Auld Lang Syne.

[**Sources:** *Swindon Advertiser* and *Salisbury Journal* 26.6.1897]

᠎᠎ஃ

Dubious Escutcheons

• •

A SNAPPY LATIN MOTTO can be a great asset, and one must admire
Andrew Riccard of Portesham (Dorset), who in a pre-Edna Everidge era
chose the single word POSSUM ('I am able') as his watchword. Since it
happened also to be the way most of the locals pronounced the name of
his village, it thereby doubled as his address.

The Wiltshire Archaeological and Natural History Society adopted a

Latin motto, which headed its magazine for more than a century, from 1854 to 1963. It ran MULTORUM MANIBUS GRANDE LEVATUR ONUS, and until 1947 these wise words ('many hands make light work' — or thereabouts) were attributed to the Roman poet Ovid. By then doubts were being entertained about the line's authenticity, and the matter was eventually settled in 1953. C.W. Pugh, while writing a centenary history of the Society, enlisted Marlborough College's help to scour the complete works of Ovid (some 22,000 lines), in what proved to be a vain quest for the bogus pentameter.

The most stylish and unusual civic motto in Wiltshire must be Marlborough's, which refers to a legend connecting the town's name with King Arthur's spindoctor, in the memorable question UBI NUNC SAPIENTIS OSSA MERLINI? ('Where now are the bones of wise Merlin?'). The earliest known use of the motto, which was adapted from a line by the late-Latin philosopher Boethius, occurs mysteriously on the title page of a history of Marlborough. Since, like pseudo-Ovid's effort, this was published in 1854, was there some classically educated practical joker abroad in Wiltshire that year? [**Sources:** Hutchins, vol.2, p.757; *WANHS Centenary History*, 1953, p.13 note; *VCH Wilts*, vol.12, p.216]

The Marlborough arms

Trowbridge-super-Mare

ONE OF THE PERILS of working at County Hall is giving out your address over the phone. The conversation goes like this: 'Bythesea Road, Trowbridge.' 'Pardon?' 'By-the-Sea Road, Trowbridge.' 'You're kidding!' 'No. I'll spell it. B-Y-T-H-E-S-E-A Road, Trowbridge. Well, I can't help it!' And so on.

County Hall was built during the 1930s in an area of Trowbridge which had previously belonged to a dynasty of wealthy clothiers, the Bythesea family. Their surname is medieval in origin (it occurs in Somerset in the 14th century), and is of a type known as topographical, describing where the family's ancestors once lived. In a list of Wiltshire taxpayers in 1332 surnames included *Bytheclive* ('by the cliff'), *Bythewatere*, *Bytheweye*, and *Bythewode*. Of course, if County Hall had been built in Delamere Road nobody would think the address odd, though the explanation would be much the same.

Many of us have topographical surnames, though less spectacular. Hill, Wood, Green, Marsh, Bridge, all derive from places in or near where ancestors lived. Some are less obvious. One of Wiltshire's most aristocratic names, borne by the Marquis of Bath, is Thynne. The family used to claim that it is a corruption of 'At th' Ynne' (which approximates to 'down the pub'). Recent scholarship rejects this explanation.

ॐ

A Girl Named Maria

AND THAT REMINDS ME, many stately homes stage open-air Shakespeare in their grounds each summer. I particularly enjoy attending the annual performance at Hazelbury (near Box). I have never seen *Romeo and Juliet* in Wiltshire, but it would be quite appropriate, if the theory is correct that Shakespeare was inspired to write the play by feuding among the county's leading families.

Sir John Thynne of Longleat and Sir James Marvin of Fonthill had been enemies since the 1550s, and their feud sucked in their descendants and many of the neighbouring gentry, including the Audleys of Compton

93

Bassett, who were related to the Marvins by marriage. In 1594 Thomas Thynne, a 16-year-old Oxford student, befriended John Marvin, a fellow-student, and through him met Maria, also 16, the daughter of Lord Audley and his wife (*née* Marvin). Their first meeting, at a supper party in Beaconsfield, resulted in a secret marriage, which was encouraged by the Marvins, but bitterly opposed and contested (when they eventually found out) by the Thynnes. By the end of 1595 the liaison had become common knowledge, and was a *cause célèbre* at court; this was exactly when Shakespeare took up an old theme (which he adapted in the light of recent events), for his tragedy of *Romeo and Juliet*.

But the real-life outcome was rather different. Despite the feud continuing, Thomas and Maria's marriage was successful. After his father's death in 1604 Thomas inherited Longleat, and Maria helped with the running of the estate until 1611, when she died in her fourth childbirth. Thomas survived her until 1635.

[**Source:** Alison Wall, in *Wilts. Record Soc.*, vol. 38, pp. xviii, xxv-xxxii]

Sir John Thynne

Clark in Holy Orders

CHURCH GUIDEBOOKS tend to be modest, moral, and uncontroversial publications, without pretensions and beyond reproach. And so indeed is the admirable guide to Seend Church. The only unusual feature about it is its authorship. It was dashed off during the 1970s by that eminent man of affairs and diarist the Rt Hon Alan Clark MP, currently member for Kensington and Chelsea. Clark once lived at Seend Manor House.

ॐ

Mind the Gap

THE SUN, as everyone knows, rises over the Heel Stone on 21st June when viewed from the centre of Stonehenge. And a lot of trouble this has caused. The actual point on the horizon at which the great luminary of the universe thus appears lies about 20 metres east of Tombs Road, Larkhill — which is, therefore, a place of awesome significance.

Aviation began at Larkhill in 1909, when a shed was built near Tombs Road by the flying pioneer Horatio Barber, to house his aeroplane. Soon another shed arrived, and then the army became interested in the strategic potential of this new technology. In 1910 three military hangars appeared, soon to be joined by further sheds and hangars (in Wood Road nearby) to house the machines of the flying school of the Bristol Aeroplane Company (now British Aerospace).

All this activity on the Larkhill skyline coincided with the beginnings of modern Druid gatherings at Stonehenge to observe the solstice sunrise. The military authorities (who were later rumoured to be contemplating the demolition of Stonehenge because it was a hazard to aviators) were at this period surprisingly condescending towards the sun-worshippers. They contrived to space the fledgling aeroplane buildings so as to leave a gap between Wood Road and Tombs Road, 'the Solstice Gap', and so allowed the sun to rise at the natural horizon (as it still does, weather permitting), rather than appearing unromantically around the back of a tin shed.

[**Source:** Mr N.C. Parker, cited by N.D.G. James, *Gunners at Larkhill*, 1983, pp.24-5]

The Quidhampton Magician

THE WILTON ROUNDABOUT, one of the busiest road junctions in south Wiltshire, does not immediately call to mind the sonnets of Shakespeare. But there may be a link, albeit a tenuous one.

Next to the roundabout that charming little church with the curious name, Fugglestone St Peter, witnessed the baptism at the end of 1552 of a certain Simon Forman, of the nearby village of Quidhampton. From this beginning Forman went on to lead an interesting life, which included apprenticeship to a Salisbury grocer, private practice as magician and concoctor of quack medicines at Fisherton parsonage (near the present Salisbury railway station), and then, after more than a year in gaol, removal to London. There, from 1580 onwards, he resumed his practice in medicine / magic (the two were barely distinguishable). He seems to have specialized in love-potions, and certainly (on the evidence of his diaries) he spent a good deal of his time personally researching their effects.

One of Forman's clients in London was Emilia Lanier (*née* Bassano), the daughter of an Italian musician, and for a time the Lord Chamberlain's mistress. She came to him during 1597 to have her fortune told, and they conducted a brief affair. The Chamberlain, Lord Hunsdon, employed a company of actors which sometimes included William Shakespeare, and from the descriptions in Forman's diaries and papers the Shakespearean scholar A.L. Rowse was able to offer perhaps the most convincing identification of the mysterious 'dark lady of the sonnets' — none other than Emilia Lanier.

Simon Forman's abilities as a fortune-teller stayed with him to the last. One Sunday in 1611 he was discussing with his wife in their London garden-house which of them would die first. He was confident that he would predecease her, and stated, 'I shall die ere Thursday night'. By Wednesday he was still in excellent health, and his wife began to tease him. Still well after dinner on Thursday, he decided to go out in his boat; and rowing enthusiastically in mid-Thames, he burst an abscess and died.

[**Source:** A.L. Rowse, *Simon Forman*, 1974]

Quidhampton No More

DESPITE AN UNPALATABLE NAME (Quid- probably derives from a word for 'manure-heap'), there were in fact two Wiltshire villages called Quidhampton. One, Simon Forman's birthplace, thrives between Salisbury and Wilton. The other lay in north Wiltshire, next to Salthrop, and close to that favourite rat-run of commuters approaching Swindon from the south.

This Quidhampton was a small settlement on the steep edge of the downs, with a chapel-of-ease in Wroughton parish, and a medieval manor house. A Tudor successor of this house still existed in 1822, when Mrs Story-Maskelyne of nearby Bassett Down made a sketch of it. Three years later, in 1825, during a violent storm, there was a catastrophic landslide, and part of the wooded hillside behind the house engulfed most of it and rendered it uninhabitable. What survived was turned into a pair of cottages, but they too, along with anything which may have survived of the medieval village, have now been swallowed up by the trees and undergrowth. [**Sources:** *WNQ*, vol.1, pp.311-14; *WAM*, vol.54, pp.411-14; *Wroughton History*, vol.4, p.66]

Quidhampton Manor House

Check-Mates

● ●

WHAT DID MONKS DO in the evenings? At Avebury in the middle
ages there was a small monastic cell, belonging to a French abbey, and
for most of the time it seems that only two monks lived there, a prior and
his companion. An inventory of their possessions was made in 1327, and
the list includes — as well as two beds, tables, pots and pans, and a couple
of horses — their one luxury, a chess set. Just as well they had something
to keep them out of mischief, because eighty years earlier, in 1249, the
prior of Avebury had been accused by a woman of murdering her brother.
[**Sources:** *VCH*, vol.3, pp.392-3; *WRS*, vol.16, no.374]

Broughton Ganders

● ●

THIS SOBRIQUET, applied to the men of Broughton Gifford, has the
honour of a mention in the *Victoria History of Wiltshire*. The proverb, 'to
shoe the goose', meaning 'to waste time by meddling or engaging in
unnecessary labour', was in widespread circulation, and can be traced
back in literature and art to the middle ages. But a version was recounted
as recently as 1934 in a local newspaper, as if the idea (of a blacksmith
shoeing geese like horses, so that they would not become footsore walking
to market) had originated in Broughton Gifford. The inventor of the
technique, according to the story, even sent the geese out on a trial run to
see how well the shoes fitted.

Like so much folklore recounted in the present century, the teller only
half-believed it, and introduced a note of scepticism. But on this occasion
his 'correction' of the story was as interesting as the story itself: 'I dwoant
spose as twer ever done, but we did used to shoe 'em in another way,
and that wur te get a mixture o' tar and sand and let 'em tread on that for
a few days. Then 'tood clot on their veet and walkin' to market din' hurt
'em.'

[**Sources:** *VCH*, vol.7, p.58; *WAM*, vol.50, p.33]

Hogwash

'THE AMAZING PIG OF KNOWLEDGE', proclaimed the newspaper advertisement, 'is just arrived from Abroad,' as Salisbury's Michaelmas fair approached in October 1790. 'This astounding Animal performs with Cards, Money, and Watches; he also tells the day of the month, and the month of the year; likewise tells the value of any piece of money, Foreign or English; he distinguishes all sorts of colours; and tells the number of ladies and gentlemen present, or any lady or gentleman's thoughts in company... He also performs many other curious feats of sagacity, which equally contribute to the pleasure and amazement of the spectators.'

Next week the advertisement was there again: 'The Question at present among the polite and Curious is, Who has seen the SCIENTIFIC PIG? And those who answer they have not, are looked on as persons that are blind to the most striking curiosity ever seen or heard of; for we know of no age or country that has, at any period, produced the like, and in all probability may never have an opportunity of seeing such another, ere the youngest of us shall be no more. Be wise then, and see it while you may.'

Perhaps the hyperbolic pig's greatest feat, as it turned out, was staying power. Far from giving his last performance in 1790, as his promoters intimated, he (or one of his descendants) was still at it more than thirty years later. Here is the *Wiltshire Gazette* in 1822:

'CHINESE WONDER. Mr Pinchbeck respectfully informs the inhabitants of Devizes, that the PIG OF KNOWLEDGE, taught by Soachanguee the Chinese Philosopher, and exhibited by Mr P. since his arrival in this country before their royal highnesses the Princess Augusta and the Duchess of Gloucester, (far exceeding their most sanguine expectations, and meriting their patronage), is now exhibiting at the Rose Inn, Devizes Green...

'This specimen of animated nature has not, and never had its equal in point of sagacity, either in the dog, horse, elephant, or any other quadruped in the world. Mr P. will exhibit the Pig of Knowledge for four evenings, in a commodious room at the Rose Inn, Devizes Green; to commence at 7, 8, and 9 o'clock: Admittance 6d. Parties waited on at their own houses during the day by giving notice.' Wisely, perhaps, the pig seems not to have visited Calne.

[**Sources:** *Salisbury Journal*, 11.10.1790; 18.10.1790; *Wilts Gazette*, 2.5.1822]

ба

More Hogwash

• •

HOW EASY IT IS, in the enthusiastic pursuit of historical enlightenment, to scribble down notes which you later find don't quite make sense. Still, when you come to write up your book, you can usually glean something plausible from them. Here is a cautionary tale.

When members of a nonconformist congregation wished to open premises for worship, between 1689 and 1852, they had to secure permission, generally from the bishop. A copy of their certificate was duly entered by the clerk in a large handwritten ledger, the bishop's register, and everything was then legal and above board. In January 1788 John Clem and three other Baptists of Imber on Salisbury Plain (one of them illiterate) duly informed the bishop of Salisbury, the suave and aristocratic Shute Barrington, that they intended meeting in two houses in the village. And their certificate was duly entered in the bishop's register, which at this period was the one started during the episcopacy of Barrington's predecessor, Bishop John Hume. And there the entry survives, alongside some sixty others, for anyone to see and make notes from.

One who appears to have done so was the author of a booklet about Imber, published during the 1970s. But he must have had trouble with his notes, for he tells us an astonishing fact. 'In 1788 Reg Hume and Shute Barrington were granted a Baptist licence in the village...' My Lord Bishop of Salisbury a closet Baptist? Surely not? And who might Reg Hume be? None other than the book in which the licence was recorded.

[**Sources:** G.S. Revels, *A thousand years of history*, p.17; WRS vol.40, no.405, citing WRO D1/2/28]

ﻉﻝ

Those Blue Remembered Hills

● ●

AS THE COUNTRYSIDE TURNS BLUISH (we're talking linseed here, not politics), and we tut-tut — 'what will the EU think of next?' — it is worth noting that *Linum usitatissimum* (flax or linseed) has often been grown in Wiltshire in the past. At least three medieval place-names — The Linleys in Corsham, Flexborough (now no more) in Manton near Marlborough, and Lyneham — refer to the crop. There is documentary evidence that during the thirteenth century Wilton was regarded as the premier linen-manufacturing centre in England, although much of the flax was probably imported. When Salisbury eclipsed Wilton linen-weaving took place there too, and was said to be the oldest craft in the city. In 1992 a survey of the remains of a group of rectangular ponds at Penleigh near Westbury concluded that they had been constructed during the middle ages for flax 'retting' (steeping the stems in water to remove the resin).

In the eighteenth century a hard-wearing cloth was produced in Wiltshire known as linsey-woolsey, which combined a woollen weft with a linen warp. But by then much of the county's linen-weaving was carried on in the south-west corner, in and around Mere. It was really a continuation of the great band of flax growing and linen manufacture which extended across Blackmore Vale in Somerset and Dorset as far west as Bridport. It continued at Mere until about 1880.

[**Sources:** *VCH Wilts* 4, 178-9; 6, 13; *WRS* 19, *passim*; *WAM* 87, 153-4, etc]

૨૦

An Enford Cottage Industry

REGULARS using the Avon valley route from Amesbury to Upavon may have noticed a roadside cottage at New Town, just south of Enford, which has a large window right down at the level of the tarmac. What was it for?

Shortly before he died, Fred Phillimore of Enford was encouraged to record his memories on tape, and they were edited by Nell Duffie and published. According to Fred the road was formerly crowded with droves of sheep each summer on their way to the fairs at Britford, Wilton, and Salisbury. When this occurred the occupant of the cottage, a man named Bird, used to leave his window open, and as the sheep passed, was accustomed to drag a couple in and slaughter them when the drover wasn't looking. Eventually, again according to Fred, he was caught, tried, and transported.

[**Source:** Fred Phillimore, *Enford Days*, 1986, pp.18-19]

૨૦

General Election Special (1997)

1. How to Rubbish an Opponent

WHATEVER SPINDOCTORS and commentators may advise, there's nothing like a bit of negative campaigning to raise the political temperature. How about this, for example, overheard in Salisbury in 1457. The speaker was John Halle, the city's MP in 1461, and his comments were directed at William Swayne, MP in 1449. The report of their confrontation is a little garbled:

'I defy the[e]; what arte thow? And I as good as thow, cherle, knave, harlotte. And I as ryche as thow and gretter of lyvelode [livelihood] than thow. And though thow sitte here in sempble [assembly] Y to contrarye

ELECTORS

OF

North Wilts

The RADICALS have been beaten in the following places:

Bath	Lancaster
Hull	Wells
Liverpool	Bedford
Cricklade	Preston
Weymouth	Ipswich
Greenwich	Kidderminster
Stoke	Guildford
Maldon	Petersfield
Rye	Hastings
Brighton	Beverley
Bridgwater	Warwick
Woodstock	Hereford
Sudbury	Berwick
Maidstone	Wakefield
Carnarvon	Wareham

Facts are stubborn things !

July 29, 1837.

SIMPSON, PRINTER, DEVIZES.

the [?I oppose you] and never to aggre to thee. And am better of byrthe than thow and have bore the worship and the astate of this cite [city] and kept it as well as thou.'
[**Source:** WRO G23/1/2. fol.31v]

2. Intimations of Immorality

IF THAT DOESN'T RATTLE HIM, the next stage may be to delve into your opponent's past. At Devizes in December 1832 the first election to the reformed Parliament involved some fairly strident campaigning between supporters of Admiral Sir P.C.H. Durham (Tory) and Mr Montague Gore (Whig). Under the pseudonym 'Olympus', a Durham canvasser published a poster (one of many) addressed to Mr Gore.

'...The Admiral has condescended to answer the pitiful trash circulated against him: perhaps you will have the kindness to answer the very serious charges which have been brought against you. To give you the opportunity of so doing, I have endeavoured to put them in an answerable form.

1. Can you unequivocally deny having shot partridges on a Sunday?
2. Can you, on your honor, deny having been busily employed, on another Sunday, in the very unsenatorial, and puerile occupation, of wantonly destroying a wasp's nest with gunpowder, or some other, and what, destructive material?
3. As there are some disreputable reports abroad, as to an intimacy between yourself and Madame Vestris, perhaps you will, for the purpose of clearing your "moral character", say *on what grounds* Madame Vestris stands, or has stood with you?
4. Can you throw any light on some disgraceful scenes which are stated to have been lately enacted at Harbourfield, near Reading?
5. Can you give "a substantial reason" why you are denominated "*A Great Wench in Breeches*"?

If you can clear yourself from these accusations, upon the strict principles of "British Jurisprudence", as laid down by your friend Mr Hook, the sooner you do it the better.'

Mr Gore responded by threatening to prosecute the printer of the poster if he did not reveal its author, but seems not to have pressed the point. His supporters came to the rescue, eliciting testimonials to his good character, and defending him against the calumny. The Gore camp were a bit cagey about questions 1 and 2 (well he may have done, sort of); on question 3 they admitted the liaison, but it was nearly ten years ago, and excusable on the grounds (apparently) that an affair with Madame Vestris was perfectly normal adolescent behaviour. Questions 4 and 5 were so infamous as to require no answer and they would not waste time replying. The following week a mock playbill appeared announcing a benefit performance for Madame Vestris at the New Theatre, Devizes.

Anyway, Montague Gore was elected MP for Devizes. And in case you're wondering, the singer and actress Lucia Elizabeth Mathews (1797-1856), also known as Madame Vestris, became an outstandingly successful and innovatory theatre manager. Oh, and gunpowder is not the best way to tackle a wasps' nest.

[**Source:** WANHS Library, folio of Wilts Election Papers, Devizes, 1818-68]

3. How to Win an Election

THE EASIEST WAY to enter Parliament in the eighteenth century (if you could afford it) was to buy up all the burgage houses in a rotten borough, fill them with tenants you could trust, and stand them a jolly good dinner just before the election. The twenty-six electors of Heytesbury, believe it or not, were represented by two MPs until 1832, and elections could not come round often enough as far as they, and Mr Snelgrove (the landlord of the Red Lion) were concerned. They did not even have to live in Heytesbury between elections. Certainly around 1780 most of the houses which conferred a vote upon their occupants were left empty until shortly before polling day, when they mysteriously filled up with the candidates' supporters.

The election dinner at the Red Lion must have been a party to remember (although most of the participants may have been understandably vague about it afterwards). In 1802, for example, £32 was spent on 160 bottles of wine, there was free beer and tobacco, for entertainment the church bells were rung and there were musicians and servants. The vast sum of ten shillings was spent on breakages.

[**Sources:** VCH vol.5, p.209; WRO 635/ 128, 131]

4. What to Do if You Lose

THE OBVIOUS COURSE, in view of my previous revelations, was to cry foul, and petition Parliament to disqualify your successful opponents. Samuel Petrie, who failed to represent Cricklade as a result of five elections between 1774 and 1790, spent a fortune on litigation, aimed not only at the corruption of the returning officer and the other candidates, but also at the electors individually. Although he won several Pyrrhic victories he was twice bankrupted and imprisoned for debt. He died obscurely abroad after 1799.

His writs caused turmoil and consternation. In order to make bribery more difficult, the franchise was extended beyond Cricklade borough to include the rural hundreds. When people complained that this was not fair on the honest voters of the borough, they were roundly told that there weren't any. The most exciting moment in Petrie's protracted disputes came on 31st May 1782, when he fought a duel in Greenwich Park with a political adversary, Lord Porchester. Petrie was hit in the stomach but not disabled. He could have killed his opponent but chose not to fire, probably because Lord Porchester owed him money.

[Source: WAM, vol.56, pp.371-87]

The Rise and Fall of the Wiltshire Carrier

TWO OF THE MANY conveniences of life which the Victorians taught us to take for granted are the rapid dissemination of news, and easy access to shops. To be forced to live in a Wiltshire village in the 18th century could be a disgruntling experience for a civilized, educated person. As Dr George Wells, rector of Manningford Bruce near Pewsey, complained to his bishop in 1783:

> 'The parochial clergy are in a manner tied down to a single spot by a multitude of restraints, some of them very irksome and disagreeable to say the least of them. They are precluded from almost every possibility of bettering their condition; being out of sight of those men who have it in their power to do something for them...'[1]

Others accepted their lot with better grace, but there were still snags. Francis Raikes, vicar of Figheldean near Amesbury, as late as the 1880s had certain problems: 'It cost me £1 to have my hair cut – 18s. to hire a trap to Salisbury, 1s. 6d. luncheon, 6d. hair cut.' He could afford it no doubt, whilst most of his parishioners had to improvize. But if for them a visit to Salisbury was essential, then, continued Raikes, 'The labourer and his wife, when they had to go, spent most of their time on the road, in a carrier's cart. Starting at 7 am, reaching Salisbury at 11 am, and not getting back till 8 or 9 pm.'[2]

Who then were the carriers who performed this vital means of communication? Like the humble motor bus of our own and our parents' generations they do not often appear in Wiltshire literature. W.H. Hudson, in *A Shepherd's Life*, mentions, 'The carriers' carts drawn up in rows on rows - carriers from a hundred little villages on the Bourne, the Avon, the Nadder, the Ebble and from all over the Plain, each bringing its little contingent.'[3] But, apart from this congregation in Salisbury Market Place, he says little more about them.

Carriers Carts, Salisbury Market

The historian's main supply of evidence about carriers comes in fact from the series of county directories which appeared from the mid-nineteenth century (1848 in the case of Wiltshire) until the second world war. This source may be pushed back another sixty years or so by the use of more selective and irregular directories, and still further into the 18th century from town guides and almanacs which appeared for major provincial centres such as Salisbury and Bath. These directories and guides appended to their descriptions of towns a list of the surrounding villages served by carriers, with names, days of the week and the town inns from which they left. From 1848 these lists may be checked by referring to the entries for villages, which often listed the resident carriers and the towns to which they carried. There are other sources of evidence as well — occasional advertisements in local newspapers, wills of carriers, stray references in broadsides — and in official sources back to the 17th century and beyond. Morgan Morse, for example, the Salisbury-London carrier, was ordered in 1625 to suspend his service as a precaution against spreading the plague then rampant in the metropolis.[4] Nevertheless it is the 19th-century carrier that we know most about, and it is our first task to try to discover whether his transport system, so meticulously (if not always accurately) depicted in the directories, was a Victorian initiative or whether it had continued unchanged from earlier times.

The 18th- and early 19th-century directories portray, in the main, two types of carrier, the long distance waggoner who lumbered across Wiltshire from London to Exeter or Bristol on a weekly or less frequent basis; and, to borrow a more modern expression, the 'inter-city' carrier, who travelled a day's journey between towns, Swindon to Oxford, Salisbury to Southampton, returning the following day. The waggoner is a well-known figure in the annals of road transport, and he of course met his end when railways revolutionized long-distance travel in the 1840s. The intermediate carrier is less well-known, but he was real enough. William Morris of Swindon, writing in the 1880s, remembered him. As a child Morris saw the London and Bristol waggons, and also:

'...carriers' carts to Cirencester, Faringdon, Newbury, Marlborough, Devizes, and Bath. All these carts made what are in America called "connections" with other carts which went to still more distant towns, so that even in those days Swindon had pretty direct communications with all parts of the country, although it very often took a considerable period of time, and involved much trouble and no small amount of risk, to make it.'

And then he went on to tell the following anecdote:

'A certain Swindon tradesman had a wife, who by some of her neighbours was "counted" rather "fast". It so happened that she became a somewhat frequent traveller by the carrier's cart to Bath. As time went on, and the visits of the lady to Bath became even more frequent, remarks began to be made. These, however, were for a time silenced by the explanation that her business, that of a milliner and dress-maker, necessitated these visits... In course of time, however, it was generally understood that pretty good evidence was forthcoming that the real object of her visits to Bath was that she might better enjoy the society of the proprietor of the Bath carrier's cart, who was also its driver. ..'[5]

The Great Western Railway, one must suppose, put a stop to this carrier's activities also.

I encountered these intermediate carriers in an unexpected source. While editing nonconformist meeting-house certificates I noticed that a number of the documents were endorsed with process notes, little jottings to remind the clerk that something was 'not paid' or 'to be collected', or the like. More than sixty such notes, mostly on documents written between 1810 and 1830, mention names, which on closer inspection turn out to be carriers, seventeen different individuals, and some names occurring up to fifteen times. These documents had all travelled to the diocesan registrar at Salisbury from various parts of Wiltshire on carriers' vans. In each case the carrier would have delivered the document with the relevant fee, and would be asked to call again later when the paperwork had been completed, so that he could take back to the senders a licence for their meeting-house. Hence the clerk's scribbled note to remind himself of the arrangement. Most such carriers travelled between fifteen and thirty miles to Salisbury: Gould of Donhead, Beams of Ludgershall, Silcox (even further) from Bath — and the most interesting, George George of Marlborough. His vehicle, described in one directory as a caravan, rumbled into Salisbury (like all the others) every Monday evening and returned the following morning, market day. Unlike the later, short-haul, carriers, they did not spend much time at the market, since they had to return by Tuesday nightfall, or else waste a third day on the double journey. George, just as Morris remembered, was part of a network of connecting carriers, since he conveyed messages from even more distant parts of Wiltshire than Marlborough, such as Cricklade, Highworth and Wootton Bassett, brought to him at Marlborough by those places' respective carriers. Quite as significant in this sample of sixty-odd documents is that the purely local carrier, as existed later in the high

Victorian period, scarcely occurs. The impression gained from directories is therefore reinforced, and we may perhaps be justified in regarding the Victorian village carrier as an innovation.[6]

But before we examine causes and implications we should perhaps look a little more closely at what we can discover about these Victorian carriers themselves, from directories and elsewhere. In general they lived in villages or small towns, and as often as not carrying was a part-time occupation, which they combined with some other livelihood in a related field. Some engaged in farming or were coal-dealers, shopkeepers, blacksmiths or publicans. Others doubtless combined their role as common carrier (public service vehicle, as it were) with that of freelance carter or haulier. They carried to the nearest large town on one, two or three days a week (or in exceptional cases daily), one journey always coinciding with market day. They arrived as early as possible and set out late in the afternoon to return home, and some at least took their timekeeping very seriously. Frederick Large remembered that in the 1860s:

'A large two-horse bus, or carrier's van, went from Swindon every Saturday morning, and the departure and return of this commodious vehicle were events of considerable interest to us lads... The owner-driver of the van was a well-known Primitive Methodist local preacher, of rather peculiar disposition, but most reliable. As a rule he drove in a thick grey overcoat, and wore a black high hat. A feature in connection with this weekly excursion was its punctuality in departing and arriving. Nothing could prevail upon the proprietor to wait even a few minutes for the most important passenger or luggage, much less to pull his horses up at other than his allotted stations on this somewhat difficult journey.'[7]

Such attention to the clock was a product, one assumes, of the railway with which many carriers connected.

If they lived in a village which looked to two or more market towns, then carrying might become a full-time job. One Highworth carrier in 1899 was visiting Cirencester on Monday, Faringdon on Tuesday, Swindon on Thursday and Saturday, and Lechlade on Friday. An Upavon carrier, meanwhile, went to Salisbury on Tuesday, Devizes on Thursday, and Marlborough on Saturday. Once they reached their destination each had his accustomed inn, which acted as his depot and parcels office, and provided stabling for his horse after the cart had been parked in the market place. Their inns were not chosen at random. The Salisbury carriers tended to congregate at inns on the side of town nearest to their approach and exit, presumably to avoid pointless traffic congestion in the centre.[8] Grouping of a sort may be seen as late as 1899 also in Devizes. By this date two large commercial inns, the Black Swan and the Crown, accommodated most of them, but seven — mostly from Pewsey Vale — used the Three Crowns in Maryport Street, five — all from Potterne and beyond — used the Elm Tree in Long Street, four the Pelican, mostly from the west, and three from Pewsey Vale the White Bear in Monday Market Street.

The Salisbury & Coombe Express, from a painting by Mr F. Brooks

Carrier's vehicles were a motley collection, ranging from horse omnibuses designed primarily for passengers, through the substantial cart for passengers and goods, to the small donkey cart, such as that of the celebrated Mrs Ridout, proprietress of the Coombe [Bissett] Express. Frank Brooks, who painted a picture of her (a version of which is now in Salisbury Museum), recalled that:

'I used to meet her at Harnham Bridge, when she was leaving the town, as she always made a stop at the old and picturesque inn called "The Swan" for a last refresher for herself and the donkeys, generally, I think, from the same jug. I often walked with her to Coombe and the pace was such that at times I was able to walk backwards and draw, hence the name she was so well known by...'[9]

As a transport system the Wiltshire carriers had by the 1880s succeeded in creating a comprehensive network of services radiating from the more important towns. If we are right to believe that the short-haul carrier was almost entirely a Victorian innovation, then he may be considered alongside other changes taking place at the same time. The first and most obvious is the railway. This, we have suggested, killed off the long-distance and some of the intermediate carriers. But where it did not offer direct competition it acted as a stimulus to the proliferation of carriers. The result was that while there were few carriers operating in the area between Swindon and Chippenham, where the Great Western Railway ran, and few serving Melksham, Westbury and Bradford-on-Avon, which were all connected by rail to Bath, areas devoid of railway lines, on the other hand, north-west Wiltshire, the Deverills, the Lavingtons, several of the valleys converging on Salisbury, all developed vigorous carrier traffic. A second factor may simply be the gradual rise in the standard of living enjoyed by some members of rural communities between 1850 and 1900, with growing sophistication and higher expectations, coupled with a great expansion in retailing and widely available luxury and fancy goods.

But the third and perhaps most interesting correlation is between the growth of the carrier and the fortunes of the town. The direction and frequency of the carriers seem to offer a good indicator of the extent of a town's hinterland.[10] This is important because it enables us to comment on the much weightier question of the rise and fall of Wiltshire towns. In

1792 nineteen Wiltshire towns held markets, including a number of quite small places — Amesbury, Bedwyn, Hindon, Mere and Wilton. By 1888 only nine remained, and of these only Devizes, Salisbury, Swindon and Warminster were significant.[11] Most of the smaller market or former market centres were not the focus of the carrier's attention; on the contrary carriers ran *from* places such as Melksham, Calne and Westbury to other, larger, towns. But, in north Wiltshire at least, changes have occurred too since the heyday of the Victorian carrier. A social study of Wiltshire in the 1940s, including shopping areas and bus frequencies, makes an interesting comparison with the carriers of sixty years earlier. It shows that by then Swindon had extended its hinterland further north at the expense of Cirencester and further south at the expense of Marlborough. Elsewhere in the county, however, once the traditional significance of the market had been lost, the smaller shopping centres — Calne, Malmesbury, Melksham — were once again establishing themselves at the expense of their larger neighbours.[12]

What then happened to the Victorian carriers? Although by 1900 they had perhaps passed their peak,[13] it was the advent of motorized transport, spurred to efficiency by the requirements of the first world war, that sounded their deathknell. Some, like Hawkins of Wroughton, changed over to motor buses, and could be found in the 1930s as, 'The Old Firm', running a service into Swindon every ten minutes. He sold up in 1955,[14] but Armstead of Newton Tony was still, until the 1980s, running his bus into Salisbury on market days, and parking in New Canal alongside other members of that multi-coloured fraternity of village buses, which somehow perpetuate the ethos of the carrier.

But the inter-war years saw the emergence of a new kind of proprietor, who ran a network of services with a fleet of motor vehicles, and who found opportunities not only in the country services, but also in serving the burgeoning suburbs of towns, and in satisfying the fashionable demand for outings to the seaside and other places of interest. Concerns such as Bristol Tramways and Carriage Company, Bath Tramways Motor Company, Western National Omnibus Company, and Wilts and Dorset Motor Services, expanded at the expense of the traditional carrier, whom they swallowed up or simply forced out of business, and almost the whole of Wiltshire was divided between these four, which were all effectively nationalised in 1948.[15]

But we shall stay with the carrier, as seen through the eyes of a child in 1897:

'Why I was being transferred to the care of Mr Jukes, farmer, and his wife, I do not now know... I must have been about five years old when I made that great journey. Passengers sat on two wooden benches facing one another. There were shelves and hooks wherever space allowed for parcels and goods. I sat with my legs stiff out in front. On the floor below me was a block of ice wrapped in sacking. The ice melted as we travelled, for it was warm in the van. Soon there was a small pool of water, and it was then that I became conscious of the looks on the faces of a fat woman and her son sitting opposite me. I knew exactly what they were thinking as they glanced from the pool of water to me... That journey of seven miles seemed to take hours. Every inn along the route was a port of call where refreshment could be taken. At every hill the men left the van and walked, to lighten the load. Before going downhill special brakes, "shoes," were fitted to the wheels. I was fast asleep long before the journey's end.'[16]

NOTES

1 Ransome, M. (ed.) *Wiltshire returns to the bishop's visitation queries 1783*, 1972 (WRS vol.27), p.164.

2 Raikes, F. *Recollections of village life on Salisbury Plain*, no date [ca.1920], p.3.

3 Hudson, W.H. *A shepherd's life*, 1978 ed., p15.

4 Benson, R. and Hatcher, H. *Old and New Sarum, or Salisbury*, 1843, p.358.

5 Morris, W. *Swindon fifty years ago (more or less)*, 1885, pp.240, 242-3.

6 Chandler, J.H. (ed.) *Wiltshire dissenters' meeting house certificates ond registrations, 1689-1852*, 1985 (WRS vol.40), pp.xx-xxi and *passim*; Pigot, J. *London and provincial new commercial directory for 1822-3*, [Wiltshire portion], p.558.

7 Large, F. *A Swindon retrospect, 1855-1930*, 1932, p.106.

8 Mullins, S. 'And old Mrs Ridout and all...' *Wiltshire folklife*, vol.2(1), 1978, pp.29-35 (at p.33).

9 Harnham Women's Institute, *The history of Harnham*, 1981 ed., p.18.

10 Chandler, J.H. *Salisbury and its neighbours,* 1987, p.l5.

11 Richardson, J. *The local historian's encyclopaedia,* 1974, p.268.

12 Bracey, H.E. *Social provision in rural Wiltshire,* 1952, pp.17, 51.

13 Greening, A. 'Nineteenth-century country carriers in north Wiltshire', *Wiltshire archaeological and natural history magazine,* vol.66, 1971, pp.162-76 (at p.175).

14 Wroughton Parish Council, *Wroughton: a guide to your village,* no date [ca.1963], p.21.

15 Chandler, J.H. *Endless Street: a history of Salisbury and its people,* 1983, pp.146-9.

16 Hart, E. *Before I forget,* no date [1984], p.12.

[Adapted from a talk given at the Wiltshire Local History Forum annual conference, September 1985]

NOTE: Since this article was first published I have discussed the geography of village carriers and their significance for determining the hinterland of Wiltshire towns. See Chandler, J.: A Sense of Belonging, 1998, pp 45-8 (map on p.46).

 え&   え&

Blood or Money: the true story of Peter Withers

HIS HORSE WAS JUMPING a wall when the hammer hit Mr Codrington on the side of the head. It was a blacksmith's hammer. He fell on to the wall, blood pouring from his face, and the terrified horse, in trying to struggle free, pulled the wall down around him. The hammer had been flung by an Ogbourne shoemaker, Peter Withers, one of more than forty men who had assembled to destroy a threshing machine at Rockley Farm on the Marlborough Downs. It was the second day of a week of rioting, which convulsed southern England during November 1830, as desperate labourers took what would now be called 'direct action' to fight for a living wage. And farmers, in fear of outright revolution, watched as their ricks burned and their machinery lay in mangled pieces.

Revolution evaporated before November was out, but the aftermath was long and bitter. In Wiltshire only one man — a labourer — was killed, and Mr Codrington recovered from his injuries after a few days. Peter Withers, his assailant, was one of eight rioters apprehended by the Wiltshire Yeomanry that morning on the Marlborough Downs, and taken to Devizes Gaol. Overall, Wiltshire's prison population was swollen by more than 300 as a result of the November riots, and a special session of the assize court was summoned after Christmas in Salisbury Guildhall to determine the captives' fate.

Peter Withers was a stocky man with a fair complexion and brown hair. A native of Chilton Foliat, he was 24 years old, and the father of twins, born soon after his marriage in 1828. They celebrated their second birthday while Peter was being held on remand. His wife, Mary Ann, was a Ramsbury girl, and the family set up home there; but the Ramsbury overseers soon took a dim view of their prospects, and sent them back to Peter's parish, which they reckoned to be Ogbourne St George.

The trial of Peter Withers took place on 7th January 1831. The court heard from the farmer at Rockley, from a local magistrate who had tried to dissuade the rioters, and from Mr Codrington, who could not remember anything that happened after the hammer blow. Evidence was taken, too, from the Ogbourne blacksmith who owned the weapon, and from Peter himself, who claimed to have acted in self-defence. This was partly true, as Mr Codrington had pinned him against a wall before he struggled free, and the magistrate had ridden through the mob brandishing a pistol and striking out with his horsewhip. But Peter, it seemed, had been the ringleader, or at least the spokesman. 'By God, we'll have blood or money', he was alleged to have shouted at the magistrate.

The jury found Peter Withers guilty of assault with intent to do grievous bodily harm. After eight days of hearings 104 men were sentenced to transportation, and 44 were given death sentences commuted to transportation. But the judges determined that Peter Withers and another man, whose crimes they considered particularly serious, should be hanged. As the black cap was donned and sentence pronounced, the newspaper report becomes melodramatic. Peter's face, we are told, became deathly white, he broke out in a cold sweat and fainted. Recovering momentarily he clutched his throat as if the noose was already tightening, and he had to be administered sal volatile. Before the prisoners were taken away the women in court, the 'rough athletic farmers', even two of the judges, were all in tears.

The execution was set for 25th January, exactly nine weeks after the hammer-blow. By then many convicts had already left Wiltshire, and were at Portsmouth waiting to embark for Australia. Meanwhile public opinion, shocked by the severity of the sentences, had come to the rescue of the two men on death row. They were reprieved, with a day to spare. Peter Withers returned thanks to the Father of Mercies, and prayed to dedicate his future life to God's service.

Their lives were spared, but they were not pardoned. Peter Withers remained in Fisherton Gaol another fortnight, and then spent two months on a prison hulk at Portsmouth. On 6th April 1831 he set sail for Tasmania to begin his life sentence of transportation. The day before he sailed he wrote to his wife.

It is a touching and poignant love letter. '...i dont think ever a man Loved a woman so well as i Lovs you My Dear i hope you will go to the gentlman for they to pay your Pasag over to Me When i sent for you how hapy i shall be to eare that you are acoming after me...' Mary Ann perhaps never received the letter. Peter wrote again, from Tasmania, but again no reply. Two years later, in September 1833, he wrote to his brother-in-law in Ramsbury.

By now he was doubting her fidelity, and hurt at receiving no news. Life in Tasmania was good, and the only punishment, he said, lay in being separated from her and their children. He did not expect to be allowed to return to Wiltshire for at least sixteen years, unless perhaps a petition to the king could be organized in Ogbourne on his behalf. But this and other letters were never answered. In May 1836, having apparently lost his wife and family, Peter Withers married again.

It was another eight years before – quite out of the blue – he received a letter from Mary Ann. She had not remarried, and she was still living with the twins in their old home. Peter took five days to compose a reply. His religious conversion in the shadow of the scaffold seems to have stuck, and the letter is sprinkled with biblical phrases. Life in Tasmania had turned sour; there was poverty and bankruptcy everywhere. 'But i must now tell you that i am marrid again and i have a stadey vertus Woman for my wife... i now that for to eare that i am maried is a hard trial for you to bare but it is no good to tell you a lye...' When things improve, in a year or two, he would try to send her money, 'a small Living about ten or fifteen Pounds a year.'

And that is almost the last we hear of Peter Withers. In 1847 Mary Ann, by now living in London, wrote to the Home Office, and was told that the latest information about her husband was that he was still alive in September 1846, but that there was nothing more recent. He would have been approaching his fortieth birthday.

NOTE

The records of the 1830 labourers' revolt hold a powerful fascination for historians, and they are a popular quarry for A level and undergraduate dissertations. New evidence about the participants keeps coming to light, from newspapers, letters and diaries, and from the family researches of their descendants. Much of the Wiltshire material has been collected by Jill Chambers into two stout paperback volumes (*Wiltshire Machine Breakers*, 1993, available in libraries), and I am indebted to her work for introducing me to Peter and Mary Ann Withers.

Our First Historian: a tercentenary Brief Life, June 1997

MASTER JOHN AUBREY was born of gentle family at Easton Piercy in the county of Wilts. (but near unto Glos.) on St Gregory's Day 1625. In infancy he was sickly, fared badly, and lived a solitary childhood (no brethren or sisters then living), much given to curiosity of nature and the scientifical arts, as well as of antiquities.

From schooling under one Latimer, a diligent teacher, at Leigh Delamere, he was sent to public school at Blandford Forum (*co.* Dorset), where he was cruelly us'd, but got his Latin and Greek. He began at Oxford, but the Civil Wars then coming interrupted his studies, and he returned with heavy heart in that dark time to his family, by then removed to Broad Chalke. The soldiery departing Oxford he resumed his term at Trinity, where he loved books and learned conversation above all else.

His father being ill, at Xmas 1648 he left Oxford for his native Wiltshire, and soon after, while hawking on the downs with friends, he happened on the wondrous stones of Abury, which years after he praised to the learned scholars at court. He was the while managing his father's estates, whose dying in 1652 brought him his inheritance, and a troublous busying time at husbandry and law.

When not about his earnest affairs, he mingled with scholars and ingeniose men at Wilton House, as well as London (where he studied the law at Middle Temple) and the Oxford coffee houses. Their thirst for learning and philosophy encouraged them to form a club wherein such matters might be debated and experimented, and this, when monarchy returned, they named the *Royal Society*.

In 1659, when the justices were at Devizes, there was a desire among some there met to make a survey of the county's antiquities, as was done elsewhere, and John Aubrey undertook as his share the task of North Wilts. This decided, his collaborators looked to other matters, or died, and never accomplish'd their design, But he investigated steadfastly his allotted portion for the space of ten years or more, as leisure allow'd, visiting houses and churches, and noting curious monuments and natural phaenomena. His great honour and pride was to conduct his Majesty (while journeying to the Bath) to observe the stupendous antiquities of Abury and Silbury Hill, with which the king was well pleased.

It was his cruel misfortune, in 1665, to woo one Mistress Joan Sumner, a headstrong, quarrelsome spinster (but rich); and was intent to marry her, on account of his estates and substance had trickl'd away by neglect, whilst he pursued his ingeniose studies. She was of Seend, and he lived a year or more in her brother's house, before she treacherously forswore their contract, and they fell to argument and dispute at law.

Each sued the other, and tho' justice lay with J.A. his fortune was us'd up and his credit gone, so that all his lands were sold. Even then, c.1670, his debts remained, and he was forced to abscond (sc. to flee the catchpoles who would apprehend him). He hid with friends in their houses, in different counties, and dared not visit North Wilts., tho' he sojourned yet sometimes at Broad Chalke (South Wilts.). He had in mind to turn to devout contemplation, and become a Jesuit, but his great socializing humour forbad it.

Through efforts of his friends (of whom he had a multitude) his circumstances better'd, and he gave himself to study and learned discourse, in the *Royal Society* and in taverns. He wrote of Surrey and then, 1679, at suggestion of Master Anthony Wood of Oxford (who had essay'd somewhat the same), he began to scribble notes on *Lives of Eminent Men*. Some were of his wide acquaintance, others he knew but by report. His method was not systematick, but (as he said) tumultuary: *sc.* he wrote just as the thoughts occurred to him, or whenever the information was discovered.

And this was how his books were all conceiv'd and executed, as a kind of chaos of curious truths and observation. For spurred by the enjoyment of his *Lives*, he set to writing much besides, on education, and superstition, and strange customs, and remarques on matters natural and scientific. In 1685 he brought to completion his notes (which for many years he had collected) on the *Natural History of Wiltshire*. This work, wherein he recorded all manner of curious facets of his native county, is accorded by many discreet judges his best work (saving only his *Lives*).

His final years were saddened by quarrels and bereavements, and unsettled by frequent changes of lodgings, but he continued diligently working on his manuscripts, especially *Monumenta Britannica*, of British antiquities. And to ensure that his labours would benefit posterity, he placed his notes and papers in Mr Ashmole's Museum at Oxford (whence they were removed to the Bodleian), whilst endeavouring also (tho' with little success) to have them publish'd.

His death chanced as following. While journeying from London to

Wiltshire, he stopt at Oxford in the lodging of a friend. Abed at night he met with an apoplectick fit which killed him (*æt.* 71), and he was buried (*'John Aubery a stranger"*) in St Mary Magdalene's church on 7th June 1697.

He was of short to middling stature, a scatter-brain'd but acute intellect, a true and endearing friend to many great and learned men. He lacked the diligence to manage business aright (whereby men accrue wealth), so that his substance and inheritance were lost. After his lifetime he was all but forgot in obscurity for many years. But he was the first to chronicle the monuments, customs, and phaenomena of his native county; and among the many who have essay'd to write histories and lives, he, *John Aubrey,* must be accounted the most engaging, amusing, and ingeniose of men.

Gastard Sunday Morning

YESTERDAY'S SNOW, delivered horizontally with venom, was mostly gone by nightfall, but we woke this morning to the real thing. It was the stuff of robins and jingle bells, and it was falling as it is supposed to — vertically, slowly, and the size of cornflakes. What is more, the weather-god obligingly switched it off as soon as we had finished breakfast.

Sunday mornings are quiet where we live and you cannot, as in towns, gauge the muffled acoustic of overnight snow from your bed. It is the visual impact here, of accustomed fields rendered colourless, a monochrome landscape.

The morning walk is different today. Yesterday, in the savage wind, we ventured no further than the garden, and the first snowfall of a young dog's life was celebrated with frenzied circuits of high excitement. But today the experienced snowdog strides out along the road, past a neighbour's step already swept (the snowing has barely stopped), past a field of dreary-grey sheep (each with a no-fun-for-us! stare), and across the field to Thingley.

The trailing edge of the snowcloud is in front of us now, and behind it blue sky and a hesitant sun are starting to paint the colours back on to the hillside beyond Lacock. The trees are already dripping.

At Thingley we reach a lane unviolated by tyre tracks. As a student of roads, I often try to imagine ancient lanes such as this before they were dressed with tarmac — rutted, grass-grown and of wavering width. Today it is easy. The snow has buried the twentieth century, and the lane greets us afresh as it would have done a medieval traveller on a winter's day six hundred years ago. We are the first of all creation to exercise this right of way today. The new snow sticks to my boots and falls off in lumps.

Ten minutes later we are playing snowballs across a field, when the Canada geese arrive. They are a noisy squadron, and we seem to lie under the flight-path of their morning constitutional from the lake in Corsham Park . I stop to count them. Fifty-nine, I think, but one of them is completely white. A snow-goose? Surely not.

We return home. Past a yesterday's snowman on a garden wall, past a cautious procession of motorists on the slushy main road, past a father with two young children dragging their new toboggan (its first outing to the playing field, their first real snow ever, perhaps). It is bright sunshine now. Already, I imagine, next year's Christmas card photographers are loading their equipment and setting off in their cars for Castle Combe.

The dog, dried-off, will go to sleep. And I shall switch the heater on in my study — but first, was it a snow-goose? Do you see snow-geese in Wiltshire? My book says that you don't, or rather, 'Anser caerulescens, Vagrant (escape)' only three since records began. But then, you don't see snow very often, these days.

S m a l l
T a l k
i n
W i l t s h i r e

wherein are Discover'd sundry *Endeavours*
(Literary and Otherwise)
by Wiltshire *Men* and *Women* chiefly
during the *Eighteenth* and *Nineteenth* Centuries,
together with certain *Mishaps* which *befell* them

Preface

IT HAS BEEN MY PRIVILEGE to have spent much of my working life so far, day in and day out, among the literature and records of local history. In doing so I have observed that, although some books on the library shelf are consulted almost daily, there are many others on whose top edge the dust thickens in desuetude. But somebody wrote them, somebody took the trouble to print them, and somebody must once have bought them, and perhaps even read them. Each has a story to tell – whether it now appears silly or earnest, misguided or dull, obsolete or obscure.

The same thought should strike anyone who scans old newspapers. In among the advertisements for cocoa, the Parliamentary intelligence and the shocking accidents, the prospector will occasionally find nuggets of pure gold. And every now and then, among some dryasdust documents in the record office, a human being surmounts the barrier of centuries to communicate, in language we all understand.

While I have been compiling this little book I have described it to my friends as an anthology, but I see now that I should rather have called it a sampler. It only scratches the surface of a vast, and largely untapped and uncharted, resource. In the manner of samplers it is intended for dipping into, and has no very rigid structure. But it does, assuredly, have a model.

Cecil Torr wrote *Small Talk at Wreyland*, he tells us, for private circulation among his personal friends. But he was persuaded to publish it, and the first part appeared in 1918. It takes the form of apparently random thoughts and reminiscences, by a genial scholar, who chose to cocoon himself in the house which he inherited in a hamlet on the edge of Dartmoor – this hamlet, incidentally (a learned friend tells me), should be pronounced 'Relland'. Much of his writing is autobiographical, but there are also long extracts from the diaries and correspondence of his father and grandfather, two canny Victorian squires. These extracts, concerning foreign travel, local events and much besides, are presented more or less at random, and are accompanied by Torr's own comments.

Such a gentle, bumbling, approach to the past seemed to me to be the perfect vehicle for presenting a selection from the kind of material which I have described; and in my own inadequate way I have tried to follow Torr's example – even to the extent of shamelessly borrowing part of his title. But there is little autobiography here, and I have neither the wit, nor the charm nor wisdom which makes Torr's book so special. In compiling it, however, I have enjoyed myself enormously; and if a fraction of the fun which went into the writing, comes across in the reading, I shall be more than satisfied.

It remains for me to thank most heartily the usual crew who never seem to complain about the inconveniences which my researches cause them. That is to say: Steven Hobbs and his colleagues in the Wiltshire Record Office; Michael Marshman, Felicity Gilmour and Wendy Bate in the Trowbridge Local Studies Library (Wiltshire County Council, Library and Museum Service); and Pamela Colman and Lorna Haycock in the Library of the Wiltshire Archaeological and Natural History Society at Devizes. I should like to offer my more formal thanks to the Wiltshire Archaeological and Natural History Society, the Wiltshire Record Office and the Wiltshire County Council Library and Museum Service for allowing me to use material in their possession. Finally, I am grateful to Ken Rogers for a number of leads, Roger Jones for his (probably misguided) confidence in publishing this collection, and my wife, Alison Borthwick, who once again has had to put up with my anti-social behaviour, and then has cheerfully and critically read the outcome.

John Chandler
East Knoyle
September 1992

[For this new edition I have made a very few alterations and corrections: JHC, 1998]

Into Print

Prefaces and Other Mishaps

Did you read my preface? I mention it only because some people tend to skip the preface and begin straight away with the book. Myself, I tend to read the preface and not bother with the book – but I imagine that this must be a bad habit picked up as a librarian. Prefaces can be a problem, certainly, for the writer as well as the reader. Take Edward Duke, for example, who in December 1836 sat down to crown the first volume of his literary achievement, *Prolusiones Historicae, or Essays illustrative of the Halle of John Halle*, (John Halle being a merchant of Salisbury) with a fourteen-page preface:

> This, almost constituent, portion of a book is presumed to be the first written, but (as in the present instance) it is, generally, the expiring efforts of the author's pen. It is, in reality, his postscript.
>
> It often serves to develope the style, and character, of the book itself, and is an index to the mind of its author...

Yes, that is where the problems begin. No-one is at their best while expiring, and a book all too candidly reveals the mind – and limitations – of its author. In this first chapter we shall conduct a little survey of some of the also-rans of Wiltshire history, and may discover some of the hurdles aspiring authors have to surmount.

Perhaps the first lesson to be learnt is that, if you are at all doubtful about tiresome matters like syntax and spelling, you ought to ask someone to look your manuscript over for you, before you send it to the printer. Good advice, but not always heeded. Take John Watts, for example, who in 1860 published his seven-page life story, *Self Help: the autobiography of*

Mr. John Watts, of Heytesbury, Professor of Gardening and Education. Here is a sample:

> daved Rose from a shepherd boy to a king and I rose from a shepherd boy to garddener. I head now eduction and if I make eney stake you must Exquese me. I do not now Eney thing bout grammer, I now more bout my granfather. My granfather wher very claver man. He meade villen [? a violin] out of old tailbord. I have herd pepel seay the did reember befre the wher born – the did rember hering the kees rattle in ther mothers pocket. I can not rember so long is theat, I can rember hering my mother seay that I was such a monster the coud Put me in to teapot. I never walk for 3 years, I walk at last From a goosbery tree to goosbery tree to fiend wich was the best, and was black one.

Once you are happy with your literary style there is the matter of illustrations to consider. There is always the danger that you may upset some of your readers if the pictures are not entirely suitable. And a hitch at this stage can disrupt the entire publishing schedule. Take this advertisement, for instance, which appeared in a local newspaper in 1767.

> This Day is Published, Price 1s. A Plain Narrative of Facts, relating to the Person who lately passed under the assumed Name of the Princess Wilbrahama, lately detected at the Devizes; containing her whole History, from her first Elopement from the Hon. Mrs Sc——t's, till her Discovery and Commitment to Devizes Bridewell: Together with the very extraordinary Circumstances attending that Discovery, and the Report of a Jury of Matrons summoned on that Occasion.
>
> In this Account will be found some Circumstances, which seem remarkably to corroborate the so much disputed Reality of the Caenean Metamorphosis and Androgynian Mystery of the Ancients; and some Hints which tend to explain the celebrated Gryph of Bononia...
>
> London: Printed for the Author; and sold by the Booksellers in

Great Britain and Ireland.

NB. Some Caracatures being thought necessary to elucidate particular Parts of this History, the Author has taken all possible Care to engage the best Artists for that Purpose.

TO THE PUBLIC – The directions given by the Draughtsman to the Engraver, occasioned some of the Caricatures in the Memoirs of the Princess Wilbrahama to be too indelicately express'd, and as there have been no more than half a dozen yet delivered out, and those too, among the Author's particular friends, hopes the public will excuse the delay of the publication, till the latter end of next month; when two other prints shall be inserted, that shall not in the least offend delicacy. NB. The Author likewise hopes, that those Gentlemen who have in possession those half dozen already published, will, for the above reasons, carefully lay them aside.

Nowadays that kind of tactic is known as 'hype', and is very effective. But there is always the danger that one of your friends with the unexpurgated version will sell the story to a Sunday newspaper. Just imagine the headline – FAKE ROYAL IN SEX-CHANGE ROW: SHOCK REVELATIONS.

ॐ

A Librarian's Treachery

No such vulgarities in the past, of course, but you still had to be careful of your friends. James Bodman, who published the first ever history of Trowbridge, in 1814, had a very unhappy experience with his librarian, a Mr Wearing. Fuelled by envy, according to Bodman, Wearing had inserted an advertisement for Bodman's book in the *Bath Herald*, but had included in it a number of misprints and errors, so as to make its author look ridiculous. So angry was Bodman, that he wrote a special poem on the subject, and included it as an epilogue to his book:

A POEM

When some of the wise heads had learn'd my intention,
To publish a work without their own invention;
To stop my proceeding, they held a consultation,
How they might succeed to stop my publication.

One said, "Twill be in vain to attack him directly,
'But if we assail him, let's do it correctly,
'And before he gets ready, we'll publish his work,
'But to accomplish our purpose, in secret we'll lurk.

'But to accomplish our work we cannot well find
'A pretext, by which we may publish his mind:
'But the way to betray him, to answer our end,
'We'll feign to applaud him, as being his friend.'

But who can accomplish this wicked intention,
To cut a man's throat by a friendly pretension?
'Why I,' says Smooth Looks, 'I'll sign my name W——g,
"'Tis part of my office, for I'm your librarian.'

A note he then wrote, pretending as friend,
To obtain such an answer as might suit their end.
'To complete my design on the man, as reverer,
'I'll employ one to publish, my friend Mr.Meyler.'

'Well said, my friend W.G., the business is done,
'Send down his own paper to Meyler and Son,
'Say, "Print it verbatim, but in any wise,
'Put many false letters, the work stigmatize."'

At length, like the panther, who misses his prey,
And leaps to his thicket to avoid a just flay;
He writes and says, 'He's not alone a hooper;'*
But if I think well, I may fall on a Cooper.

---

* Where the panthers inhabit, they are called Hoopers, because they betray the traveller by imitating the human voice.

Early nineteenth century view of Trowbridge

All a Matter of Confidence

• •

One cannot help feeling that James Bodman was quite capable of making himself appear ridiculous, without any assistance from Mr Wearing. Perhaps part of the trouble was that he lacked confidence. This comes over in his preface:

> But let me take leave to say, that to write a first History, is like a mariner going to sea without a rudder or compass, or one travelling by night in some trackless country, who has a certain object to go to, without light or path. But if I am so fortunate as to bring but a glimmering light out of this gross darkness, I hope the next attempt will be exceedingly visible; especially if undertaken by an abler hand. I do not expect to fare better than authors who are well qualified for publishing – I do not expect to escape the sneers or reproaches of the envious man, or the find fault reader; who (to use the words of a great writer) is like a growling dog over his viands, who very often snarls and growls over that very food by which he is satisfying himself, and filling his stomach...

What he needed was a stirring title-page, something to intrigue and impress the potential reader. How about this:

Warminster Common: shewing the steps by which it has advanced from its former state of notorious vice, ignorance, and poverty, to its present state of moral and social improvement... to which is added, an account, never before published, of numerous and important cures performed by that wonderful agent, Medical Electricity. By W. Daniell... 1850.

Or, even better, something to show that you are an author of considerable accomplishments:

Swindon Fifty Years Ago (More or Less). Reminiscences, Notes, and Relics of ye Old Wiltshire Towne, by Master William Morris, Author of 'France and the French', 'Ireland and the Irish', 'In Search After Ozone and Oblivion', 'Out and Home Again by way of Canada and the United States', 'What a Summer's Trip told me of the People and the Country of the Great West', Etc., Etc. Reprinted from ye Swindon Advertiser. Swindon: Printed and Published by the Author, at the 'Advertiser' Office, 10, Victoria Street.

No-one is left in any doubt that Master William Morris was a man of the world. But William Morris (not to be confused with his more famous namesake) was a journalist, you see, and journalists are concerned to make an impact.

Some authors, however, no matter how important the things they have to say, shun all publicity and live the life of a recluse. John Legg of Market Lavington published two important treatises in 1780, on bird migration and on the grafting of plants. Both appeared anonymously, and Legg's achievements would never have been credited to him at all were it not for renewed interest in his work during the 1890s, and the quest to discover his true identity.

The help of Alfred Smith, doyen of Wiltshire ornithologists, was enlisted, and after considerable frustration he not only discovered a memorial tablet to Legg in Market Lavington church (he died in 1802, aged 47), but also made contact with surviving members of his family. As a result he was able to paint this vignette of a private, tortured soul:

He lived and died a bachelor, and for some time at least, if not to the end of his short life, his sisters lived with him. He appears to have had no profession, but to have devoted himself in his early years to the study of Nature; and he is reported by his descendants to have practised the art of grafting and inoculation of trees in his own garden at Lavington: but in the latter part of his life, for he died in middle age, he was absorbed in religious speculations; and he appears to have latterly given way to melancholy thoughts and unhappy broodings, to which he was doubtless predisposed by much infirmity of body. Family tradition reports that towards the end of his life he shut himself up almost completely, seldom moving beyond his garden, where he indulged in reveries, and mused in solitude: nay, so persistently did he shun the society of his fellows that he objected to be seen in the village street, and to avoid observation he is said to have made a private path to the Church, by which he could go unseen by any: and even when a young relative was taken by her mother to visit him, all she ever saw of the recluse was his pigtail as he darted upstairs to avoid the interview. His nephew, too, recorded that he never saw him but once, and that then he never spoke to him.

ﻉ

A Cynic

A few months before John Legg's birth, and a few miles away in Devizes, an author of a very different kind published an anonymous book. *Origines Divisianae, or the antiquities of the Devizes: in some familiar letters to a friend, wrote in the years 1750, and 1751*, was probably the first 'spoof' local history ever written, and I can only think of one other since, Osbert Lancaster's *Drayneflete Revealed*. The author's cynical approach is summed up in an anecdote, with which he opens his second letter:

An old woman, who shew'd Lord Bathurst's fine place by Cirencester, was ask'd by a Gentleman that came to see it – Pray what building is that? – Oh, Sir, that is a ruin a thousand years old, which my Lord built last year; and he proposes to build one this year half as old again.

The book's author was a certain James Davis, a Devizes physician, and its printer claimed that by the time it was published in 1754 the author was dead (although the *Dictionary of National Biography* states that he died on 13th July 1755 – so perhaps that, too, was just his little joke).

Davis was a cynic, and the target of his book was the improbable antiquarian speculations of William Stukeley and his coterie.

He was well aware of their learned footnote technique, so he includes his own parody:

(a) The uncommon advantages of Etymological knowledge you will find very handsomely handled by a Friend of mine in his ingenious treatise on Barley Wine; who is a merry Greek, and sensible even when Carotic or Carybaric; and indeed always, but when he is delicate, v. Oinos Krithinos, p.23, and a dissertation upon Close-stools.

A close-stool, incidentally, was what we should call a commode. But the most cutting satire is kept for the list of contents, which is printed at the end of the book:

LETTER 1: A Preamble of a School-boy — A peep at a Town and a Castle — A doubt whether it be British, Roman or Saxon — Julius Caesar knew nothing of it, that's poz — Musgrave mistaken, St-k—y mistaken, every body mistaken but the Author — Monks were good scholars — Roman coins and Penates found here — Why they were hid — Mr. Wise hinted to be otherwise.

LETTER II: A Speech of an old Woman on Ruins — Roger Poor Bishop of Salisbury. suddenly metamorphiz'd into poor Roger — King Stephen a Pretender — Alexander Bishop of Lincoln a son of a whore — Henry Blois Bishop of Winchester an ecclesiastical Bully — His brother King Stephen a pickpocket.

LETTER III: Fitzhubert an errant Freethinker — Dy'd in his shoes — The Castle not heard of for 100 years, being hid all that time in a mist — A pause in the narration for a muzzy description — A long tedious Story about Hubert de Burgo Lord Chancellor — How he had like to have been kidnapp'd and how he conjur'd himself thro' a Keyhole into a Monastry — Henry the third out at Elbows —

Account of a Trap-door near the High-Altar in Merton Priory very convenient for prime Ministers in the Suds [i.e. in trouble] — A dispute between Captain Geoffry Crancomb and an honest sturdy anonymous Blacksmith — Henry the third not quite so bold a pickpocket as King Stephen — Hubert had nothing to live upon, but bread; water, and his beads, for he would not eat his own words — Peter de Rupibus Bishop of Winchester had a heart as hard as a stone — Robert Bishop of Salisbury sent some Constables to the Devil — Hubert conveyed miraculously to Wales and never heard of after.

LETTER IV: A pair of new fashion'd spectacles recommended to all Antiquarians — Cambden an old fashion'd wary precise Antiquarian — A description of a fine place of ruins — Digressions of use to Authors and booksellers — Castles dye of consumptions — The most antique pair of scales, ever known, try'd — St—k—y almost lost in a Roman ditch of his own making.

And so on, and so on.

But whether such a display of wit and erudition impressed its audience and damaged its victims is hard to assess. Davis is virtually unknown now, and his book very scarce, whereas Stukeley figures large in every history of archaeology – even though much of what he believed was absurd, as Davis realized.

こ

A Two-edged Sword
● ●

And here's another matter which the budding author should bear in mind. If you wish your books to be a publishing success you should try to include somewhere an indication that they will impress their audience. Choice snatches from as many favourable reviews as possible is the best way.

But do make sure that they are favourable. Edward Duke published a prospectus for his book on John Halle, which included the following reviews:

This work deserves a place amongst the curiosities of literature – *John Bull*.

We know not when we have met with a more amusing publication than the first volume of a work entitled the Halle of John Halle – *Bristol Journal*.

This work will be esteemed by those who like to make the history of manners auxiliar to the history of events and persons. Most heartily indeed do we 'throw our old shoe' after it – *Literary Gazette*.

It is probably a mistake to publish extracts from reviews of your work, unless you are absolutely sure that they are meant to be genuinely complimentary. Anyone who has experience of reviewing local history books, and who has tried to be gentle on a second-rate work so as not to discourage its aspiring author, will know what I mean, and will be able to read between the lines of a review. The back-handed compliment is a favourite device, and I remember once having it done to me: 'The author analyses his material in ways that a modern historian would approve of...' – and I too made the mistake of quoting it on the fly-leaf. Since then I have paid similar compliments to others.

Edward Slow, the dialect poet from Wilton, whose work we shall sample later, was fond of including press notices in his books. But when we read this accolade of his poetry from *Public Opinion* – 'his skill with the West country lingo is curious and interesting' – or this, from the *Durham Chronicle* – 'It is not high-class poetry, certainly; but it does not come below the average...' – we may comment 'Two cheers'. Worse, from Slow's point of view, is his use of the review in *Court Circular*, which he quotes thus:

His poems are certainly very amusing, * * * Mr Slow also writes in English, and his verses have the true ring of feeling in them.

The trouble is, that it does not take a great deal of imagination to guess the gist of the comment concealed by * * *.

❧

Envoi

• •

So, now we have covered the title page, the list of contents, the preface, the illustrations, the problems of editing, and all the publicity. There is just one more thing – the ending. Here is the closing passage from Edward Duke's epic volume, with which we began:

> 'Oh! my book, what shall I say unto thee? Oh! *mi ocelle*! thou apple of mine eye! thou little knowest the troubles, which too probably await thee! Thou art about to enter into life – about to encounter the passing remarks of those, who might meet thee in thy wandering path; and whilst, mayhap, some may kindly take thee by the hand, and send thee on thy way rejoicing, others may be intent on spying out all thy faults, and yield thee a more unfavourable reception. Thou mayest, in thy adventurous course, fall in with the grim critic, who, eyeing thee askaunt, *torvo vultu, truculentoque corde* [with a scowling face and a ferocious heart], may cleave thy skull with his literary tomahawk, or mercilessly plunge his sharpened knife into thy very heart. Thou art about to sail on a sea beset with rocks, and quicksands, and liable to encounter the tempestuous gale, which may hurl thee to inevitable destruction. Oh! my book! my anxious heart beats heavily for thy fate. Fare thee well! I can only add, in the words of Martial, '*I, fuge, sed poteras tutior esse domi*'.

Martial was probably right. His line can be roughly translated: 'Go, fly, but you could be safer staying at home.'

Actually, this passage is only the end of volume one... But volume two was never published.

❧ ❧

S u p e r s t i t i o n s

A Donkey to the Rescue

Among the reminiscences of William Morris, the worldly wise newspaper proprietor, was the following little story:

> I once had a donkey.
>
> The other day I passed in the High-street, Swindon, a woman who once had a baby.
>
> I always think of my donkey and her baby when I see that woman.
>
> It is not very many years ago when, one day, I was called away from my books and papers to a woman with a baby in her arms at my door. The poor child was black in the face, and its body and limbs were perfectly rigid as it lay in its mother's arms in the throes of a fearful phlegmatic struggle.
>
> 'Oh please sir, I hope that you won't be offended by my asking, but would you let me pass my baby under your donkey's belly? It has the whooping cough so bad, and I am told that is the only way to cure it,' piteously exclaimed the woman as I neared her.
>
> 'How many times has it to be done?' I asked in reply, as it at once occurred to me that I had previously heard something of this remedy, with some vague idea that the ceremony had to be performed altogether nine times – three days in succession: then an interval of three days: then another passing for three days, and so on, until the child had been passed nine times under the donkey's belly on nine separate days, extending over a period of fifteen days, which, it must be admitted, was long enough time to either kill or cure the unfortunate patient.

'Only once, if you please, sir; but I must pass it under the belly three times. You won't mind my doing it, will you, sir?'

In this year of grace, eighteen eighty-five, the mother of that child is, probably, still under forty years of age. I often see her in our streets, but I have never had the heart to ask her what the effect of her passing her child three times under the belly of my donkey had.

૨ð

The Medicine Chest

William Morris was not alone in his concern to record old customs and beliefs. In the case of his native Swindon the contrast between old and new was more pronounced than elsewhere, naturally, since in 1885 most of Swindon was less than fifty years old; but similar attempts to collect information about the 'old ways' were made in many places. Folk cures were a case in point, because everywhere they were succumbing to the onslaught of scientific medicine.

Well, not quite everywhere. Here is Alfred Smith again, the ornithological detective, wearing a different hat, as he describes a bit of medical misunderstanding:

But to mark the supreme indifference to reason, and the mere working of a charm, which is really the light in which many of our rustics regard the prescriptions of medical men, I will give the following case, which occurred within my own personal knowledge, within the limits of the borough of Devizes. A labourer, being confined to his bed with a rather sharp attack of pleurisy, was visited by the parish doctor, who, together with other remedies, said he would send a blister [i.e. a poultice], which should be at once applied to the patient's chest. On the following day, when the medical gentleman visited his patient, he was met at the door by the sick man's wife, who, with great glee, expressed her admiration at the effects of the blister, which had done wonders; and said that her husband was in consequence much the better. The doctor of course expressed his satisfaction, but when he came to examine the sick man, he was surprised to find no trace of a blister, and on enquiring how that was, the wife with great readiness explained, 'You see, Sir, he hadn't got no chest, but he's got a good-sized box in the corner, and we clapp'd en on that': and there, sure enough, on a deal box, was the blister which had worked such a magic cure, to the no small merriment of the doctor.

ë

Who needs a Doctor?

Such were the wonders of Victorian medical science. But to return to the older, traditional, treatments, we find that between 1893 and 1897 a series of cures was sent in by correspondents to the editor of a new journal, *Wiltshire Notes and Queries*, with a view to preserving and comparing them:

For the Gout, Rheumatism, or any other Defluction. Take polipody of the oak, hermodactyls, China root, sarsaparilla, of each four ounces, guaicum six ounces. Bruise these and infuse them 24 hours in 9 pints of water and 3 pints of white wine, in a pot close cover'd, haveing stood infusing 24 hours on a moderate fire; then let them boil gently to the consuption of a fourth part, and strain for use.

The same ingredients will serve again to make two more decoctions, pouring on them each time 6 pints of water and 2 of white wine, boiling and straining the liquor as before.

Drink for 3 days as much of this as reasonable as you can, the more so as not to be offended at it, the sooner will be the cure effected; while you drink of it abstain from broths, salads, sauces, fruits, fish, milk or anything made with it. N.B. You may eat of any sort of well roasted meat which is right easy of digestion and not salted. On every fourth day take a gentle purge, and while you take the decoction forbear all other liquors.

If you follow these directions exactly, you'l not fail of a cure in either gout or rheumatism or a sciatica; be sure you neglect not purging, otherwise you'l be apt to break out into boils.

This medicine greatly purifies the blood and only works by urine, and is an alterative only, and can be of no ill consequence to the patient. N.B. This has at once taking cur'd the most inveterate gout.

Observe: Not to put in the wine as menc'oned in the first paragraph, but filter the decoction and then put in the wine and give it two or three gentle boils.

Now, just wait a minute – that's not fair. Forgive me for interrupting, but you really cannot change your mind at this late stage in the recipe. We had enough trouble finding the hermodactyls, and by now we have been infusing our decoction for 24 hours.

Oh, well, you had better carry on with the next one, I suppose:

Snail Broth:- I knew two persons who were dosed with snail broth; it was used as a cure for consumption and wasting complaints. One of the patients was a young woman living at Bishopstrow, the other was a lad whose home was in Wales. The black, shell-less slugs that come out at night when the dew falls on the grass were also recommended to be eaten for the same disease, and I have been told by old folks now living in south Wilts that they have known many who partook of them. But for the snail broth I can myself vouch. The broth was made by boiling the snails, shells and all, in milk, straining it, and giving it to the sick person fasting, generally before breakfast. It was very slimy and jellied when cold. As children, we used to amuse ourselves by picking up the snails and singing-

Snail, snail, put out your horns,
Or else I'll kill you.

Or-

Snail, snail, come out of your hole,
Or else I'll beat you as black as a coal.

A Cure for Neuralgia:- Walking through one of the adjacent villages the other day I came across a farmer that I knew – a genuine son of the soil – and in response to his kind inquiries for my health, I complained to him that I had been sadly troubled with neuralgia of late. 'That is a sort of toothache,' said he, 'a thing I never had since I was a boy, and I will tell you what cured me. Old John, who has been dead this forty years, told me of it. Cut a piece off each finger- and toe-nail, and a piece off your hair, and get up on the next Sunday morning before sunrise and with a gimlet bore a hole in the first maiden-ash you come across and put the nails and hair in, then peg the hole up.'

A maiden-ash, for the benefit of your readers who would like to try the experiment, is an ash that has not been pollarded or topped.

Curious Recovery of Speech. ...a curious case is given by Archdeacon Squire of a person who, after having been dumb for years, recovered the use of his speech by means of a dream of this description:-

'One day, in the year 1741, he got very much in liquor, so much so that on his return home at night to Devizes, he fell from his horse three or four times, and was at last taken up by a neighbour and put to bed in a house on the road. He soon fell asleep; when, dreaming that he was falling into a furnace of boiling wort, it put him into so great an agony of fright that, struggling with all his might to call out for help, he actually did call out aloud, and recovered the use of his tongue that moment, as effectually as he ever had it in his life, without the least hoarseness or alteration in the old sound of his voice.'

を

Garden Warfare

●●●

And here are a few gardening tips, supplied by Samuel Cooke of Overton, near Marlborough, and published in about 1747 in a useful volume, the *Complete Gardener*. A contributor to *Wiltshire Notes and Queries* possessed a copy, and described it thus:

> The advice at the end of the work on general topics is certainly curious, and throws rather a lurid light on rural Wiltshire life of the time. After giving some instructions for the destruction or prevention of vermin, he says, sage and rue will keep toads from the garden; a lanthorn set on the side of the water will prevent the croaking of frogs; polecats and badgers, as also foxes, are numerous enough to require special traps for their destruction; bullfinches and goldfinches are to be exterminated; under 'bat-fowling, the manner of it', the author says, 'observe where these birds roost, as they do in shrubs, hedges, and trees'; mole-catching is a simple matter – put a head or two of garlic or onions in their holes, they will run out, as if frighted, and you may with a spear, or dog, take them; adders will fly from the smell of old burnt shoes in a garden.

ॐ

Rooted to the Spot

●●●

Meanwhile, in a village a few miles away, none of these potent nostrums seems to have had any effect on the predicament of a certain Mr Dean. A very early (1724) press report tells the strange story:

> We hear from Collingbourn Kingston in Wiltshire that there is now living there one John Dean, who for three years past has been in one Posture, leaning in a Partition Wall between two Chambers; at first his head rested against the Wall, but by Degrees forc'd a Way through, as likewise for his shoulders, his Breast resting upon an Inter-joist; his Legs by long standing begin to mortify, so that he

cannot live much longer; he eats very hearty, and is always craving for Victuals; his Excrements are voided in the Place where he stands, which contributes very much to the Disagreeableness of the Object. Several People have endeavour'd to persuade him to move from the Place, but in vain, alledging that he cannot be easy in any other Posture, and if they go to use Violence, it puts him in a raving Madness; he sometimes talks very sensible, at other Times like a Lunatick, and believes that he is bewitch'd, which Opinion has prevail'd over the greatest Part of the Parish.

٭

Wilkinson's Questionnaire

Forty years before the first issue appeared of the glorious ragbag of similar antiquarian culs-de-sac, *Wiltshire Notes and Queries*, a county society was formed at Devizes under the name 'Wiltshire Archaeological and Natural History Society', and this began to publish a magazine (as it still does). Folklore and folk customs made an appearance in the very first issue, and seem – very much to the society's credit – to have been regarded from the outset as an integral part of local history.

A leading enthusiast in the early years was John Wilkinson, who was rector of Broughton Gifford, near Melksham, from 1848 until his death in 1876. He was keen to encourage local clergy to write histories of their parishes to a common format, and he set out a detailed framework of 'heads of information' to be collected. Several, including his own on Broughton Gifford, were published, and some others remain in manuscript at the society's library. A detailed questionnaire was sent, on the bishop's authority, to each incumbent, and about seventy responded. Four of the questions concerned traditions and customs current in the parish at the time (the 1860s), and although most forms were left blank on this subject, there was a handful of replies. So far as I am aware, none has been published up to now:

Avebury: Mummers at Christmas. Eating cakes with honey and 'Lent-figs' on Silbury on Palm Sunday. Possibly an adaptation by the medieval church of some heathen custom to the act [account?] of the cursing the barren fig-tree on the Mount of Olives on the Monday in Holy Week.

Beechingstoke: It is said that one of the Raymonds of Puckshipton offered to rebuild the church if the lead of the roof was given to him. The parish accepted the offer and the church was rebuilt, and the roof covered with shingle tiles (1693). By this transaction Mr. Raymond is said to have netted a good sum of money. This must have been Charles Raymond who died in 1716.

Chilton Foliat: A loaf baked on Good Friday always remains good. And grated into clean water is a great cure for fevers, etc. Rain water caught on Holy Thursday is a cure for bad eyes.

Durrington: The only superstition which has come under my notice is that an aged woman nearer 90 than 80 told me – perhaps five years ago – that she had gone out the night before and had shaken her apron to the moon, because no-one had given her any gift for some time, and that a present had come to her within a few hours.

Fittleton and Haxton: The people here think much of keeping Christmas, when some of the village youths come round, and act as 'Mummers'. They also speak of 'Tide Times'.

Heddington: When I first came here there was a very abominable custom of treating with rough music newly married couples. The boys and young men furnished themselves with old pots and pans, and amused themselves by beating them for half the night in front of the house. I believe the custom is now quite discontinued.

North Tidworth: I believe the common people 'blow away warts' to the moon. This they do for one another. I am not allowed to stand at the foot of the bed of a dying person as it hinders the departure of the spirit.

᛭

Oram's Grave

Presumably in the 1860s the rector of Heddington's attitude prevailed, that such superstitions were abominable. He seems, incidentally, to have witnessed a skimmington (a communal punishment for marital irregularity) and assumed that it was a wedding custom. By the 1890s, although fewer traditions would have survived, the questionnaire might have been more productive, since by then the study of folklore had become more respectable as a pastime for clergymen. Even the bishop took a personal interest, as this contribution to *Wiltshire Notes and Queries* reveals:

At the intersection of the old track from Salisbury to Warminster across the Downs, with that from Maddington to Codford St Mary, on the boundary line of Maddington and Chitterne St Mary, is a barrow marked 'Oram's Grave' on the Ordnance 6in. Map. The Bishop, on his visit to us (23 March 1893), pointed out this name to me, of which I was previously ignorant, and suggested that it was the corruption of some British or Saxon name, which I doubted. Afterwards, on looking at the map, it occurred to me that as the grave was situated at the cross roads, Oram was probably the name of a suicide, buried there according to the old custom and law.

A conversation with widow Sarah Cook (aged 81) on 28 March 1893, proved that this was the case. She told me that in 1849 she and her husband were living in one of the Maddington Manor Down Barn Cottages, and in the other the shepherd lived, James White and his wife Elizabeth (formerly Windsor), a very good woman, aged 61, both of Chitterne. Elizabeth White told Sarah Cook that when she was a child she was coming home with her father from Salisbury (or elsewhere) and when they were near the crossways by the Clump, they saw many people coming from Chitterne to bury Oram in the barrow there, for he had hung himself with his own rope, and was to be buried there. Her father told her that 'her maunt be vraughten at what she saw for they wouldn't hurt she', and so she saw Oram buried. She did not tell Sarah Cook whether his body was in a coffin or not, but Sarah Cook thinks there was a coffin; certainly there was no parson and no service. The barrow has ever afterwards been called 'Oram's Grave', and the name is now perpetuated in the Ordnance Survey.

8 May 1893. – The Rev. A.C. Pinhorn, Vicar of Chitterne, told me the circumstances of Oram's burial are forgotten in Chitterne, except that the cause of his suicide was disappointment in love, and that a stake was driven through the body, which I think proves that though he may have been carried to the grave in a coffin, he was not buried in one. There is no record of the funeral in the Register, nor any charge for it in the parish accounts.

⁊ ⁊

Clergy

Broughton Gifford

John Wilkinson's interest in folklore during the 1860s puts him ahead of his time, and must have seemed odd to many of his fellow clergy. But he had discovered from his own parish registers a kindred spirit in the person of one of his predecessors, a certain William Hickes, rector of Broughton Gifford from 1689 to 1733. 'We are most thankful to him,' wrote Wilkinson, 'he certainly provided for, if he did not anticipate, the demands of the parochial historian.' Near the end of his incumbency Hickes wrote the following note on a fly-leaf of his register:

> In Novemb. Anno Dni. 1732. A house called the Church House, which had two chimnys, one at each end, was pulled down and the stones and timber used in the Rebuilding the House near the Parsonage House. (This House reached from the Lower Stile going to the Brook) to the Rails eastward as may from the Stoone wall left for Bounds of the Church Yard.
>
> This Church House was Built by one Thomas Cookson, as appeared by a Stone in the outward Wall of the sd. house next the Churchyard Side, in which was Engraven a Pedlars Pack and on Each Side a Cock.
>
> Some Poor people lived in it in the memory of a man who livd in the year Sixteen hund. eighty and nine and in particular (as I have been informd by some that could remember it) the Father of John Oatridge, which John Oatridge had a leg cut of and mended Shoos, in a house belonging to Esq. House in the lower end of the field near the Brook and was Buried in May 1703 which House was pulld down about year seventeen hundrd. and eleven or twelve.

About this Church House after it was pulld down were noises heard in the night like throwing the Timbers about one upon another and upon the Stones that Lay near by Mrs. Hunt and her two daughters that livd just by.

Likewise in the Farm House (lying by the Parson's House in wch. then livd one Robert Newman) while the Church house was Pulling down and after they heard the treading of one going up and down Stairs.

Also a Noise of throuing the Stones that were brought from the sd. Church House into their Barton, from one heap to another.

Over the years Hickes had many observations to make on the weaknesses of his flock. He was forthright in recording 'reputed' and 'pretended' wives, and 'illegal' marriages. One or two couples left things until the last moment:

John Tomkins of the paroish of Holt and Ester Stevens of the paroish of Broghton were maryed by licence. The man was about 65 years old, and was sick 3 or 4 weeks. The woman about 25 years. He scarce ever saw her till they came to Church to be married, nor spoke a word to her above his sign to mary her, but by another person, and it was agreed upon but the night before mariage, and were maried the next day, and he dyed the next day after mariage. So that the woman was a maid, wife, and widow within 24 hours, and supposed to be a maid as well as Widow and own'd to me she was a maid still.

Wilkinson, when he transcribed that entry for his history, coyly omitted the last observation, with the remark: 'The further revelations of the plain-spoken Rector concerning Mrs. Tomkins, do not admit of publication.' Why not, one wonders? But then one realizes that it is just one of many examples of the Victorians' knack of titillation, achieved by omitting an innocuous remark and then referring to it by innuendo. Of course the same code precluded any mention of another entry, by the next vicar, in 1735:

Jacob Bull married Miriam Bull, both of Broughton. The woman was delivered of a male child the same evening.

The moral tales which pepper Broughton's register are not only about matters sexual. [In fact the practice of an old man marrying a very young woman shortly before his death was quite widespread, and was generally intended to prolong a copyhold tenancy for the deceased's family. See J.H. Bettey, 'Manorial custom and widows' estate', *Archives*, vol.20, 1992, pp.208-16.] Here is a sad story from Hickes about anger:

Isaac Bull was buried, Aug. 13. He was thrown of his hors on Lansdown and dyed the next day. His mother he curs'd at his going out and she wish'd that he might break his leg or nec before he came home. He threw his mother downe and he mockt her, calling her snecking bitch and other reproachfull words.

No, we can't have that. Wilkinson omits the word 'bitch', and inserts three dots in its place. But when describing his own times Wilkinson is more candid and forthright. Here, in 1859, he describes housing conditions, marriages and amusements:

The labouring population are very indifferently lodged. The cottages are abundant, but the dwelling rooms are few and small (the weavers devote the best lighted and largest apartments to their shops [i.e. workshops]), the sleeping accommodation is not such as to admit of the decent separation of ages and sexes. Wells are infrequent (notwithstanding the excellent water within a few feet of the surface), nor are the offices [privies] convenient or proper. The drainage is defective. This state of things is no more than might be expected in a parish, where the landed proprietors, being non-resident, want that interest in the people, which would naturally arise from personal communication. The poor here are not neighbours to the rich. In this respect we are no worse off than a large proportion of out of the way parishes, but we have disadvantages of our own. With hardly an exception, the cottages (originally for the most part encroachments on the commons) belong either to the poor occupiers themselves; or to proprietors, who are hardly removed from the labouring class; or to the farms, with which they are let. The owners or the managers want either the means or the will (generally both) to promote domestic comfort. Though there are so many cottages and some vacant, yet rents are not low; three small rooms and 10 or 15 perches of garden ground fetch £4 a year. The explanation is, that a large proportion of the cottages for hire are owned by one person, who also keeps a beer shop and general store of such articles as the poor require. He works the rent against the shop, and the shop against the rent, so that he is able to keep up prices in both commodities.

St. Mary's Church, Broughton Gifford

The marriage ceremony is conducted about here in a manner which is not pleasing. It is a ceremony and no more. [Wilkinson's observations on marriage are discussed on pp 89-90 above].

The same remark applies to games and amusements; we have next to none. There were indeed, ten years since, the remains of a

Michaelmas revel. Bushes were hung out at unlicensed houses, and the whole thing had degenerated into a mere drinking bout. The excise officers and the police extinguished it. Bull-baiting lingered here longer than elsewhere: there is a tradition of it on the common. So there is of cock-fighting: the pit is said to have been where the Rector's cucumber frame now stands. The moral odour of the place still hangs about it: the only thing he ever missed were five cucumbers stolen one Sunday morning. The chief village dissipation takes place at the Whit-sun meeting of the Benefit club. The neighbouring fair at Bradford Leigh used to be much frequented, and was generally accompanied by mischievous midnight revelry. This holiday gave a mnemonic date to 'the simple annals' of domestic life. I have heard old people reckon events, 'come next Bradford Leigh fair'. I have known a skimmington. A mob, with tongs, gridirons, saucepans, or anything they could get, surrounded the house of one who was said to be an unfaithful husband, and made most unmelodious music. Kattern cakes are carried about for sale on St Katherine's day, November 25th. It seems a pure matter of vulgar merchandise. There are no rhymes, no bowl, no jollity, no maidens making merry together and looking out for good husbands by help of the patroness of spinsters. We have no 'merry wakes, May games, and Christmas triumphs', of course no christening customs, but not even a harvest home. We are rather dull.

The 'we' is important. Wilkinson was one of that priceless band of clergymen who settled into their parishes and became totally bound up with the affairs of their parishioners. He was no detached observer, gone tomorrow, but an intimate historian.

He wrote his history as a model for others to emulate, and it is arranged according to the scheme which he had devised for parochial histories. His ideas were in turn derived from the *New Statistical Account of Scotland*, which had been compiled by local clergy.

⁂

A Temperate Vicar ...

• •

But if Wilkinson failed to spur all his colleagues into producing copy for a comprehensive published history of Wiltshire, that did not mean that they were unwilling to chronicle their own parish events in private notebooks, for their own and their successors' reference.

John Augustus Lloyd was one such chronicler. His volume of parish notes begins in 1877, when he became vicar of Broad Hinton, high on the downs south of Swindon, and continues through the 1880s until his departure for Mere in November 1890. His successor, Vere Awdry, kept it going with rather less gusto for a few years, but then it gradually fell into abeyance.

Awdry's short incumbency was marred by tragedy. A widower, on 21st June 1891 he records that his little girl died suddenly of convulsions aged two years and one month, and was buried with her mother at North Bradley. For two months Awdry was absent from his parish on doctor's orders, but on 29th October he remarried, and brought his bride back to the village. They were, he reports:

> ... accorded a most hearty welcome by the villagers, the horse being taken out of the carriage, and the carriage with its occupants drawn into the vicarage grounds and up to the door by hand.

The following January the notebook records that:

> ... a small hand fire pump has been presented to the vicar for a wedding present. It stands in the vicarage hall always ready for use, and is at the service of all who need it.

A more protracted episode of parish history was chronicled by his predecessor. Lloyd was the son of a Bath magistrate and physician, and it was perhaps not surprising that he should espouse the cause of temperance. It was some eighteen months after his arrival that, in November 1878, he chaired a public meeting which inaugurated the Broad Hinton Church of England Temperance Society and Happy Home Union.

Its minute book has survived, and shows that, as in the case of so many local initiatives, it was carried on with great enthusiasm for a few years, but then the regular meetings ceased. The last entry describes a public tea held in the village in May 1891, and attended by about 100. Lloyd had left the village by this date, and Awdry had taken over. The assistant diocesan secretary of the temperance society spoke – predictably – on the evil of drink and the dangers which might follow. His talk was preceded by a few half-hearted words of introduction from Awdry, who said that he had no experience himself but should be glad to hear concerning it.

But in Lloyd's time, when it was set up, the society had chalked up a famous victory. It was Lloyd's idea to revive the old patronal feast, held by the medieval church each year on the day of the saint to whom the church was dedicated. Broad Hinton's saint's day, St Peter ad Vincula, should have been on 1st August, but for temperance purposes the revived feast was held later in the month. The first festival took place on 18th August, 1879, and involved an afternoon service and sermon by a visiting rector, followed by a temperance tea and school feast. The minute book records that it was, 'quite a success', and includes a newspaper cutting which begins:

> We have to record the success, in spite of some little difficulties, of the first annual festival of the village temperance society.

A fortnight later we learn what those 'little difficulties' might have been. Lloyd's parish notebook has an entry for 30th August:

> The licence of Henry Witt landlord of the Bell Inn in this village was taken away by the Marlborough bench of magistrates for being drunk and riotous on Sunday 17th instant. Broad Hinton Feast! How has a church festival degenerated and fallen through.

Sure enough, the *Marlborough Times* reports that:

> Henry Witt was charged with being drunk and disorderly at Broad Hinton, and fined 10/- and 18/6 costs.

His licence was not renewed, and the decision on its renewal was deferred.

Whether this was an isolated protest by the publican, or the result of an 'alternative' feast organized at the pub, we are not told. But there is an irony in the plight of Henry Witt. In reviving the patronal feast the vicar imagined that he was recreating a medieval church festival. What he forgot, or chose to ignore, was the alternative name for such events, the church-ale (because ale was brewed and consumed in great quantities in order to raise funds for the church fabric), and the fact that at the reformation such feasts were outlawed on account of the drunkenness and debauchery associated with them. It was Henry Witt who had revived the old tradition, and he might with more justification than the vicar, have exclaimed, 'How has the festival degenerated', when he discovered that only tea was being served at it.

But such was the Victorian perversion of ecclesiastical history. The temperance movement, having taken away the publican's livelihood, was now in the ascendant. In November 1880 Lloyd recorded in the parish notebook:

> The Bell Inn – Loveday having had possession for about one year became bankrupt, and John Austin a tee-totaller took it. He gave up 10th December finding it could not be made to pay honestly.

In January 1881 there is a note that it had changed hands again, and the census of April 1881 records that Henry Hopkins, a thirty-year-old carpenter and licensed victualler from Calne, was at the Bell; so it presumably reverted to being a conventional pub, as indeed it is today. But not to be outdone, the temperance society on 6th June 1881 opened its own alternative place of refreshment, a coffee tavern, in a cottage a few doors down the village street.

There were two classes of adult temperance society members, those who asserted that they were willing to do something towards the suppression of drunkenness, and those who were total abstainers. The latter signed the pledge:

I hereby agree, by God's help, to abstain from the use of intoxicating drinks, except at the Holy Communion, or under medical order, as long as I keep my card of membership.

At the inaugural meeting twelve joined in the former category, and six in the latter, but there were many new members, and not a few ignominious departures, during the first few years of the Broad Hinton society's existence.

From the vicar's point of view there was one most satisfactory convert to the temperance cause, and this warranted a special entry in the parish notebook:

Dec.10th 1879. The Rev.J. Campbell gave a temperance lecture at the schoolroom. Henry Witt late of the Bell Inn signed the pledge, which he has not yet broken (Nov.1880); he is quite altered for the better.

Lloyd kept up the momentum. In June 1880 he presided at a temperance meeting, by reading extracts from the *Temperance Chronicle* and afterwards the humorous piece, 'How to cook a husband'. Then in August preparations were under way for the second annual feast. This too proved to be a bittersweet experience, as the parish notebook records:

Monday 16th Aug.1880. Temperance festival and tea service at 3 pm. Rev.J. Campbell preached. Day fine and numbers present large. The late landlord of the Bell Inn kept a stall for the sale of non-intoxicating drinks in the vicarage field. As if to counter-balance this one of the members of the fete committee who had previously broken his pledge very brutally beat his wife the day previous.

This was not the first lapse. As early as 16th April 1879 the minute book records:

The name of Charles Pickett was removed, he having declined to try to keep the pledge for the future, offering no apology to the society for the disgrace cast upon it, and neither communicating with the president nor returning his card.

But we are not told what that disgrace was, and there is probably no way of ever finding out. The last of the regular entries in the minute book also has an intriguing aspect. It refers to a meeting on Boxing Day, 1884.

> A very enjoyable evening was spent – the proceeds just covered the expenses, including some unfortunate accidental breakages.

ॐ

...And an Intemperate Curate

Not all clergymen, however, were so concerned to promote good living and counter the evils of drink. Henry Hunt, the radical demagogue, recalled the brief career of a curate of Enford (near Pewsey) at the end of the eighteenth century:

> The Sunday arrived, and my father, as the principal person in the village, always anxious to be the first to shew his attention to a stranger, and particularly when that stranger was clothed in the dress of Pastor of the parish, waited upon him at the Inn or Pot-House, where he had taken up his quarters, and not only invited him to dine, but also offered him a bed and a stall for his horse till he was better provided at the Vicarage. I, of course, accompanied my father, and we had little difficulty in getting over the first introduction. He was a young man of easy manners and address, and without the least ceremony, accepted the invitation to dine, etc; but he informed us, that he had made a bargain, and had taken lodgings and intended to board, with the landlady at the Swan, as he could not bear the thoughts of living in a dull country Vicarage House by himself.
>
> We went to Church, where he dashed through the service in

double quick time, and 'tipped us', as he had previously informed me he would, a *Rattling Sermon*, as a specimen of his style of oratory. He appeared a clever thoughtless youth, of twenty-five; but the rake, as my father said, 'stood confessed in his eye', and its effects sat visible upon his brow. After dinner he took his wine like a *Parson*, and before he had finished a bottle he was as drunk as a *Lord*; so much so, that he was utterly incapable of performing the afternoon duty without exposing his situation to the whole congregation. My father was shocked at his indiscretion, and sent a hasty excuse to put off the afternoon service... I took the hopeful and reverend young gentleman, who had been so recently inspired by the Holy Ghost to take priest's orders, a walk into the fields, to recover him a little, as my father thought him a very improper guest to introduce into the drawing-room to his daughters. In the course of our walk he professed a very sincere and warm friendship for me, and promised himself a world of pleasure in my society; and he frankly and unblushingly informed me, that he had brought with him from Oxford a bad venereal complaint, which, he added, was most unfortunate, as he was fearful that he should inoculate all the pretty damsels belonging to his new flock, which would be a *cursed Bore...*

He lived but a short time; having soon fallen a victim to his profligate course of life. He was little more than a year, I think, the Pastor of the Parish, and he administered the sacrament, and performed all the other offices of the Curate, when the effects of his drinking did not interfere with it, and during this time he always lodged at the public house. This was a sad example for the people of the parish!

ஃ   ஃ

L i f e ' s   R i c h   T a p e s t r y

Great Native Stamen

Clerical irregularities have always been a fertile source of prurient gossip, and we shall stumble across another instance (from Keevil, this time) later on. But if vicars were capable of the occasional over-indulgence, that was as nothing compared with some of their parishioners. Here is an obituary notice:

> EXTRAORDINARY POWERS: The late Mr Joshua Dixon, of Downton, in this county, who in 1801 died suddenly at the age of 103, had all his life been a remarkably free-liver. According to his own calculation he had consumed two thousand gallons of brandy, without taking into account a variety of other kinds of liquor. He moreover enjoyed his faculties to the last. He was twice married, and of his numerous offspring by both wives, the oldest had died at the age of 70, while the youngest was only 18 at the father's death. Had this man practised the temperance of some patriarchs he might probably have attained the age of 150. The question is a difficult one. He doubtless lived longer as an habitual drinker, than he could have done as an immoderate feeder. The two seldom go together. The very strong men live on in spite of everything. It will be an interesting spectacle to see (as doubtless the world will yet see) to what amount of longevity, great native stamen will conduct the strictly temperate and virtuous man.

But then perhaps, as the old joke runs, the virtuous man would not actually live longer – it would just seem longer. And in any case I am not sure that we should trust the calculations of a man who claimed to have drunk two thousand gallons of brandy, however enjoyable his faculties. Here is another eccentric – an eighteenth-century aristocrat this time – out and about enjoying himself:

Bampfylde Moore Carew [the son of a Devon rector, who adopted the lifestyle of a gipsy and wrote books], disguised as a shipwrecked sailor, on nearing Longleat fell in with another in the same plight as himself; after having been successful in obtaining alms and food at the mansion, they adjourned to a public house, and, having had a good carouse, separated.

Shortly afterwards Carew was overtaken by two horsemen sent by Lord Weymouth to bring back the two sailors. When ushered into the great man's presence Carew was treated very roughly. He was then removed to await the capture of his comrade, and soon that ragged gentleman entered the room where Carew was confined. They had just time for a hurried consultation together before they were again separated, and Carew was once more brought before the Lord of Longleat, who thereupon, to the unbounded astonishment of the prisoner, disclosed the extraordinary fact that his ragged shipwrecked comrade was none other than himself! It seems that he was in the habit of thus playing the vagabond, partly to relieve a natural ennui, and partly to learn what was really going on in the neighbourhood of his vast estates. I should add that he insisted on Carew staying with him at Longleat some time.

It would be interesting to know the name of Lord Weymouth's 'local'. The most appropriate would perhaps have been an establishment recorded at Monkton Deverill, a few miles from Longleat. In August 1877 members of the Wiltshire Archaeological Society, meeting at Warminster Town Hall, were treated to a lecture on 'Some account of the tavern signs of Wiltshire and their origin', by our old friend the Rev. Alfred Smith (who seemed to be able to turn his hand to anything). The subject generated considerable interest, and there seem to have been a number of contributions from the floor of the meeting, which were included as footnotes when the paper was subsequently published. But that was not the end of it:

> On the day following that on which this paper was read before the Society, at Warminster, the archaeologists, in the excursion to Stourhead, halted at Monkton Deverill, and here it was discovered that the village hostelry, now denominated the 'New Inn', was once designated by the far less commonplace, if somewhat eccentric sign of 'The Tippling Philosopher'!

I came across this reference some years ago, and subsequently discovered that there had been an inn of the same name in London. Still it seemed odd to find it in such an out-of-the-way place as Monkton Deverill. I wondered, in fact, whether someone had been pulling the archaeologists' collective leg. But then one day I found in the Wiltshire Record Office that the alehousekeepers' recognizances for the Warminster area in 1751 include, most unusually, the sign of the house as well as the name of the licensee. And there, at Monkton Deverill, was 'The Tippling Philosopher'.

Our next eccentric also haunted the Warminster area, and probably could have regaled us with a fund of stories about tippling philosophers. But she fell on hard times, as this newspaper obituary from about 1777 tells us:

> Lately died at Bishopstrow, her native place, near Warminster, in Wilts, the celebrated Juliana Popjoy, in the 67th year of her age. In her youth, being very handsome and genteel, she was taken notice of by the late celebrated Beau Nash, a gentleman noted for his gallantry, dress, and generosity; when he soon prevailed on her to tread the flowery paths of pleasure with him, she was accordingly ushered into the blaze of the world, was mounted on a fine horse, and had a servant to attend her. This seemingly happy state continued some years; but at last, Mr Nash's finances being low, a separation took place, when poor Juliana experienced a sad reverse of fortune, and was driven to almost the lowest ebb of misery.

However, she did not, like too many of her sisterhood, take to parading the streets for a livelihood, but to a very uncommon way of life. Her principal residence she took up in a large hollow tree, now standing within a mile of Warminster, on a lock of straw, resolving never more to lie on a bed; and she was as good as her word; for she made that tree her habitation for between thirty and forty years, unless when she made her short peregrinations to Bath, Bristol, and the gentlemen's houses adjacent; and she then lay in some barn or outhouse. In the summer time she went a simpling, and occasionally carried messages. At last, worn out with age and inquietude, she determined to die in the house where she was born; accordingly, a day before her exit, she reached the destined habitation, where she laid herself on some straw, and finished her mortal pilgrimage.

ε&

Death's Rich Tapestry

Of course, the pithiest obituaries are to be found on tombstones, and witty epitaphs have been collected and copied for centuries. Charles Dickens, who during the 1850s published a magazine, *Household Words*, was responsible for popularizing this one, which he attributed to Pewsey. It still turns up, incidentally, in present-day anthologies.

> Here lies the body of Lady O'Looney, Great Niece of Burke.
> Commonly called the sublime. She was bland, passionate
> and deeply religious, also she painted in water colours and
> sent several pictures to the Exhibition. She was first cousin
> to Lady Jones, and of such is the Kingdom of Heaven.

One consequence of its publication was that the rector of Pewsey at the time, Thomas Ravenshaw, was, as he put it, 'much worried by incessant applications for "correct copies"'. The fuss, one imagines, soon died down, but Ravenshaw continued to be interested in the subject, and in 1878 he published a collection under the title, *Antiente Epitaphes*. There is a presentation copy in pristine condition in the Library of the Wiltshire Archaeological and Natural History Society at Devizes. In an appendix to his book he finally laid the ghost of Lady O'Looney, who had never been at Pewsey at all, and showed up Dickens (or whoever Dickens had copied it from) as guilty of considerable poetic licence.

The original, in fact, relates to a Mrs Jane Molony, who died in January 1839 and was interred in St George's Burying Ground, Hanover Square, London. Her epitaph runs to 483 words, and describes in confusing and tedious detail the estimable achievements of most of her relatives. For the record she was not 'bland, passionate and deeply religious' at all, but 'hot, passionate and tender, and a highly accomplished lady...'. How she came to be linked with Pewsey is not explained. [However, it appears that a tombstone which included some similar wording to that quoted for Lady O'Looney did exist in Pewsey churchyard as recently as 1965 (information from Mr Wilfred Offer).]

Ravenshaw's book prints epitaphs from all over England, and includes many medieval examples. But here are two from eighteenth-century Wiltshire. The first, from his own church at Pewsey, is rather touching; the second, from Potterne, is facetious:

SAMUEL AUSTIN
Stay awhile and spend a tear
Upon the dust that slumbers here
And while thou readst the fate of me
Think on the glasse that runs for thee.

MARY wife of the above
I grieve to think I cannot grieve no more
To think my dearest Friend is gone before
But since it pleased God to part us here
In Heaven I hope to meet my dearest dear

> Here lyes MARY the wife of JOHN FORD,
> We hope her soule is gone to the LORD;
> But if for Hell she has chang'd this life,
> She had better be there than be John Ford's wife

Ravenshaw's successor, Bertrand Bouverie, wrote *A Few Facts Concerning the Parish of Pewsey*, which was published in 1890. It is probably the worst local history of a Wiltshire parish published around that time – or should that distinction go to *A Sentimental and Practical Guide to Amesbury and Stonehenge* by Lady Antrobus? Anyway, despite Bouverie's imperfections he does include an anecdote and an epitaph recorded in a letter sent to him in 1885:

Upon one of my visits we were told that there were three men drinking together at the Phoenix, who were named respectively – Deadman, Coffin, and Ghost. The last was a pedlar, who used to carry about silks and haberdashery; who the other two were I forget.

Sometime before – about 1815 perhaps, or earlier – there had died a certain Mr E—— in Pewsey, upon whom was written an epitaph, the author of which was not known, and I forget the name of the subject, but I have heard him spoken of as a most unhappy, fretful man. There was a schoolmaster in the village, a Mr Strong, who may perhaps have written them. He conducted the singing in the church, and was, though rather pedagoguish and pompous in manner, a clever man and a very good teacher:

> *Here lies, to rest for evermore,*
> *A body ne'er at rest before;*
> *To an early grave untimely sent*
> *By physic, wife, and discontent;*
> *The oddest mortal, while alive,*
> *That Nature ever could contrive;*

Where he is gone is hard to say,
And we will hope the better way;
If soar'd above, 'tis ten to four
He's tired of Heaven in an hour:
If down to hell, the devil grim
Will quickly be as tired of him.

And here, to round off our little collection of epitaphs, is another, also first published during the 1890s:

Among the combatants on the Parliament's side at Edgehill was a Wiltshireman who afterwards attained celebrity by extraordinary longevity. This was William Hiseland (Hazeland?), born in the year 1620 during James the First's reign, and dying in 1732, in the reign of George II. He commenced his military career at the early age of 13, probably in the Earl of Pembroke's militia; he fought his way all the way through the Civil Wars, and was with William of Orange's army in Ireland, and closed his foreign services in the Flanders campaign under the renowned Duke of Marlborough. Either in active duty or as an invalid he bore arms for the extraordinary period of eighty years. The Duke of Richmond and Sir Robert Walpole, in consideration of his long services, each allowed him a crown a week for some time before his death. The old man helped himself in another way, having had three wives in the course of his life; his last marriage was contracted the year before his death, viz. 9th August, 1731. A picture of him taken at the age of 110 is said to be still extant. His epitaph, given below, is on his tombstone in the burial-ground of Chelsea Hospital:

Here rests WILLIAM HISELAND,
A veteran if ever soldier was;
Who merited well a pension
If long services be a merit:
Having served upwards of the days of man.
Antient, but not superannuated,
Engaged in a series of wars
Civil as well as foreign;
Yet not maimed or worn out by neither.
His complexion was florid and fresh,
His health hale and hearty,
His memory exact and ready.
In stature he excelled the military size;
In strength surpassed the prime of youth.
And what made his age still more patriarchal;
When above one hundred years old,
He took unto him a wife.
Read – fellow soldiers, and reflect
That there is a spiritual warfare
As well as a warfare temporal.

Born 6 August, 1620
Died 7 February, 1732, aged 112

This remarkable career was noted by a Devizes antiquary, James Waylen, to whom we shall be further indebted when we delve into crime and punishment.

More Ham – less Calf

Waylen was interested in collecting examples of longevity in Wiltshire, and he also pasted into his scrapbook oddments on all kinds of related subjects. Here is an undated piece of anthropological nonsense:

Peculiarity in Wiltshire Men – I have noticed that in Wiltshire, as in some other counties west of London, the men have no calves to their legs. All of them, young and old, wear knee-breeches, and a sort of tight leather legging, and this exhibits more palpably their thin shanks. Otherwise they are generally handsome men, mostly a middling size, thin and wiry. I was told by a gentleman, who seems to know the rural population of England well, that in all the counties where bacon is eaten as a staple article of diet, the men have small calves. I cannot see any reason for this: but whether it be bacon, or whether it be that a bacon-eating race have invaded these counties, and have brought a peculiar formation of legs with them, it is a fact that they have calveless legs, no matter how well fed or how starving they may be. The jolly-faced farmers have the same kind of legs as the lean labourer. – Adam Brown.

Calfless Wiltshireman approaching Devil's Den, Clatford, near Marlborough

Dabchicks, Gudgeons and Dogs

What a strange thing to write to the newspaper about! But this kind of attempt to categorize inhabitants of an area by physical or mental characteristics has a long history. John Aubrey's thoughts on the differences between the peoples of north and south Wiltshire, which are included in his introduction to *The Natural History of Wiltshire*, are too well-known to bear repeating here. Another manifestation of such interests is the coining of nicknames, and some of these in the middle ages turned into family surnames which are still in use today. 'Fulljames', for example, derives from French *fol jamb*, or 'bad leg', 'Pettigrew' is *petit cru*, 'small growth', 'Smallbone' and 'Armstrong' are self-explanatory.

At a more local level nicknames have often been applied by one community to a rival one, usually in derision. An excellent example, supplied in Ida Gandy's book, *The Heart of a Village*, is Ramsbury people's nickname for their neighbours at Aldbourne – 'dabchicks'. A dabchick, apparently, arrived one day on Aldbourne village pond, to the great mystification of the villagers, who had never seen one and could not identify it. Their ignorance amused the Ramsbury folk, who watched dabchicks every day diving in the River Kennet, and so they taunted anyone from Aldbourne by shouting 'dabchick' after them. This association, Mrs Gandy points out, became respectable, and was commemorated by a dabchick emblem engraved on bells cast at Aldbourne before 1757. It is, therefore, a sobriquet of long standing.

Along the Wiltshire-Somerset border disdain for one's neighbours was expressed in a little ditty:

Trowbridge knobs,
Bradford gudgeons,
Hilperton tiedowns,
Bradley donkeys,
Road waspies,
Beckiton bees,
Frome dumbledories, and
Warminster fleas.

This was collected by a lady from Purton, Ethel Richardson, who also preserved a rhyme along similar lines about the church bells in the villages around Shrewton:

Shrewton brave bells,
Ma'anton ting tang,
Rollestone frying pan,
Upper Ar'ston besom stick;
Lower Ar'ston candlestick.
Stoke slats,
Barwick strails,
Stubbleford rats,
Without any tails.

Notice, incidentally, the dialect forms of Maddington, Orcheston and Stapleford.

Deeper still into the heart of Salisbury Plain, here is one more nickname, the subject of an enquiry to *Wiltshire Notes and Queries* in 1896.

I have heard it said that there is nothing which upsets a native of Imber so much as the sobriquet of Bungey, or Bungay, and that they obtained the nickname by roasting a dog so named. Can anyone supply me with further information as to this?

Lock up at Bradford on Avon, surmounted by gudgeon

Nobody replied.

But while on the subject of dogs, let us end this chapter with a touching story of canine loyalty. It is recorded in the diary of Captain William Owen, of Glansevern in mid-Wales, who was travelling home through Wiltshire in December 1751:

> The 13th in the morning walked from Heytesbury to Warminster, and stayed there the remainder of the day. One Jacob Dunn, that kept the Packhorse Inn, gave me a little dog, of the Dutch-mastiff breed, which I took with me into Wales, and left with my mother. After her death in August 1754, it accompanied my niece, Molly Owen, to her father's at Tanycoed, where she kept it for her grandmother's sake. When I returned into the country after an absence of ten years, this dog was grown decrepit, grey, and blind with old age. Upon my entering the house it ran with the utmost fury and open-mouthed at me, as I thought to seize me by one of my legs, but upon coming up to me, stopping, suddenly jumped up and fawned upon me, and it was with difficulty I could prevent its following me wherever I went.

ॐ   ॐ

C r i m e ...

The darker side of Cherhill

Notebooks, diaries, and minute books, of course, later become the stuff of the village historian. Here the skilful author of an exhaustive history of his village, James Blackford of Cherhill, near Calne, is turning his attention to the life of crime. Three paragraphs are taken from local hearsay, but the fourth is supplied by the notes of a former rector, William Plenderleath, who served the parish from 1860 until 1891:

Many years ago one of the Cherhill farmers noticed his stack of firewood was disappearing but was unable to find out where it was going. One day he took a piece of wood from the stack, cut three holes in it and then filled it with gunpowder, afterwards rubbing dirt over it to cover the marks. He then replaced the piece of wood in the stack. A few days later the piece of wood was missing; shortly after the report went round the village that a cooking pot had been mysteriously blown off the fire at a house in Greens Lane. The farmer then knew where his wood was going.

Many are the tales told about the large elm trees which used to line the main road at Cherhill. One of them stood near the Bush Inn and wagoners used to draw their teams of horses and wagons under this tree whilst partaking of refreshments inside the inn. If the old inhabitants' tales are correct, many are the sides of bacon, sacks of corn and cheeses that have been lifted off wagons by ropes manipulated by men up in the tree. On one occasion a side of bacon was missed; next day persons were surprised to see a stick lying on top of the chimney of a thatched cottage at the bottom of Labour-in-Vain Hill. Someone in authority became curious and wanted to know why it was there. The replies not being very satisfactory he decided to investigate; the missing side of bacon was discovered hanging up the chimney by a rope attached to the stick.

On another occasion two men wanted a cheese. It was decided that No. 1 should go in and entertain the carter while No. 2 moved a cheese from the wagon to a safe hiding-place known to both. Having completed his task No. 2 returned to the inn to help entertain the carter. After a little while No. 1 left the inn for a few moments and removed the cheese from its hiding-place to another known only to himself. After the carter had gone both men went to divide the cheese, but it had disappeared. Little did No. 2 suspect that No. 1 had moved it to another place so that he could retain it himself.

My own uncle, [wrote Plenderleath] who was born in 1776, when he heard of my having accepted a living in Wiltshire, solemnly exhorted me never to think of driving across the downs without my servant and myself being provided with firearms. There was also a band of footpads known as the 'Cherhill Gang' who relieved many a traveller of the pence which he had intended to pay his scores owing at the Bell or the Black Horse. Two old men who were said to have been members of this Society lived on into the period of my residence, and anyone noticing their venerable white heads bowed over their big prayer-books would have taken them for very Village Patriarchs thus ending their simple and blameless lives. One of these men is reported to have sometimes gone out upon his marauding expeditions in the summer time without a stitch of clothing, as he said that not only did such an apparition frighten people on a dark night, but also that a naked man was less easily recognised than one who appeared in the ordinary costume of the period.

Yes, I suppose so, but it must have been rather difficult to conceal the stolen goods.

In fact, having written that remark, I now find that Plenderleath had pondered the same problem. In a piece entitled 'Cherhill Gleanings',

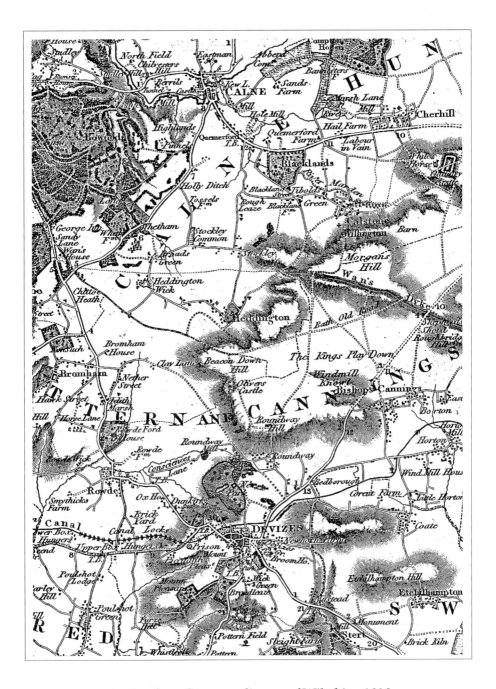

Section from Greenwood's map of Wiltshire, 1820

which he published in 1889, he included a version of the same story, and ended it thus:

The usage must, however, I should think, have entailed some practical inconveniences with regard to the disposal of booty if trade was brisk; and also, if the victims did happen to show fight, it would have been apt to hurt!

And then, for good measure, he recounts another anecdote:

I remember a story that our late neighbour, Mr Henry Merewether, was very fond of telling of how he was returning one dark night from Devizes, where he had been defending a man charged with highway robbery. So clearly had he shown the jury that, notwithstanding the existence of suspicious circumstances, his client was a man whom it was impossible for one moment to suppose capable of such a crime, that the latter was triumphantly acquitted, and left the dock, as the newspapers say, 'without a stain upon his character'. But the same night, alas! on the top of the downs, Mr. Merewether was himself requested to stand and deliver. And, still more sad to relate, the author of this request was his maligned client of the same morning! Those of us who remember Mr. Merewether will feel sure that the tale must have ended happily, and that whether by reason of his strong right arm or his persuasive tongue – (I think, if I remember rightly, it was the former) – he came off triumphantly, scot free.

ॐ

Mine Host

• •

But if, unlike Mr. Merewether, you had not the stature to defend yourself, a journey across the Cherhill Downs on a dark night in the eighteenth century must have been a nerve-racking experience, and the comforting light of the Black Horse Inn a welcome relief. Why, incidentally, is it called the Black Horse, when it stands beneath the Cherhill White Horse cut on the hillside? And why, for that matter, is the perfect place to watch the sun set over West Wiltshire the garden of the Rising Sun at Bowden Hill? No matter. The point is, that the cheery inn meant safety and good fellowship.

The Black Horse Inn opposite the Cherhill White Horse

Or did it... Here is a newspaper report from January 1842:

About three weeks since a perfect male skeleton was discovered in a field attached to a brickyard, in the chapelry of Stert, a short distance from Devizes. It was within two and a half feet of the surface of the field, and was found by a young man, whilst digging for clay; and who, attaching very little importance to the circumstance, took the bones up, and in the course of the day reinterred them. The fact, however, having been communicated to some of the clergymen of the neighbourhood; and those clergymen having been previously informed that murders had been committed near the spot, and that within a few years other skeletons had been dug up in the same field, felt very anxious to obtain any information that could throw light on the affair; they therefore caused the bones to be disinterred, and sent for Mr Whitmarsh, the Coroner, who held an inquest on them at the Bell Inn, Lydeway, on Monday last, when several aged persons were in attendance to give evidence...

It appears that about eighty or ninety years ago, there was a public house called 'The Shepherd and his Dog, kept by Thomas Burry, near the three mile stone on the Salisbury road; that Burry himself was of ill-repute, and his house of worse; that at that period large numbers of pedlars travelled the road; that many of them sought shelter at the Shepherd and Dog, but that few left the house alive, or if they did, it was only to be murdered on the road, and that the road then ran near the brick field. An old man named Sutton, of Urchfont, 88 years of age, recollects when he was a shepherd boy, threescore and ten years ago, that a person named Withers, whilst drinking at the house, overheard some persons concerting the murder of a Scotch pedlar then there, and that Withers went to Urchfont, and gave information of the fact, when the Urchfont people came and rescued the pedlar through the window. The cry of 'Murder', this old man said, was then very frequent in the neighbourhood of the Shepherd and Dog; and he has known several persons dug out of the brick field. There is also a tradition that when old Burry died, the bell would not sound, and that there were such noises as had never before been heard. The license was afterwards withdrawn from the house. A person named Edwards, said he knew an old man named Mower, a smuggler, and a friend of Burry's, and that sometime before his death, he heard him say that he had killed many a man between the Charlton Cat and Wedhampton, and buried them at Wroughton Folly. Edwards also said that when he was a boy, persons used to be afraid to pass the corner at the Shepherd and Dog. The owner of the brick field said that some years ago he discovered a skeleton in the same field, and from its position, it was evident that it had been pressed by force into a hole not large enough to contain it; and that a twelvemonth ago another skeleton was dug up.

A descendant of Burry's – an old man verging upon fourscore years – was also examined, but nothing could be elicited from him, farther than that he was not answerable for what other people did. He was repeatedly asked whether there was not a trap door to the cellar, and whether he himself had not very recently filled the cellar with gravel, but he evaded the question, and would give no direct answer. He lives in the very house that was the Shepherd and Dog.

W.D. Barker, esq., surgeon of Devizes, examined the skeleton, and said he had no doubt, from the size of the thigh bones, that it was that of a male person. On the top of the skull there was a perforation, which must have been effected by some sharp instrument, and which was sufficient to cause death. In his opinion this perforation was made prior to interment, and the person of whom the skeleton was the remains came to his death by violent means. The jury therefore returned a verdict to that effect.

૨▲

To Bournemouth for Tea

Smugglers and highwaymen have acquired a romantic image, even to the extent that the exploit of the 'moonrakers' – cunning brandy smugglers – has become the symbol of Wiltshire one-upmanship, and a matter of local pride. In reality smuggling was a nasty, shadowy business which is seldom well-documented. But Wiltshiremen were certainly involved, as a tombstone at Kinson (now a Bournemouth suburb) darkly commemorates:

> To the Memory of Robert Trotman late of Rowd in the County of Wilts, who was barbarously murdered on the Shore near Poole the 24 March 1760.
>
> A little Tea one leaf I did not steal
> For Guiltless Blood shed I to God appeal
> Put Tea in one scale human blood in t'other
> And think what tis to slay thy harmless brother.

The tradition, it was said, was that he was a smuggler, and met with his death in an affray with the coastguard.

More Problems on the Road

Of Wiltshire highwaymen there is a great deal more evidence, thanks largely to the Devizes antiquary of the nineteenth century, James Waylen. He kept a scrapbook (now in the Wiltshire Archaeological and Natural History Society's Library) into which he pasted newspaper cuttings about highway robbery, and anything else that took his fancy. In 1856 he wrote a series of articles for the *Wiltshire Independent*, and these were subsequently published, anonymously, in book form. The Stert inquest, printed above, comes from his scrapbook, as does the following short account, which illustrates one misfortune for the gentlemen of the road which had not occurred to me before. There you lurk by the roadside, black cape, loaded blunderbuss, curious hat – 'Stand and deliver', you cry,... But no-one answers:

> Wednesday evening three coaches were stopt between Devizes and Marlborough, by two highwaymen. There being no passengers in the two first, they desired the coachmen to lend them a shilling each, for they were quite broke down, and they would pay them well for it another night. From the third coach they took about six pounds.

That little episode probably dates from 1782. Six years earlier, prompted by news of an archaeological excavation at Silbury Hill, a correspondent to the *Salisbury Journal* sent in a story about a less violent, but more subtle, form of highway robbery – daylight robbery might be a better description:

To the Printer of the Salisbury Journal:
SIR. As the attention of such gentlemen as have a taste for antiquities is, I imagine, at present fixed on what passes in digging Silbury Hill; I thought that the following anecdote, which was told me long ago by one who was a party in the transaction, might serve to amuse the antiquarians till their workmen at Silbury had finished their search; and if you can find room for it in your paper, 'tis at your service...

A poor boy was carrying a pitcher of milk along the road near Silbury-hill, and unluckily fell down and broke the pitcher; a taylor, who lived at Abury [Avebury], just by, met the boy crying for the loss of his pitcher and his milk; and at that instant a coach came in sight. The taylor, who was a man of humour, bid the boy be comforted, and told him he would try to get something for him of the gentry in the coach, and for this purpose bid him cry out lustily as the coach was going by. The coachman was, as was expected, ordered to stop on hearing the boy's cries, and the people in the coach enquired what was the cause of the boy's lamentations; the taylor stepped to the coach side, and told them that the boy had reason to lament, for that he was carrying home an urn which his father had just dug out of one of the barrows; that as a piece of antiquity it was of great value; that Dr Davis, of Devizes, who was known to be a great antiquarian, would have given a guinea for it, etc. This excited the curiosity of the gentry in the coach to examine the broken pitcher, and thinking that the pieces might be joined together, they offered to give a crown for it, which was accepted: the taylor gave the boy a shilling to make good his loss, and put the remainder in his pocket. The gentry in the coach drove away with the broken pitcher, supposed now to be a Roman urn, and probably is now shewn in the musaeum of some antiquarian as such, and much admired by the Virtuosi. WILTONIENSIS.

But Dr Davis (remember him from chapter one?) was not to be fooled so easily. He was presumably the source of the story.

Another rather unusual traffic incident occurred some fifty years later:

In July, 1829, Sir Goldsworthy Gurney made his famous journey in a steam carriage from London to Bath and back. Gurney was a surgeon in Marylebone, greatly given to the working out of inventions in his spare time, and it took him some years to complete his first 'motor' in his back yard in Albany Street. He accomplished the journey to and from Bath at the rate of fifteen miles an hour, and there was only one disturbing incident, when a crowd assembled at Melksham set upon the machine, and having burnt their fingers, threw stones and seriously wounded the stoker.

Gurney's Steam Carriage

Rising again

Well, maybe that was just a touch of xenophobia, or an understandably hostile reaction to alarming new technology. But when it came to thieving, that was a different matter. Nothing was sacred, as this story from Purton illustrates:

> It is surely well to impress upon the young the spirit of reverence, and that the Church and God's Acre which surrounds it are hallowed ground. In the old days this was unhappily not the custom, for we are told that when any parishioner wanted a good flat stone, he repaired to the graveyard to pick out one which might suit his purpose. It is even said that someone in Purton wanting a new bottom for his oven upon which to bake his bread pressed a tombstone into the service, and when the bread was duly baked, plainly upon the bottom of the large loaf could be read the words, 'Here lies the body of...'.

When a story is considered particularly good there is always the danger that oral transmission and improvement will not be sufficient. It will be turned into a poem. Is this a rustic equivalent of the Homeric epics, which were couched in verse as an aide-memoire to the bard? Or is it the less remote legacy of the ballad seller? 'The Village Baker', as reported by Ethel Richardson, Purton's historian, extends to 63 lines, but we shall join the action at the point where the baker is showing the parish mason, whom he had employed to mend the oven with tombstones, the result of his handiwork:

> *He took him to the bakehouse,*
> *Where a curious sight was seen,*
> *The words on every loaf were marked*
> *That had on tombstone been,*
> *One quartern had 'in memory of'*
> *Another 'here to pine',*
> *The third 'departed from this life*
> *At the age of ninety-nine'.*

A batch of rolls when they were done
Had on the bottom plain,
The trusting words distinctly marked
'In hopes to rise again,'
A batch of penny loaves came next
Which said 'our time is past,
Thus day by day, we've pined away,
And come to this at last.'

࿇

A Poet who lost his head

Stealing tombstones is bad enough, but the Trowbridge historian can cap that story. The town's most famous rector was the poet George Crabbe, who is best remembered now for the tale of Peter Grimes. Crabbe died in 1832, and a monument was erected to his memory in Trowbridge parish church, where he was buried. Fifteen years later, in 1847, repairs to the church were necessary, and his grave was disturbed. It was then that his skull disappeared; and a mystery remained over its whereabouts for the next thirty years. The *Trowbridge Advertiser* takes up the story in 1876:

> Strangers are inclined to question the correctness of the story of the lost skull, but as we have had it from the lips of the gentleman who has been the means of restoring it, we give it:- Thirty years ago, I was standing by the open vault of the Poet Crabbe, with the then Rector of Trowbridge, the late Rev.J.D. Hastings. The church was then undergoing thorough alterations, and the floor of the chancel was up, for the purpose of lowering it. The removal of the surface disclosed the vault of the Poet Crabbe, where he was buried fifteen years before. It was his wish to be buried in a plain coffin, hence the rapidity of decay... The workmen tossed up a skull, and Mr. Hastings said, 'That is the skull of Poet Crabbe; this is where he was buried'. I was a student of phrenology then, and said, incidentally, 'I should like to take a cast of that skull'. Nothing more was said, and we left.

George Crabbe

That evening a dirt-begrimed labourer presented himself at the side door of my father's house and enquired for me, saying in a sepulchral voice, 'I've got it'. 'Got what?' I said. 'Old Pa'son Crabbe's skull! and we should like a drop o' beer on the job, please Sir.' 'I don't want it; I can't have it; put it back; don't let my father see you here with it; where is it?' I said. The man replied, 'I put it in my tommy-bag when you was gone, as I heard you say you should like to take a cast, and now I can't put it back again, for the floor is all rammed down and cemented, and the stones laid, and if you don't have it I shall destroy it, that's all', and he was proceeding to tie up his 'tommy-bag', and to depart to fulfil his threat. To save the skull from such a fate, brought about by the simple remark I had made at the graveside, I decided to take care of it, and carried it indoors, but my father would not have it there, so I tied it up in a silk pocket-handkerchief, and hid it in a dry place for seven years, when I removed it to my iron chest, and there it has been ever since. I offered it to the late Rector for re-interment, but there was no opportunity for raising the chancel floor... I have shown it to the poet's son, before he went to Australia, and have since, at his request, forwarded him photographs of it in four different positions.

In 1876 the skull was placed in a polished oak box, and re-buried near Crabbe's vault in the chancel of Trowbridge parish church.

... and Punishment

A Gruesome Business

Justice seen to be done had a rather more literal connotation when public executions took place at or near the place where the crime was committed. The hanging of William Jaques for murder at Stanton St Quinton in 1764 was one of many such awful warnings which lingered on years after the event. John Britton, a Wiltshire antiquary who made his name in London and wrote his autobiography, was not born until seven years after the hanging, but he knew all about it nevertheless:

> An event connected with this locality, and noticeable, as illustrating the superstitious opinions which prevailed amongst nearly the whole population of the time, may be narrated; as the relation of it made an indelible impression on my young mind, and indeed impressed me with the belief that the phenomena of lightning, thunder, and storm always accompanied human executions. When a boy, I often passed a gibbet, in Stanton field, on which a man had been hung in chains for murdering a negro in Stanton Park, a large wood so called. The two had been seen together at Malmesbury, and at the village of Stanton, and the murderer was noticed on the same day by some of the inhabitants of Kington, walking at a quick pace through that village inquiring his way to Chippenham. He had killed his companion, rifled his pockets, and was on his road to Bristol. Within an hour after the murder was committed, the body was discovered by a woodman, who communicated the intelligence to the inhabitants of a neighbouring farm: a hue-and-cry was raised, the man was traced through Kington, and arrested at Chippenham on the same day. He was conveyed to Salisbury,

John Britton

tried, and condemned to be hung. According to my father, who often repeated the tale (one story forms a staple article for retailing in a country village, for a long space of time), he, with almost all the inhabitants of Kington and the neighbouring villages, went to see the murderer hanged on Stanton Common. As the culprit approached the place, a small black cloud was observed over the gibbet: it increased, and at the time of the execution had extended over a wide space. When the man was 'turned off', there was a vivid flash of lightning, with thunder, and a violent storm arose, and continued during the remainder of the day.

ぇ๑

More Hanging About

Britton, no tittle-tattler, was quite right about the potency of such stories. They passed into folk memory and endured centuries of retelling. In the burial register for Maddington (which is now part of Shrewton on Salisbury Plain) an entry reads:

> William Lawne, sonne of Giles Lawne, barbarously slaine neere the Windemill, Sept. 23rd, and buryed the 24th of the same, 1666.

In September 1900, 234 years later, a contributor to *Wiltshire Notes & Queries* was able to fill in the details:

> Canon Lowther informed me that the old clerk of Orcheston St George, whom he found in office when he took the Rectory in 1830, told him that the man who was murdered at the Gibbet, had taken a large sum of money at Warminster market. The ostler of the inn where he put up knew this, and after he had left Warminster followed him, and shot him at the place where the Gibbet now stands, making off with the money. The murderer was apprehended, and hanged in chains at the crossways of the London and Warminster, and Shrewton and Devizes tracks. Old people

remembered the stump of the Gibbet when I came to Maddington, and there is still a tradition that where it stood, 'on a place like a grave (which I could never find) nothing will grow'. Canon Lowther told me that the story was stated to him by the clerk in Orcheston St George churchyard, who pointed out a place to him, saying, 'And here, sir, lies the man that heard the shot fired'. The Canon had no idea that it took place so long ago as the entry in Maddington Register Book proves it did, and he believed that the clerk claimed to have known the man who heard the shot fired.

ᔥ

Incident at Watkins' Corner

It is in the nature of anecdotes and oral traditions, such as these examples, that they are improved each time they are given an airing. The parish historian uses them for light relief, but must learn to spot a tall story when he or she finds one. Ethel Richardson, the historian of Purton, near Swindon, amassed a fine collection (including the token thunderstorm) when she looked into the origin of Watkins' Corner:

> One of the last horrible gatherings of this kind took place in the year 1817, at a corner on the high road between Purton and Purton Stoke, when people flocked from Gloucestershire and distant parts of Wiltshire to see John Watkins hanged. He had been convicted of a murder, no paltry theft this time, he had killed Stephen Rodway of Cricklade, and so well deserved to suffer.
>
> A small boy, aged but seven years, son of the Vicar of Purton was there, and in charge of his father's gardener, who, horrible to relate, held the child up, so that he should get 'a better view'. This fact was told to the author by the daughter of this boy, quite 100 years later.
>
> Many stories are still remembered in connection with this particular hanging. The church bells were tolled as the murderer was taken past Purton Church to where the scaffold had been

erected, and a small prayer book, still to be seen at Purton, was placed in his hands, from whence to read the 108th Psalm, beginning, 'Awake up my glory, awake lute and harp'; the concluding verses, 'Oh help us against the enemy for vain is the help of man', were truly more suitable to so dread an occasion. Souvenir hunting, it is said that the murderer's collar, boots and braces were eagerly seized by spectators, and carefully preserved to show to friends for many a long day afterwards. Gruesome too were some awful stories told later. It was said that one night two men were drinking at the inn at Stoke, and that one bet the other he would not dare to crawl down a ditch near Watkin's Corner, and say, 'Well, Watkins, how are you feeling?' The man took up the bet and went; crept into the drain and asked the question. The other, unknown to him, had placed himself within reach in the darkness, and replied promptly, 'Very cold and miserable'. This reply so alarmed the first man, that, having a weak heart, he promptly died of fright. Then people say that the hangman, on his way home that day, was thrown from the trap, and broke his neck; while a fearful thunderstorm raging, seemed a protest from the sky, but which certainly may have frightened the horse, and so upset the cart! Further, years later, the very shed at Blunsdon where the gallows were stored, caught fire, and consumed them to ashes. So poor Watkins became more famous in his end than he had been in life; for the corner is always known by his name, and the story of his end told to strangers.

❧

A Final Twist

Victorian journalists were perhaps more cautious about checking their sources, but they were never coy about crime and punishment, as they were about sins of the flesh. Frederick Large was a Swindon journalist who worked on the same paper, the *North Wilts Herald*, and in the same office, as he tells us, for 54 years 9 months (think on that!). In 1931 he published a volume of reminiscences, and from it this sad little story will, I think, bear repeating:

I remember a case in which a burglar had been apprehended for an extensive robbery of jewellery in Wood Street. Some remarkable facts were brought to light in this case. The culprit, who was of most gentlemanly appearance, with a long frock coat and high silk hat, had made himself acquainted with a Post Office official, the Post Office being immediately opposite the jeweller's premises. By this means he became acquainted with the habits and customs of the jeweller, and noticed that he was in the habit of visiting the Postmaster most evenings for friendly intercourse. Watching the jeweller leave the shop on one of these visits, the thief seized his opportunity to enter the premises and take away a large quantity of jewellery, to the value of several hundred pounds.

Shortly after this the Post Office official, who had become friendly with the criminal, fell upon evil ways, with the result that he was committed to a long term of imprisonment. During his incarceration he supplied information to the prison authorities which enabled them to trace and bring the jewellery thief to justice. The ex-Post Office official, clad in convict's clothing, was brought to give evidence, with the result that the prisoner was committed to the Assizes, where he received a sentence of 14 years penal servitude. As a result of turning Queen's evidence, the ex-Post Office man's sentence was reduced from five years to three, this being the closing chapter of a most sensational case, which caused much excitement in the whole district. Strange to say, on the day in which the ex-Post Office official was released from Portland, he fell down some steps and broke his leg. He was taken back to his quarters and the broken limb was set, but the injury turned to mortification, and proved fatal. He was buried in a convict's grave.

Fiendish Devices

●●●

It was a subject which appealed also to the Victorian antiquaries, who sometimes appear to have taken a slightly unhealthy interest in ancient modes of punishment. The very first issue of the *Wiltshire Archaeological and Natural History Magazine* has an article about the cucking stool (ducking stool or tumbrel) at Wootton Bassett. Its author, Frederick Carrington of Ogbourne St George, near Marlborough, drew on his legal background and contacts to collect parallels from other parts of England, and so explain this unpleasant device. He included a description by a French lawyer, which was first published in English in 1715:

> *Cucking Stool* – the way of punishing scolding women is pleasant enough. They fasten an arm chair to the end of two beams, twelve or fifteen foot long, and parallel to each other, so that these two pieces of wood with their two ends embrace the chair which hangs between them on a sort of axle, by which means it plays freely, and always remains in the natural horizontal position in which a chair should be that a person may sit conveniently in it, whether you raise it or let it down. They set up a post, upon the bank of a pond or river, and over this post they lay almost in equilibrio the two pieces of wood, at one end of which the chair hangs just over the water; they place the woman in this chair, and so plunge her into the water, as often as the sentence directs, in order to cool her immoderate heat.

Coming round for more

A few years later Carrington contributed a much longer paper to the magazine, entitled 'Facts and observations as to the ancient state of Marlborough'. That indeed describes the first fifteen pages of his article, but then he warms to his subject, and the remaining twenty-nine pages are given over to hanging; the pillory; whipping the poor; the cucking stool; and the brank, or scold's bridle. A lively and good-humoured speaker, by all accounts, such was his enthusiasm that he took along his own brank, a nasty piece of restraining headgear for scolding women, to display to his audience when he delivered the paper. He would certainly have been interested in the following contribution to *Wiltshire Notes and Queries* which appeared some thirty years after his death:

> In a copy of the *Statistics of Crime in Wiltshire*, 'formerly belonging to Mr Alexander, for many years the Governor of the Gaol at Devizes, and previously the Keeper of the Bridewell at Marlborough', a sentence is recorded at the Wilts General Assizes, 1807, against a man named Benjamin James, of two years' imprisonment, and to be twice exposed in the pillory. In a marginal note Mr Alexander writes:
>
> 'This man was confined in the Bridewell, and stood in the Pillory at Marlborough, once at the commencement and once at the expiration of his sentence. The mob, by whom the sentence of the law was inflicted, was very merciful to him on the first occasion, and the man was foolish enough to say that he would stand another such a punishment for a pot of beer, which was not forgotten when the time came for him to undergo the second operation. Preparations were made by the people a long time beforehand. Rotten eggs, dead cats, cabbage-stumps, and everything that could be thought of, was plentifully prepared, and he received a most dreadful punishment. A cabbage-stump was thrown at him which stuck in his cheek, and the machine went round several times with the stump sticking in his face. When released he presented a most horrible spectacle, and his life was despaired of a long time.'

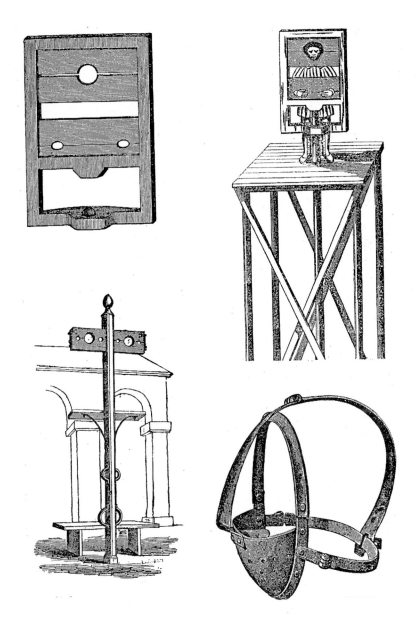

Fiendish Devices
Top: Marlborough Pillory with and without victim
Bottom Left: Whipping Post
Bottom right: Brank

The pillory was a machine which kept revolving, the prisoner was fastened to the upright pole, and the populace pelted him for one hour with anything except stones or other hard substances.

ॐ

A Barbarous Villain
• •

Occasionally, in spite of whatever punishment was dictated by the law, public opinion regarded a crime as so heinous as to brook no mercy. Here is an example reported in the *Gentleman's Magazine:*

> Feb.25th 1764: Henry Timbrell, a petty farmer, near Malmesbury, in Wilts, was committed to Salisbury gaol for castrating two lads whom he had undertaken to breed up for a small sum. These unhappy youths the barbarous villain had before endeavoured to destroy by throwing them in the way of the smallpox; but not succeeding, his rapacity at length suggested to him this operation, by which he thought to qualify them for singers, and to dispose of them at a good price. They are both alive, and their wounds healed. For this fact he was tried at Salisbury assizes, found guilty of a misdemeanour, the Coventry Act not reaching his case, as lying in wait could not be proved against him; his sentence was four years imprisonment, a fine of 26s. 8d., and to find security for his good behaviour during life. The sentence was thought so unequal to his crime that it was with the utmost difficulty he was preserved from the rage of the populace.

ॐ

Salisbury Water Torture
• •

On other occasions, especially when the offence had not affected them, and was not perceived as a threat to society in general, people might take a more detached view, and look on with amusement. Here is a newspaper cutting collected by James Waylen. It dates from about 1780:

Thursday last we were entertained with a trial of an uncommon kind, at a military tribunal under our Council House in the Market Place. – Two of the dragoons now quartered in this city had been guilty of petty thefts or frauds on their comrades, and instead of a court-martial, the officers left the conviction and punishment of this trivial offence to the men. Accordingly they were drawn up; one of them, dressed as formal as a judge, with a knapsack round his head, came escorted by a guard, took his seat in an elbow chair, with his clerk attending to take minutes – the two culprits brought by a file of musqueteers – a jury of twelve, collected indifferently from the men, and a charge given – the evidence then heard, and on conviction the Judge, with great solemnity, after observing on the evil of their offences to their society, sentenced them to undergo the punishment of booting and bottleing, and which was inflicted immediately, by each juryman giving a dozen blows with a jackboot on the posteriors of the criminal, and then pouring bottles of cold water thro' the sleves of his coat, the arms being extended, which produced something equivalent to the fit of an ague, from the trickling of cold water down his sides.

᠎

A Courtroom Drama

This, of course, was child's play for the reporter. But when we start to browse among the late Victorian broadsheets we encounter columns – whole pages sometimes – devoted to individual trials. It is probably not generally known that the first published book (really little more than a booklet) by the Wiltshire naturalist, novelist and 'prose-poet of the countryside', Richard Jefferies, was a practical manual for journalists. *Reporting, editing and authorship: practical hints for beginners in literature,* was published in 1873, and displays some of its author's frustration with his lot as a reporter, as well as his aspirations for a literary career. It deserves closer scrutiny from devotees of Jefferies than it has so far received. [It has now been reprinted in *Richard Jefferies Society Journal,* vol.2, 1993 and vol.3, 1994].

But I am digressing. Jefferies gives detailed instructions to the cub reporter about how to cover a trial – how to organize his papers, what pen to use, who to approach for details of names and charges, all the practical details which his own experience had taught him. Later on in his booklet, however, he tackles the broader issues:

> The principal rule in editing a paper is to insist upon every line being readable. The public want no solid cleverness, no prosy compilations, however good in their object, they require amusement. Men will read an 'Extraordinary Discovery in California' who would contemptuously pass over long speeches and dull leaders. With the vast flow of news that now comes in there is a constantly increasing impatience of long accounts – a constant tendency to condense everything.

During the first half of 1881 readers of local newspapers in Wiltshire had to contend with lengthy accounts of two trials, and public interest was maintained because of the salacious nature of the accusations, and the 'fresh revelations' (as modern tabloids would regard them) which kept coming to light. The first was a libel case brought by the vicar of Keevil (near Trowbridge) against a fellow clergyman, arising out of allegations that he had misconducted himself with various parishioners. The second was described by the *Wiltshire Times* as 'the fracas between noblemen'. Lord Edward Thynne brought a charge of assault against three men who had accosted him while driving his pony carriage between Laverstock and Salisbury. We soon discover that there was more to it than that. But the best Victorian journalists whet our appetites not with vulgar headlines; instead we are treated to sparkling dialogue, apparently reported verbatim, though in reality carefully edited and selected for dramatic effect:

> Did you not know at the time that it was the Marquis Townshend who struck you? – No.

> If you had known it was Lord Townshend you would not have been astonished at it? – Yes I should.

I am sorry, but I am bound to ask you this question: 'Were you not in 1872 a constant visitor at his house, enjoying his hospitality?' – Not hospitality. I was frequently in his house, but not to see him.

Mr.Powning [counsel for Lord Edward] protested against questions being asked relating to events that occurred nine years ago. He advised his lordship not to answer any further questions relating to the subject.

A legal argument ensued, the result being that the Bench ruled that the questions were admissible either in extenuation or aggravation of the assault.

Mr.Tatlock [barrister for Marquis Townshend]: You were a constant visitor at Lord Townshend's house in 1872? – Yes.

And you eloped with his wife? – Yes.

Have you, from that time to the day of the alleged assault, ever met Lord Townshend face to face? – Never.

Did you ever get a beating from Lord Macduff? – I was assaulted by two men, one of whom was Lord Macduff.

In consequence of this same affair? – Yes.

That was the *Wiltshire Times* reporting the first hearing of the case in May 1881. When it came up before Quarter Sessions at Warminster in late June the facts were rehearsed once more, and on this occasion the *Salisbury Times* reporter showed that he too could write dialogue worthy of Oscar Wilde:

You, I believe, saw Lord Townshend some years ago? – Yes.

I think, in those times, he had the pleasure of receiving visits from you at his house in Dover-street? – Yes.

What year was that in, Lord Edward? – In 1872.

How long did those visits last? – From the beginning of 1872 till November.

Then, I believe, it was in 1872 you were kind enough to take his wife away from him? – It was (laughter).

At this time you were married – and I am not going to say anything further about a lady now dead? – Yes.

Before you took her away did you write her several letters asking her to go? – I don't recollect whether I did or not.

Will you be pleased to tell us? – I can't recollect; I might have done.

You can't recollect! Did your wife unfortunately find one of them – do you remember that? – Yes.

And she sent it up to him? – Yes.

Mr.Swayne [the presiding magistrate]: I don't think this is necessary.

Mr.Tatlock: Sir – on this point I shall not say another word. (To Witness) When you took her away from Lord Townshend's did you meet her in a cab in the street going to see her sister? – No.

That is false? – It is untrue.

Did you take her from Dover-street? – No.

Will you mind being kind enough to tell me where you took her from? — I don't see what that has got to do with the assault ('Oh, oh,' and laughter).

Mr.Tatlock: But I am going to ask you (laughter).

And so it continues, column inch after column inch. And at the end of it all Lord Edward won his case, at the expense of losing all vestige of self-respect in a blaze of humiliating publicity. And we are left suspecting that greater issues and darker secrets remain to be discovered.

This, of course, is the stuff of the novelist and the playwright. Hence the progression of Richard Jefferies' thought: reporting – editing – authorship. And in the following year, 1874, he published his first novel..

N e w s p r i n t

Unexpected Arrivals

'Every line being readable', was Jefferies' stricture to newspapermen. Sometimes the news was, almost literally, heaven-sent, as the editor of the *Swindon Advertiser* was pleased to discover in May, 1869:

> About two o'clock on Friday morning last, as P.S. [Police Sergeant] Stephens was standing in Taunton-street, New Swindon, he was startled by a very brilliant white light overhead. On looking up he saw a globe of perfectly white fire apparently about a foot in diameter descending towards him. When it came within about one hundred yards of him, it suddenly turned red throwing out a number of sparks like a rocket. It continued red until it came within about thirty yards of the ground and then turned green; finally disappearing when about fifteen yards from the earth and apparently in the middle of the street. The light was so brilliant that everything around was distinctly seen, and the sudden change to darkness produced a very peculiar effect. He went to the spot where the fire appeared to fall but could find nothing.

But wait, I think that I may be able to help him with his enquiries. I seem to remember reading in a footnote somewhere – yes, here it is, in a book on early motoring:

> The first road traffic signal in this country appears to have been a semaphore erected in Westminster in 1868. It had red and green lamps lit by gas. Its short life terminated abruptly in a violent explosion.

I wonder whether the explosion could have been so violent as to propel the apparatus to Swindon. I suppose that we shall never know.

Swindon was not the only place in Wiltshire where things fell out of the sky. In July 1892 another 'unidentified flying object' landed near Devizes:

Fall of a balloon at Bulkington.– The aeronauts missing.– A large balloon with a car attached passed over Devizes about 7 o'clock on Tuesday morning, and shortly after came down in a field at Bulkington. A young farmer named William Hillier, who was mowing grass, narrowly escaped having his horses struck by the car, which passed directly over him, only a few yards high. It next struck the hedge, and bounding up for about twenty feet, descended two fields off. He at once made for the spot, and found men running from all directions. After first securing the balloon to a tree, he made a survey of the car, but found in it nothing but a card and a clasp knife opened, which had evidently been used to sever the ropes as one was cut through, and another gashed in several places. The car, which smelt of seawater, had at the bottom of it a quantity of shingles and small shells, and had apparently been dragged along the sea shore, besides being dipped in the sea. There was also nearly half an inch of snow in the car when first discovered, showing that it must have mounted to some high altitude before descending. The car also bore the appearance of having been dragged on rocks, as it was grazed and one or two ropes torn off. The inscription on the card was:— 'L. Demeyer, 96 Rue de l'Ourcq, 96, Paris, Membre d'Academie, d'Aerostation Meteorologie, et Fabricant de Vannerie en tous genre.'

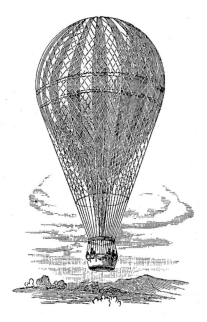

P.C. Osmonde was soon on the scene, and with the aid of several helpers the gas was allowed to escape, and the balloon was packed in a cart and taken under his care.

For the newspaper editor this story had the additional spice that, when he went to press, the mystery remained unresolved. His readers had to wait until the following week to discover that the outcome was happy, and that the three French 'aeronauts' were safe and well.

ح٭

Fillers

● ●

In fact, there is a good deal of news in Victorian local newspapers which leaves us crying out for more. The weekly paper did not carry only local news. National and international events were also carried, sometimes of audacious triviality. Here, for example, is a one-liner from the *Wiltshire Times* in August 1881.

> For throwing cayenne pepper at Oldham a woman has been fined £5 and costs.

But you cannot leave it there, with us readers in suspense. Why did she throw cayenne pepper at Oldham? Did she have a grudge against the town? From where did she throw it? How much did she use? Did she hit Oldham, and if so what was the effect? Was anybody hurt? Was £5 the usual fine for throwing cayenne pepper, or was it considered lenient or excessive? Were the costs for clearing up the pepper?

I suppose that it just goes to prove what we all know, that a little cayenne pepper goes a long way!

– Ah, now that is the kind of joke that our Victorian newspaper readers would definitely have enjoyed. It would have appealed to their sense of humour.

Indeed, when, as often happened, there were not enough readable local and national news items and advertisements to fill the Procrustean bed of an eight-page broadsheet, the editor would resort to a column of puns and clever remarks, headed 'Wit and Humour' or 'Facetiae'. Here are some examples, supplied by the *Trowbridge Chronicle* to its readers in 1879:

Coming to the point – Sharpening a pencil.

Most people are like eggs – too full of themselves to hold anything else.

What is the difference between a poor gun and a masquerade costume? –° One is fired and doesn't hit, and the other is hired and doesn't fit.

Nothing is so fatal to the romance of a kiss as to have your girl sneeze at the very climax of osculation.

A great many men are of the opinion that a certain quantity of wine is good for a man. It is the uncertain quantity that hurts him.

An unsuccessful vocalist went to a country poor-house, and delighted the inmates with his singing. He said it was a natural thing for him to do, as he'd been singing to poor houses ever since he began his career.

'With all thy false I love thee still,' murmured a young man as he calmly handed his girl the artificial teeth that she had sneezed into his lap.

Satisfied at last – A contented shoemaker.

First irate female: 'I'd hate to be in your shoes.' Second ditto: 'You could not get into them.'

A new nation seems to be rising in Europe – consternation.

A young couple were returning from the theatre, where they had witnessed a love scene acted. 'I can do better than that myself,' the young man remarked. – 'Why don't you, then?'

Well, I don't know about you, but Victorian jokes never did much for me – except for the last one, but I think that 'love scene' meant something rather different in 1879. And what is this obsession with sneezing while snogging (oops, sorry – osculation)? Is it some kind of omen, as the Romans believed, or has it something to do with the lines from the nursery rhyme, 'Sneeze on Tuesday, kiss a stranger... Sneeze on Saturday, see your sweetheart tomorrow'? Or are we still in Oldham?

Another device for filling space and amusing readers which was occasionally tried was the riddle. The crossword puzzle in its present form is a twentieth-century invention, but here, as early as 1775, a contributor came close to using the cryptic clues beloved of crossword compilers:

ENIGMATICAL LIST OF TOWNS AND VILLAGES IN WILTSHIRE:

1. Half a large fish, a vowel, a consonant; two-fifths of a celebrated orator, and two-thirds of a grain.

2. Three-sevenths of a bigot, a vowel, the last letter in the alphabet, and two-sixths of respect.

3. Half a noted perfumer, three-fourths of an aromatic herb, and four-eighths of a bird.

4. Three-fifths of an infant, a consonant, what is used in writing, and a much-esteemed dish.

5. Half a useful firing, half an amphibious creature, a weight, three-fourths of treacherous, and what the sun does.

6. Four-fifths of a character in the Irish widow, and a passable river.

7. Two-thirds of a domestic animal, the initial of a tender passion, a liquid letter, and a vowel.

8. Half a large bird, two-fifths of a wedge of gold, and a title of distinction in Spain.

9. Half an excursion, a consonant, and what we do with the dead.

10. Not low, and merit.

11. Five-sevenths of an insect, a youth, and a vowel.

12. Three-fifths of a month, a liquid letter, and what a member of parliament represents, will make known the native place of-

NANCY I———s.

Now you may need a little help with that. If I tell you that there was an eighteenth century London perfumer by the name of Richard Warren & Co.; and that *The Irish Widow*, a play of 1772 by David Garrick, features a character called Martha Brady – you should not have too many problems. Mind you, there seems to be a mistake in clue 3 — for 'starling' read 'sterling'.

❧

A Whiff of the Orient

If to our way of thinking the Victorians were not very successful when they were trying to be funny, when they were in earnest their quest for self-improvement through knowledge has a certain piquancy. Here, for example, is another filler from an 1879 *Trowbridge Chronicle* which caught my eye:

IN THE HAREM. When a Turk has disposed of his visitors he goes into his haremlik to dine or breakfast, first removing his babouches. This custom of removing one's shoes before entering a room is not a religious superstition, but comes of the necessity for keeping carpets clean, seeing that they fulfil the purpose of chairs, tables, sofas, in other countries. The bedroom of a harem may be furnished like Parisian boudoirs: but custom is stronger than fashion, and Turks of both sexes like to recline or sit cross-legged on the floor. Their carpets are curiously soft and thick, and the carpets over the doors shut out all draughts and noises. Through the open windows that look out on the garden come a scent of roses and the hum of bees, mingled with the laughter of children, who are playing on a well-trimmed lawn, under the eyes of the dark-eyed Circassian nurses. The mistress of the harem — the Buiuk-Hanum (great lady, to give her full title) — dresses much like an English lady nowadays, reads French novels and plays the piano, though she dons upon state occasions, such as the chalvas, when she entertains other ladies. Chalva means a cake, but has come to designate a party at which that dainty is eaten, just as we say tea for tea-party in England. When a Turkish lady gives a chalva, her husband is perforce excluded from the harem while the strange women are in the house. These guests begin to arrive towards six, accompanied by their maid-servants and negroes carrying lanterns, and bringing their children with them. Closely muffled, they divest themselves of their burnouses and babouches in an ante-room, and put on delicate slippers, which they have brought with them in bags. The reception-rooms are brilliantly lighted up with pink wax-candles and scented with fragrant pastilles. There is no kissing or hand-shaking between the hostess and her guests; but each lady, as she comes in, lifts her hand gracefully to her heart, her lips, and her brow, which means, 'I am devoted to you with heart, mouth, and mind'. This mode of salutation, when smilingly performed, is very pretty. The greetings being ended, the company seat themselves on chairs if there be any Frank ladies present; if not, they betake themselves to the divans and carpets, and the cake-eating begins.

I am sure that it must come as a great relief to all my right-minded readers to learn that this – and not what they thought – was the kind of excess that went on in a harem. Indeed, after reading that reassuring note respectable parents in Victorian Trowbridge need have had no more qualms about allowing their daughters to visit Turkey, than they might about them attending a Wesleyan tea meeting – unless, that is, too much cake was considered bad for their complexions. I wonder whether any Trowbridge girls ever did end up in a sultan's caravanserai.

ٿ

The Rustic Polymath

Reading some of these fillers, one cannot escape the conclusion that the editor has made them up during his lunch break. Here is a dubious piece, originally published in the *New London Magazine* long before most local newspapers had begun, in May 1786:

The following is an exact copy of a sign, hung out at a village in Wiltshire:

ISAAC FAC TOTUM, barber, perr-wig maker, surgeon, parish clerke, scool mester, blacksmith, and man-midwife.

Shaves for a penne, cuts hare for toopence, and oyled and powdered into the bargin. Young ladys genteely edicated; lamps lited by the hear or quarter. Young gentlemen also taut their grammor langwage in the neetest manner, and great cear takin of their morels and spelin. Also salme singin, and horce shewine by the real maker. Likewise makes and mends all sorts of butes and shoes, teches the ho! boy [hautbois or oboe] and Jews harp, cuts corns, bledes and blesters on the lowest terms. — Glisters and purges at a penny a piece; cow-tillion and other dances taut at home and abroade. Also deals holesale and retail perfumerry in all it's branches. Sells all sorts stationry wair, together with blackin balls, red herrins, ginger bred, and coles, scrubbin brushes, treycle, mouce traps, and other sweetmetes. Likewise Godfrey's cordiel, rutes, potatoes, sassages, and other gardin stuffe.

N.B. I teaches joggrafy, and them outlandish kind of things. A bawl on Wensdays and Frydays; all performed (God willin) by me, ISAAC FAC TOTUM.

The Man in the Moon

Another way in which an editor, short of copy, could fill out his paper was by running a kind of gossip column, obliquely poking fun at people and places under the cloak of anonymity. Nowadays such 'in-jokes' of a century or more ago generally fall flat, either because the innuendoes have been lost, or because of the changing taste in humour which I noticed earlier. But here are a few of the better contributions (all from 1883) to a column which ran during the 1880s in the *Trowbridge Chronicle*. The supposed correspondent was none other than the 'Man in the Moon', who was able to look down bemusedly on the Trowbridge area, and pry into all sorts of personal goings-on. This conceit was maintained to the extent of poking fun at an amateur astronomer who, he alleged, was prying back again:

What is it on the move in Chapmanslade that makes every man so watchful of his neighbour's interest, as for each to be a detective of the other's acts? A man has been too free at Christmas, gets fined for it at Warminster, and a few days afterwards he is summoned before the Westbury bench to answer the same charge for the same offence, on the same day, in the same street. It seems that one side of Chapmanslade street is in Warminster magisterial division, and the other side in Westbury division. The offender seems to have imbibed on one side too freely and afterwards, in that state, crossed to the other side, and this is said to have constituted the double offence. The magistrates very wisely refrained from punishing the man twice for one and the same offence. It shows how watchful the Chapmanslade folks are of each other's welfare.

Valentine's Day, that annual outlet for spite and spleen of the most reprehensible kind, was again characterized in Trowbridge – I hope not elsewhere – by the faithful postmen seen labouring along bearing most curious missives. What connection a dip candle, a wooden monkey on a stick, a box of cockroaches, and other tender trifles have to do with St Valentine, I leave your readers to judge. The spiteful and splenetic senders, moved by the most pitiable of motives, somehow or other do it so clumsily that they cannot conceal their animosity; for postmarks and clumsy attempts to mystify handwriting are sometimes eloquent.

What is the meaning of sending candle-ends as valentines? I am told the piece of dip candle that has been sent from one to another around this town, through the post, each one mistaking the right party who sent it. How much farther it will go is not known. Perhaps a vigorous blow from the P.O. stamper will flatten it out of all semblance, and terminate its career.

The parties who, the other night, carried off some choice rhubarb from a garden in Waterworks Road, can, I am informed, have a valuable recipe how to preserve it, on calling at the owner's residence.

More Trivia

Nothing, it seems, was too inconsequential or too remote to be printed in the local newspaper when there was space to fill. Following the Oldham pepper scoop the *Wiltshire Times* continued through the silly season of 1881 with more information which the good people of west Wiltshire had previously done without:

The electric light has been introduced into the smoking room of the Junior Carlton Club.

According to an Arkansas paper, an intoxicating spring, whose waters taste like apple brandy, has been discovered in that State. A Missouri journal notices the statement, and sarcastically adds that Nature knows where her gifts will be best appreciated.

On Tuesday, as a Birmingham auctioneer, Mr. Fellows, was conducting a sale at Garrison-lane, Birmingham, and was saying 'Going, going, gone' previous to knocking down some articles, the floor gave way, and precipitated a number of persons, including several brokers and women, some with children in their arms, into the cellar beneath. Several of the people were hurt.

Luminous paint is being used for country post boxes in Cambridgeshire, so that they may be seen in the dark.

The stamp duty of 3d a pack on playing cards amounted in the last financial year to the net sum of £14,652.15s.9d.

Yes, I know what you're thinking. Actually, that comes to 1,172,223 packs of playing cards – perhaps more, as the figure was net. No television, you see, and nothing much in the newspaper.

F a i r s

Selling a Wife
● ●

Journalism is a hurly-burly world, and the scramble to meet a deadline can lead to tawdry prose. Richard Jefferies was aware of the pressures:

> The editor should never argue. He will have twenty people, of twenty different minds, to see him on a market-day, all bursting with their own ideas. Physical exhaustion would be the result of an attempt to convince them, besides every one would be offended. His object is to acquire information, he has merely to listen, and to put forward no view, except to help the speaker to a better comprehension of his own ideas.

But later there would be time for reflection. We have already been introduced to Master William Morris, who went 'In Search after Ozone and Oblivion' (what a modern ring that title has!). He was the founder of the *Swindon Advertiser*, in 1854, and he remained its editor until his death in 1891. He had plenty of opportunity to pick up unusual stories during his career. This one will have a familiar ring to readers of Thomas Hardy, as it foreshadows the action at Weyhill Fair upon which the plot of *The Mayor of Casterbridge* hinges. Morris published the following in 1885 – serialization of Hardy's novel in *The Graphic* began in January 1886:

> Among the poor, however, in some parts of the country at least, there existed a tradition that a man might rid himself of a faithless spouse in an equally legal but far less expensive manner – by putting a halter round her neck and leading her by it from the home to the public market place, and there publicly disposing of her by

auction. The parties to whom I have referred not only believed in this tradition, but they made all the necessary arrangements for taking practical advantage of it. The halter was bought, such notice as was considered necessary of the intended sale was given, and the day and hour fixed when the sale was to take place in the Swindon Square or Market-place. It was, of course, also arranged that the young navvy was to be there and to become the purchaser, for the sum, I believe, of sixpence and a pot of beer. At this time, no doubt, there was a very general impression on the minds of the ignorant and unlettered that such a sale of a wife as that contemplated was legal, and that the liability to maintain her was thereby transferred from the vendor to the purchaser. For some reason, which I never heard, the sale did not take place, although there was a large gathering of persons in the Square at the time appointed to witness it. Although at this time the schoolmaster had not come in, the policeman had, and I have always entertained a grave suspicion that it was through his interference that so many persons were deprived of the sight they went out to see, and the town spared the disgrace of having a woman led into the public square with a halter round her neck for public sale.

ॐ

Salisbury Fair

When there was plenty of time and too many column inches to fill, the reporter might indulge himself in what may best be described as a little essay. Here is a cutting of 1892, anonymous but not without literary skill, and quite satisfying in its balance of information, description and humour:

> At Salisbury Fair, among the sights and sounds. A person passing through the Market Square today would hardly realise, in the garb of peace and quietness it now wears, that it was, during the first three days of the week, the scene of a queer mixture of confusion, noise, and delight, which are its characteristics during the annual

pleasure fair. If you were to ask the youngsters, who have lightened the weight of their money-boxes with rides on the hobby-horses, or in beholding the marvels of the waxworks, or who have a confused idea of 'music' emitted from the discordant orchestra of wailing and blaring organs, they would probably tell you that never was there such a glorious gala in the history of the world.

But if you were to speak to those who have watched the progress and decline of the Salisbury Fair year after year, and are therefore entitled to give an idea on the subject, you would listen to the universal opinion that this year's fair was not to be compared with that of previous years – though not much worse than last. The only difference of view would be that whereas some with a sneaking regard for old time amusements – and the writer pleads guilty to being in that category – would sigh and regretfully murmur 'Worse luck', whilst others, with a gleam of satisfaction in their eyes, would exclaim, 'The fair is dying out, and a good job too'.

But the purpose of this article, for the moment, is not to deal with regrets for the past or speculations as to the future. For though some of us cannot help looking upon the din created in the proximity of a leading business part of the city as an intolerable nuisance, yet there is associated with the round of pleasure a certain charm which cannot be resisted. It was in vain that the writer determined the other night to reach Castle Street from Fisherton Street by the circuitous route of round Silver Street, the Canal, Milford Street, Brown Street, Rollestone Street, Salt Lane and Scots Lane, in order to be far from the madding crowd. When he reached the vicinity of St Thomas' Church, some irresistible impulse drew him round by the 'drangway'. A moment or so later he was in the thick of the 'fun of the fair', and he would not perjure himself by saying he was altogether disappointed.

It was an animating scene, in sooth. The gorgeously decked proscenium of the waxwork show, the glitter of gaudy colour on the switchbacks and roundabouts, the drolleries of the showmen straining their lungs as they touted for customers, the brazen-throated organs grinding away simultaneously at different tunes

Salisbury Cathedral, west front.

with deafening discord, the roar of the multitude in the square, the shouts of half merriment and half fear of some of the youngsters (aye, and some old'uns, too) as they swirled round the undulating track of the aerial railroad, or galloped around the endless circle on the, 'firey untamed steeds', that bobbed up and down with the semblance of racing, as they spun onward to the 'music' which we have before mentioned but have not attempted to describe – all these things, combined, produced upon the mind a nameless bewilderment of delight.

The first thought was one of pity for the unfortunate tradesmen whose places of business this hubbub was in the very midst of, but that was, after all, supplanted by a stranger feeling of gratification of the fact that it seemed to be the means of giving hearty and earnest enjoyment to hundreds of folks who perhaps never have any other chance of obtaining it. Those who can find a warm corner in their hearts for the little ones, must have been in a state of high pleasure at the evidences presented of the delights in which the youngsters were positively revelling. Never to them did sweets taste so dainty of flavour as those bought by a thoughtful parent at one of the many stalls; never were toys hugged so closely to the little breasts, with a sense of anxious pleasure; never was man so funny as the droll clown who fooled and capered on the platform outside the show; never were wonders so great and marvellous as those to be seen inside the show; and never did the little heads whirl so much with the intoxication of the babel and pandemonium of delight.

It was thus that the juvenile mind was struck, the children of older growth did not fail to recognize in the fair the usual elements of comicality. It is true, we suppose, that a man on pleasure bent can extract humour from almost anything. In the ordinary course, there is nothing diverting in the extraction of corns – especially when personally struggling with an old and longstanding friend and adherent – and one does not always laugh at the administration of medicine. But the crowd who thronged round the chiropodist in the Market Square, who had extracted corns 'from all the crowned heads of Europe' (though he probably meant their feet) – and watched his operations on customers from among the throng, could not help laughing, partly because there was something droll about the operations, and partly because they were 'out to enjoy themselves' and must laugh, whether they would or not. The quack doctor, too, did a brisk trade, but perhaps with him his wonderful volubility and terror-striking vocabulary of expressions proved the greatest attraction.

But oh! the watch seller! What a lot of infantile credulity there is in the pleasure-seeking British public! To think that there are people gullable enough to imagine that for the twentieth part of the value of a Waterbury they can get a brand new English gold lever! Yet, by remarkable dexterity and bamboozling, the 'auctioneer' throws his line, the credulous fish (with a readiness that would shock the hungriest Avon trout) swallow the baited hook and part with their shillings. When the time is ripe the gold levers are distributed, a moment later the trick is discovered, the crowd roars with merriment, and the victims throw their gilded cases of useless tin on the ground, and dance on them with vexation.

At the boxing booths, too, similar scenes are enacted. A broad, burly-looking customer makes his appearance, and in a voice, as loud as his hide was apparently thick, challenges the world of pugilism to combat, and would give worlds to have only a round or two with Sullivan or Slavin or Corbett (or 'any of the lot'). The knot of lookers-on are awe-stricken – nobody dares take up the gauntlet and face so terrible an individual. The consequence is that the spectators are outside and not in, and business for the moment looks bad.

Just, however, as the crowd begins to move away in disappointment, a very little man (supposed to be from the country, but really an accomplice) suddenly presents his wiry form and breathes defiance to the challenger.

'Look 'ere, young man,' says the latter, 'I would advise yer to go home and ax yer mammy ter whack yer. I could lay sich as you with the tip of my little finger.'

'Could yer', says the supposed 'yokel' in a tone of assumed anger and disgust, 'Try it on, yer great bully, and let's see.'

'Go on away, lad, go away,' says the other deprecatingly, 'I want to fight men and not boys, but if yer doant mind coming inside I'll box yer ears for 'ee, just to satisfy yer.'

'I can't stand these hinsults any longer,' says the 'abused' one and rushes into the booth with a veritable leap, and the crowd flock in after him, expecting to be the witnesses of a fine piece of impromptu, but really carefully rehearsed, fun.

In the midst of so much robust enjoyment there are very few causes of complaint, the chief of these being that that execrable nuisance, the 'squirt', or 'Lady's teaser', as it is sometimes called, was in evidence during the fair. The police cannot be expected to do everything and be everywhere at the same time – indeed, they kept admirable order, thanks to Mr Matthews' capital arrangements. But it is really to be hoped that another year steps will be taken to put down the pest, which would soon have an ending, if the plan were adopted in Salisbury, which is in vogue in other places, viz., that of prosecuting both those who use and those who sell the abominations. It only remains to be added that the fair people cleared out on Thursday afternoon, and that the Square now wears its wonted appearance.

Personally, my sympathies are with the chiropodist. 'Crowned feet of Europe' just wouldn't have sounded right. But notice how carefully the essay has been constructed, and how well the writer has struck his course between serious comment and frivolity. Only at the end, when advocating the prosecution of water-pistol vendors, does the conventional Victorian psyche put in an appearance.

But, at the risk of labouring a point, I must make two more observations in favour of this piece. The first is that deep undercurrents lie beneath it. A royal commission had sat in Salisbury four years earlier to take evidence about the fair, and many harsh words and dire predictions were made about it. There were calls that it should be abolished.

The second, quite different, point is that a short story by Thomas

Hardy, 'On the Western Circuit' (which was probably written in 1891 and was published in 1894), uses Salisbury Michaelmas fair as its backcloth. The present essay, we recall, dates from 1892. I find it intriguing to read the two descriptions, and imagine that perhaps Hardy and our anonymous reporter unconsciously brushed past each other in the 'madding' crowd, as both their heads bristled with the words they needed to transfer the scene to paper.

ॐ

Curiouser and curiouser

The popular culture of the Victorian funfair had evolved over centuries, and details had been carried by local newspapers since they were first printed. Here is a notice about a forthcoming fair, and dates from 1774:

INTELLIGENCE EXTRAORDINARY: As the 25th of September happens this year on a Sunday, Shrewton Fair will be held on Monday the 26th instant; there will be the usual entertainments, but the nobility and gentry are in expectation of a Fete Champetre, where masks are to be admitted: We hear, a Miller in Plush will make the first appearance, and shew some odd tricks; but will be greatly outdone by one in a short fustian jacket, who will dance an hornpipe on a furze faggot from France, with ten thousand five hundredweight on his head: he will be introduced by a little Doctor, who will read a lecture on silence. – Some pretty diversions will be shewn by a man at Hyde and Seek; – A laughing figure in the shape of a Pumpkin, will bring all sorts of hot-house productions, and a sprig of the old tulip tree in a tray, made of the famous Damory Oak; he will try to make a Greyhound swallow a purse of guineas. The company will all be entertained with blamange and plenty of French wines – Franky Peggs, in the chair. NB. The roads are made very good.

Strange the things which pass for entertainment, and grotesque some of the food on offer:

On Tuesday evening last one Scarlet, a noted cock-fighter, at Burbage, in this county, eat [i.e. ate], at an inn in Marlborough, a raw cock, of 4 lb weight, which had been killed that day in fighting. He eat it with bread, pepper, salt and vinegar. After Scarlet had done, another canibal, his companion, eat a cock of 5 lb weight, without any bread. The latter, worse than savage, not content with displaying his first brutish feats, afterwards eat a raw rat that had been dead four days.

❧

Up to no good

That was in 1773, according to James Waylen, who pasted the cutting into his scrapbook. And if you think that that was unpleasant, just listen to what went on, according to the Clerk of the Works, after the Whitsun Fair in Salisbury Cathedral Close:

And here it may not be foreign to the subject, to mention a custom, which had prevailed time immemorial, because the consequences of it must contribute to the fractures here mentioned; viz. in the Whitsun holidays, a fair is kept within the Close of Sarum, at which time it is customary for people to go upon the spire, there having been sometimes upon it eight or ten persons at a time.

The late bishop, dean and chapter, put a stop to these fool-hardy practices, by which many lives were hazarded without the least advantage to those who attempted it: and the danger was the greater, because these people never went up but when heated with liquor, which furnished them with that unnecessary courage. It seems they had certain sports in their passage up and down, viz. those who were the highest had the pleasure of discharging their urine on those below. Whoever considers the effect of urine upon lead, stone, and timber, as likewise upon all materials used in buildings, will own, that a great mischief must ensue, and hasten the natural decays. Besides this, there is reason to suppose, that the weather door and some of the eight doors were left open, and so the rain and snow was conveyed into the very connections of the timber, and the iron that was to assist and strengthen the joints. There was always, at these times, another injurious practice, viz. that of people rambling all over the roofs of the church, and particularly in the gutters, where, besides their usual discharges, they frequently cut their names, the date of the time, and other foolish devices; and by vying who should make the deepest impressions, they frequently cut through the lead, and of course the water was let in upon the timbers, and hastened their decay.

D i a l e c t

'Leabourin' volk'

How uncouth they were, the Wiltshire peasantry! That, at least, is the impression we are given by the commentators of the day. But they, of course, were looking down on popular culture as something inferior and laughable. And we are in danger of making their prejudice our own.

Some years ago I edited a little book of Edward Slow's dialect verse. He was a carriage-builder in Wilton, who rose to become the town's mayor and a respected alderman. During the 1860s, as a young man, he discovered an aptitude for writing dialect; and between 1864 and 1918, a few years before his death, he was the author of at least thirty-five small books and pamphlets, in dialect verse and prose.

By no stretch of the imagination can his work be described as great literature, or even good poetry. But the historical interest of his productions lies in the fact, as I wrote in my introduction, that he was no mere observer, but a participant in the things he described. 'And, unlike most writers of humble origins, he did not try to rise from the ranks of the working classes, or... try to interpret working-class ways to his intellectual friends.' He was writing for the 'leabourin volk', of whom he was one.

One of the poems which I included was 'Ower Girt Zeptember Vair'. It paints an evocative picture of Wilton sheep fair, in a way quite different from the journalist's account of Salisbury fair. Here is part of his treatment of the quack orator:

> *Zee yonder Quack begins his clack,*
> *Like a maniac he spouts till he's black;*
> *Zays he, mines tha tack,*

If ya've pains in tha back,
Ar any wur else, I'll cure tha attack
Why do ee remain za long in yer pain,
Wen I stoutly maintain
That if you obtain my medicines plain
Good health you'll regain, yes! an retain,
An never agean complain;
Dwont think ta meak wills,
Bit teak my pills, and be rid of yer ills,
Eece an 'tis zaprisan, wieout disguisin,
Ow many putts vaith in thease Quacks advisin...

Edward Slow, as we saw in our first chapter, printed complimentary reviews of his work in some of his books. They were taken from various magazines and local newspapers, including the *Durham Chronicle, Court Circular, Middlesbrough News, Carriage Builders' Gazette,* and the *Richmond and Ripon Chronicle.* Presumably the reviews had been syndicated to these far-flung periodicals, and Slow did not actually send out complimentary copies all over the country.

Perhaps not, although we have it from Edith Olivier that he did send a copy to Alfred Lord Tennyson, because he felt that poets should always be ready to exchange their works. The poems of Tennyson duly arrived in return, with a note: 'I thank you for your meritorious volume of poems.' And I can testify to having found, in a second-hand bookshop in Ripon (one of the places from which reviews emanated), three small pamphlets of Slow's works, dating from 1902-6. One of them is so rare that I do not believe that it exists in any library in Wiltshire. Here is a short piece of dialect prose from it:

TRAVELLEN ATHOUT AR TICKET. When tha new Zouth Waastern Railway wur aupend vrim Zalsbury ta Wilton [in 1859], there wur a main lot a Wilton bwoys as wur prentices in tha Zity, who waaked backurds an verreds nite and marnen; zometimes some on ess manidged ta muster up the tuppence apeny ta pay var a ride in tha train, which wur conzidered a bit of a luxury, an a girt trate in thic em there days. Tha ticket collector at Zalsbury Stayshen wur a main crotchety zart of a feller, an a got it into he's yead that zome a we bwoys did offen av a ride in athout ar a ticket an slip out weout bein zeed. Bit twur never done as I knaas on, at laste I never tried it on. Houzemever just var a lark, an ta get thease yer jealus minded Collectors back up a bit, Ben Binks zaays ta I one marnen, jist loud anuff varn ta hear, 'Diss knaa Jack I da offen come vrim Wilton ta Zalsbury, athout ar a ticket'. The Collector hearen on it, collar'd un be tha ear, led un into tha Booken Office, and zent var tha Stayshen Measter; who axed what wur the matter. 'Why zur, zaays tha vussy Collector, I auveryears thease young scamp tell he's companion there, that he offen comes vrim Wilton ta Zalsbury athout ar a ticket'; 'Is that true', zays Stayshen Measter. 'Eece zur I do,' zaays Ben. 'Well how do you manidge ta do it?' says he. 'Why I da waak in,' zays Ben.

A coose Stayshen Measter cooden help smilin as a let ess bouath off. Bit thic ar Ticket Collector wur down on Ben an I, as longs he lived.

ટ▲

Edward Slow's Novel

Slow's undoubted talent for mimicking his own, and his friends', way of speaking brought him considerable local celebrity around the turn of the century. But in his largest and most ambitious project I cannot help the feeling that he overreached his abilities. This was a full-length novel of 260 pages, *Jan Ridley's New Wife*, and was published in 1913. The plot is thin and contrived, and the characters only appear in order to serve as mouthpieces for Slow's attempt to contrast Wiltshire and Cockney dialects, with a dose of public-school English thrown in for good measure. In this extract a picnic is about to take place at a well known national monument about ten miles from Wilton:

Well, upon my sacred wod and honnah,' says Dick [a Cockney], 'these are really some monsters and naow mistike! I've seen a few big blocks of stoan in my time at various plices in London, but, by jove, these giants beat em oll holler, anyhaow. And the puzzle of it is, Tribbet, how in the nime of thunder did they get em heah, seeing there were no railroads or machinery either, when them hoff-civilized old fogies they call Druids fixed em up. Well, its a bloomin conundrum, that's what it is, and oll the learned and knowing ones as ever existed, who have studied em, examined em, and wrote abaht em, cawn't mike em out any more than you or I can. Well, as I syes, heah they aw, and heah I suppoas they'll remain, a bloomin mystery, and its naow use form you and me to puzzle our brains as to how they kime heah, or for what purpose they were fixed up; sow let's gow and have some inside lining, for I begin to feel a sinking just here,' says he, tapping the lower part of his waistcoat. 'This heah air down heah seems to set a fellaw's innwards longing or something to do pretty often.' The party were soon busily engaged making short work of the ham sandwiches, bread, cheese, and ale. 'Upon my sacred wod and honnah,' says Dick, after he'd finished, 'never in oll my blessed life have I ever relished such a snack as that; them sandwiches were a real treat, and as for Uncle's hoam brewed ail, it's really like imbibing Moet's best sparkling Phizz.' 'Ah, it's tha hayer, my bwoy,' zays Jan Ridley [a Wiltshireman], 'ower good woold country vresh hayer; that's the zart a saace to go we yer grub, as da meak ee relish it zoo.'

'No doubt about that, Uncle,' says Tom Tribbet [a public-school type], 'for although your good, wholesome, homely fare is relishable anywhere and anywhen, yet when a fellow gets an appetite hightened and sharpened by this beautiful bracing air, it is doubly so.' 'Heah, heah!' says Mister Daisher, 'thems my sentiments exactly, Mister Tribbet.'

What do ee think a tha Stounes, Dick?' zays Missus Ridley. 'Think of em, Haunt? Well, to sum it up quick, I think em a bloomin mystery as nobody ever have, or ever will unravel. What's the good of all them bookworm fellas, archeological and antiquarian, coming here, spoutin and lecturin, and suggestin this, that, and tother, and writin books and pamphlets about em enough to stock a library, and awfter oll, they knaow naow more abaht em than you or I do, Haunt; thats my private opinion. It's oll a matter of theory and speculation on their pawts.'

'I tell ee what it is,' zays Jan Ridley, 'I've a bin visitin thease yer Girt Big Stounes dozens a times, ever zunce I were a bwoy, at ael sazons a tha year, an at ael times, marnen, non an night. I've a studied em, rade about em, an dramed about em in bade an out a bade; run em auver in me mind in wirk an out a wirk; Zundys an week days, an atter ael this, I've come ta tha clusion that they were stuck up be the Devil, an nabiddy else, an twur about tha time as he wur draved out a Heaven be Zaint Michael, as we da rade about in Scripter. Atter bein turned out, ya zee, a diden knaa where ta goo, zoo at last a wandered ta Zalsbury Plaain, an stuck up thase yer Girt Stounes var a house ta bide in.' At this very quaint suggestion the company all burst out laughing. 'Well, ya mid ael laugh, bit now let's hear what you've got ta zay about em ar bit better, will ee?' zays he. 'Well, I for one,' says Tom Tribbet, 'certainly lean to the prevailing opinion, that, they were erected by the Druids as a Temple to worship the Sun, for as you're aware, even to this day, on the 21st of every June, the summer solstice, people come from all parts to see that luminary cast it's first ray on rising, across the 'Friar's Heel' yonder, on to the Altar Stone just here.'

Yes, writing dialogue is a gift not given to us all; and the confusion is only made worse when, as you may have noticed, the narrator keeps changing his accent as well. But if that took you a long time to read, I can assure you that it took a great deal longer to type into my word processor. Spare a thought for the printer's poor compositor who in 1913 had to set the whole book.

A Parish on Wheels

Having seen how not to do it, let us turn to someone who did it rather well. Howard Swinstead was a priest employed by Salisbury Diocese from 1892-5 as itinerant minister to the gipsies and travelling population of the area, and in 1897 he published an account of his work, which he called *A Parish on Wheels*. It is a scarce book which I have never seen anyone refer to, so I propose to give it an airing. In this passage Swinstead describes a theme by now familiar to us, the activities of the quack orator at a country fair:

> His complete kit is a shiny hand-bag, containing illustrations on calico of dreadful fractures to limb and skull, and oddments. These are spread before him, with mysterious precision, guarded by a bottle or two, which the orator by turns patrols and handles with affection.
>
> During these ostentatious preliminaries a small audience of velveteens and sky-blue ties assembles.
>
> The speaker delivers himself with slow, deliberate, perhaps bibulous, hauteur, as if he expects to catch a new auditor with every syllable.
>
> 'My name is Pro-fessor Chunk, chiropodist and taxidermist' (the nearest listeners look terror-stricken as the orator clears his throat). 'In order to ass-ure you, ladies and gentlemen (the gentler sex are entirely imaginary), that I am not a quack, but a bonyfide 'erbalist of twenty years' study and standin', I will give you my card stating the postal address, to which letters of hevery description will be delivered – if correctly addressed – to me by her Majesty's post officials: Pro-fessor H. Chunk, General Practitioner and Bird-fancier, Yeovil Road, Sherborne.
>
> 'The reason for which I have the honour of addressing you in this field to-day is, as you will see, owing to the loss of my arm from causes connected with my past 'istory.' (Here he puts his whole conceited soul into the narration, and if he lacks an arm, his eyes do their best to dilate and make up for the loss.) 'I was a faithful

soldier in her Majesty's service in the Ashanti Campaign in the year 1870, and it was my privilege to lose my arm for my Queen and country while dashin' heroically at the black but comical enemies of our nation. Their 'air was made of feathers. But they scraped my arm off, I will give them that credit, and retired ignerminously defeated.'

(How often have I wished that I could arrest and keep my congregation's attention as this man did; but perhaps his subject permitted of the more varied treatment and the less exactness of statement.)

'Since that date, my friends and fellow-countrymen, I have been withdrawn from active service, and therefore you see me now living still to benefit my nation. It is to do you all good that I came. Now, I am prepared, by means of this compound of 'erbs, which I now 'old between my forefinger and thumb, labelled with my hown trademark on each bottle, which will cure all the natural ailments that the body is suffering – except a broken leg. Stand back, if you please!

'And so, if any gentleman here is afflicted with rheumatism, asthma, gout, peritonitis, neuralgia, or a slow liver, he has only to give me current coin to the amount of one shilling and a penny halfpenny (by post to the registered address, threepence more), and he will receive instant attention from headquarters, who will send him this bottle. I have only a dozen, so be quick, if you want them now; the chief ingredient is *aqua pura cum grano salis*, which, if taken in large enough quantities, will relieve anyone of indigestion caused by too liberal feeding at his last meal. (All right, young man, you can 'ear just as well if you step back off my dispensary carpet. Thank *you*!)

'I was myself troubled with excrescences on the chin; my barber allowed this razor to go through these, instead of passing over them. The result was apocryphal: the blood was abysmal, and the warts were quite irreplaceable.

'But if any gentleman 'ere is covered from 'ead to foot with bubukles, whelks, or pimples, let him step forward, and with my elixir for the preservation of the cuticle in all forms, I will cure him.'

(The challenge is not accepted.)

'There was a lady come to me last week, tremblin' with beauty like the flower-garden in her 'at. And I said to her, "Good madam, pray be seated – and how are you? Have you taken the medicine I gave you?" She replied, "I am takin' it. I am as I am, and I can't be no ammer." Now that, I conceive, is the right spirit in which to take medicine.

'Do your best and leave the rest with Nature. (A wave of pious but resigned approval here passed over the faces of the bystanders.)

'You say you believe in my medicines (this was quite gratuitous as a true quotation, for no one had opened his lips). Well, I reply, believe in them one and three halfpence. Thank you, sir – only one bottle, you said? And you another? Yes: you don't look too well, my lad; try two doses at a time, and then send for more when you've finished – that's what you want, and so do I.'

I knew not how near I was to danger while being entertained by this stranger unawares.

'Won't you come and see a great curiosity I have, sir? It is marvellous; we only show it to a few gentlemen quite private – not a public show.'

With that he led me into a frail booth, whose calico walls flapped feebly in the wind, and with great show of doing me an enormous kindness in the strictest secrecy, he unlocked one box after another, until he produced the most degrading and nauseating show I have ever been entrapped into seeing.

'What do you think of it, sir? isn't it marvellous?'

'Yes, I allow that; but –'

He was off, had mounted the steps in front of the booth, signalled silence to the man who had by banjo beguiled a wavering audience to pause and look at nothing particular, gave the assistant the keys to lock up his show, and just as I came out of the curtained entrance, shouted in a raucous voice:

'The clergyman who is now standin' before you at the entrance to my show declares it is the most marvellous and soul-stirrin' sight he ever beheld. It is a reg'lar tail-twister! He is from the Bishop of Salisbury, and all the clergy and noblemen of the county agree with his recommendation that I have now to show you,' etc. – but by this time I was quite out of earshot.

He afterwards replied to my remonstrances:

'Well, you see, sir, public speakers like you and me – we has to gull the public, hasn't we, sometimes?'

But I got 'upsides wi' un" within three months. It was to an August crowd under the Weymouth Jubilee Clock that he was spouting his first-quoted moving address (or something like it), when he spied me coming along, and with great gusto appealed to me for a recommendation of his goods.

'There's a gentleman – a clergyman too – will tell yer the same.'

Several heads turned my way in the direction indicated by his demonstrant finger, and by an inspiration which has always since seemed unaccountable, I turned my own head with the rest, to look for the advertisement he was pointing out.

The effect was a most desirable one: the unpaid advertisement fell flat, the public felt duped, and I chuckled at the score paid off three months after date.

Lost Causes

The Art of Flying

The Salisbury Diocese Itinerant Mission continued for another twenty years after Swinstead had left it, but seems to have been killed off by the First World War. Its work was highly regarded by both churchmen and travellers.

But the clergy's brushes with itinerants and wonder workers had not always been so cordial. Here is part of a letter about an event which occurred in a village near Devizes in 1735:

> Mankind, not satisfied with travelling on the elements of earth and water, have attempted to invade the air, from the days of Daedalus downwards. 'Pennis non homini datis', ('with wings not given to man') they have hitherto essayed, unsuccessfully, the Art of Flying: notwithstanding Bishop Wilkins's prediction that the time would come when a man setting out on a journey would ring for his wings, as heretofore for his boots.
>
> About 100 years ago, an adventurer of this kind travelled the country, making for money at different places the exhibition of a flight from towers and steeples. His method was to have a rope fixed to the top of the place from which he was to descend, and strained to a convenient place where he was to alight. A board, with a groove to receive the cord, was fixed to the breast of the 'aeronaut', and by this he was to descend headforemost to the point of alighting. Amongst other places he visited Bromham, and having solicited permission to 'fly' from the steeple, some idle people of the place, without consulting the clergyman, who was indisposed, gave him leave to perform. A time was appointed, the apparatus

was fixed, and a mob assembled. The flyer ascended the steeple, made his plunge, and was half way down the rope, when some persons employed to strain it pulled it too hard. The top of the spire gave way, and came down. The aeronaut, luckily for himself, fell into a tree in the churchyard, and received but little hurt. Had he fallen to the ground he would have been dashed to pieces. This event probably put an end to steeple-flying; but as the inhabitants of a country are often ridiculed for the foolish acts of their neighbours, the story of pulling down their own steeple was for a long time a standing joke against the people of Bromham. It was repaired; but some years afterwards was struck by lightning, and shivered near the same point where it had been broken before.

Bromham Church

The Wiltshire Coalfields

The pages of history, of course, are littered with human follies of every kind, and I had long been intrigued by a reference I came across in Dr. Hunnisett's edition of eighteenth-century Wiltshire coroners' inquests. On 6th May 1776 at Longbridge Deverill (near Warminster), we are told:

> Thomas Coward was in the bottom of a pit digging for coal and had just sent up a thing full of earth called by the miners a cart when the rope broke and let fall the cart and earth with great violence and killed him on the spot.

But why should he have been digging for coal at Longbridge Deverill? The parish lies on chalk and greensand, with the Oxford clay outcropping not far away at Horningsham. But the nearest coalfield is in the Radstock area, nearly fifteen miles away, and the coal measures at Longbridge Deverill must be thousands of feet underground. The mystery remained, until I came across a short article by Professor J. Buckman, entitled, 'On some coal mining operations at Malmesbury', which was published in 1855:

> The little town of Malmesbury is well-known to the antiquary for the remains of its once glorious abbey, its interesting market-cross, and, if I recollect rightly, a cozy hostel, formed out of the ruins of an old conventual building, besides other reliques of great interest. Its inhabitants are a primitive race who derive great satisfaction from a charter, and still better, from a large piece of rich land bequeathed to them by King Athelstan. Now, whether the king with his bequest gave the assurance that, by digging deep, those into whose hands the said land might fall would realize great treasure, or whether some person in digging a well suddenly came upon a black coaly-looking substance in the stratum of clay, does not appear; but we incline to the latter opinion. However this may be, certain it is, that about a century ago, operations for coal-mining were commenced on Malmesbury Common; the timber of the estate

was felled to pay the expenses of a shaft that was sunk and, as report said, coal found. Indeed this latter assertion had been verified over and over again, as young natural philosophers (and they were very young in it) had from time to time collected lumps of carbonaceous matter, black as coal, and which on being brought to the unerring test of experiment – the trial by fire – burnt like coal; in short, were the true 'black diamond'.

Still with this evidence the mining had been abandoned after the sinking of a shaft – and of some money. The latter article, by the way, was supposed to have been raised again by the wary ones whom rumour asserted to have been bought over not to prosecute the work any farther by the coal-masters of another district, in order to prevent the competition which this new mine from its contemplated riches must inevitably produce. Now as this opinion still prevailed, it was not long since deemed advisable to re-investigate the matter, but this time it was determined that such investigation should be intrusted to a geologist, and as such I was requested to undertake the inquiry.

Having therefore gone to this most interesting district to prosecute my mission, I was soon in communication with some intelligent gentlemen who represented the estate, when the evidence connected with the opening of the shaft was laid before me. About two pounds weight of the previously-mentioned black substance brought from the shaft, was submitted for inspection. This black matter of course proved to be lignite or carbonized wood, thin deposits of which will be found in most thick clay deposits, and very frequent in this which is the Oxford clay. Such appearances, however, have frequently led to fruitless mining experiments, the usual argument for which is, 'here is a good burning coal got a few feet from the surface; it is true it is but a thin seam, but how much thicker will it become the deeper we descend.

On going to the site of the old shaft, I soon found that it had been commenced in the Oxford clay formation, and from examining the exposed debris of the shaft, I became convinced that the opening of nearly one hundred yards in depth as stated by my guide, had not pierced through the Oxford clay bed.

Here, then, the question of obtaining coal on this spot was at once set at rest, inasmuch as we should have many thick formations to penetrate before arriving at the usual position of coal-bearing beds. [Since] the aggregate thickness... would not fall far short of 3,000 yards,... it became evident that it would be rash in the extreme to recommend any operations in search of coal, as even if it were proved to exist... it would be far beyond a mining depth, and besides we are quite without evidence of its quantity or value.

'He that diggeth a pit, shall fall into it,' we are told in the Bible. Many of the pits which people dig for themselves are less spectacular than that which disappointed the 'primitive race' of Malmesbury (I must say, by the way, that I have always found them most hospitable and sophisticated); nor are they so traumatic as the pit which carried off Thomas Coward.

ϩ

A Cracked Existence, or ... Swindon is flat

But the most heroic champions of lost causes are those who, having been proved to be misguided, persist in their beliefs. One such who never flinched from defending his philosophy was John Hampden. The *Swindon Advertiser* takes up the story:

What first brought Mr Hampden to Swindon was never generally known. What was known was this. He came with the remnants of issues of a number of pamphlets he had published crammed into boxes and other receptacles, and also with his pockets and hands full of copy of other pamphlets he wanted to publish. Shortly previous to Mr Hampden's advent, Swindon had been visited by another pamphleteer and lecturer; one who had sought to tell the public something new by disputing the old theory of the world's rotundity through the medium of a lecture, followed by the sale of a book in which the whole proofs were to be seen at a glance. Like many another venturesome adventurer, this gentleman met with such ill success at Swindon that he could not pay for his printing in cash, and he therefore paid for it in kind. The printer took out his bill in his customer's books. When John Hampden appeared the printer sought to turn one of the books into cash by inducing him to become a purchaser. John Hampden bought the book, and the circumstance became the turning point in what at best had been but a cracked existence. He became positively cranky over the credulity of mankind in believing that the earth was round and not flat. He at once abandoned all his old studies and theories. Old pamphlets and new copy all went into the fire or elsewhere, and from that moment onward John Hampden went forth, like another Don Quixote refreshed, with the Swindon printer doing duty as his Sancho Panza, to maintain the great truth of the age – the earth is flat and not round. Hitherto John Hampden had lived an ideal life in the realms of theory. He was a student, we have been told, of prophecy, and the purpose of most of his voluminous pamphlets and fly sheets had been to prove from the Jewish prophet Daniel that the termination of the times of the Gentiles would come shortly, when the second advent of Christ takes place, and the Jews with the lost ten tribes are restored to their pre-eminence as a nation at Jerusalem. He looked for startling events between 1891 and 1894.

In fact, a truly startling event (for him) did occur towards the end of January 1891. He died.

Here is his obituary, from the *Wilts and Gloucestershire Standard:*

The death is announced of a well-known former resident in Swindon, and at one time a frequent contributor to our columns, Mr.John Hampden. The death of Mr.Hampden, says the Standard, of Wednesday last, the sturdy upholder of the theory that our earth is flat, if it has no other effect on the world at large, will at least be a distinct loss to the Postal revenue. For his correspondence, if rather one-sided, was unwearied. No astronomer of any eminence but has, at some period of his career, been favoured with a more or less abusive missive, and though these 'demonstrations of their ignorance' were never answered, the fact in no way cooled Mr.Hampden's ardour. For, if silence did not give consent, passive resistance to his arguments regarding the flatness of the earth, and unfulfilled prophecies, were accepted as proofs that his 'facts' were unanswerable. Some savants, indeed, were singled out for peculiar distinction. They had pamphlets, and even little volumes, penned to their dishonour. 'Ignorance', 'credulity', 'deliberate attempts to deceive a trusting world' — such were the mildest of the charges which were brought against the teachers of the accepted system of cosmogony. Now and then, indeed, when the turpitude of believing in the rotundity of the earth became more than usually intolerable, Mr.Hampden issued a special journal to denounce the knavishness of the latest 'Newtonian impostor'. His life was devoted to such kicking against the pricks, and the saddest feature in this worthy man's delusion was that he firmly believed in the truth of his paradox, which is, perhaps, more than could be said of some who pandered to his harmless craze.

In private life Mr.Hampden is understood to have been a reasonable person, and as a man of business, endowed with decided acuteness. But once touch, in even the remotest manner, on the 'so-called' oblate-spheroidicity of the earth, and you were doomed to a verbal avalanche. Yet it is erroneous to suppose that Mr.Hampden was the inventor of that exploded hypothesis. Though his writings were most numerous, and his map, with the North Pole in the centre of a plain, and the South Pole running all around it, was best known, it was another paradoxist, writing and lecturing under the name of 'Parallax', who first led Mr.Hampden into the error, which cost him so much time and money, and, one might think, worry, were it not certain that controversy in which the talk was all on one side was the salt of his life. 'Parallax' was a surgeon in North London, and though he died a few years ago without abjuring his absurdities, it is always doubtful how far Mr. Samuel Rowbotham quite swallowed his oft-exploded arguments.

But just as the inquiring intellect of Sir Richard Phillips, bereft of sufficient knowledge to keep its speculation within reasonable bounds, was a victim to the paradox in his day, so Mr. Hampden, who then lived at Swindon, found something attractive in the specious talk of the latest earth-flattener. But what was worse still, he accepted in an unquestioning spirit the experimental basis of 'Parallax's' theory, that on a part of the Bedford Canal where there is an uninterrupted water line of about six miles, the fullest tests had proved that there were no signs of curvature. Unfortunately for Mr. Hampden, he wagered five hundred pounds on his opinion as to the correctness of this statement, which, if true, would have gone some little way to substantiate a view negatived, however, by a score of far more conclusive facts. And the result was that, though he remained as unbelieving as ever, he lost his five hundred pounds, and got himself into endless trouble.

An eminent naturalist, in fact, accepted his challenge, and 'staked' the money with the conductor of a sporting journal. Perhaps it would have been wiser to have refused to degrade a scientific question to the level of a vulgar bet; since no one whose opinion was worth considering was at all likely to espouse Mr. Hampden's heresy. However, three boats were moored in a line, three miles or so apart. Each carried a mast of a given length, the conditions of the experiment being that if, when the tops of the first and last masts were seen in a line through a telescope, the summit of the middle mast was not found to be above the level, the earth-flattener was to be adjudged the money. The result may be anticipated. Mr. Hampden returned from 'the Level' a poorer, but not a wiser man. On the contrary, his wrath knew no bounds; but, instead of expending his indignation on the paradoxer who had led him astray, he devoted it to those who 'still believed' in the earth's rotundity. The subsequent history of the affair was, indeed, extremely unpleasant, for it landed the loser in the Law Courts, and estranged from him much of the sympathy which might otherwise have been bestowed on the ignorant victim of so unequal a contest. Mr. Hampden became plaitiff in an action to recover his five hundred pounds from the hands of the stakeholder, on the technical ground that the transaction was in the nature of a 'gaming or wagering contract', and, as such, null and void by the Statute 8 and 9 Vict. c.109 s.18. Upon this ground the late Lord Chief Justice Cockburn, and the late Justices Mellor and Quain, decided in favour of Mr.Hampden. Still, Mr.Hampden did not abate his ardour or spare his printer's ink; he went further, and added to his leading foible very pronounced views of the proper interpretation of the Book of Daniel. His mind was, in truth, so constituted that no facts could convince him of his error.

To such a damning indictment of a man's life-work there can be little to add, except to reveal that the 'eminent naturalist' was Alfred Russel Wallace (1823-1913), a most distinguished scientist and humanist, who many people credit with anticipating Darwin's theory of natural selection. The outcome of the 1870 experiment was in fact less clear-cut than Wallace had imagined, because Hampden insisted on using a theodolite rather than a telescope, and then interpreted the result differently. Successive bouts of litigation left Wallace a great deal poorer than the £500 he had wagered, and perhaps led him to modify his view on the stage within the evolutionary process occupied by Mr.Hampden.

But to us, passive observers a century and more later, it all seems to have been a storm in a teacup, just like James Bodman's dispute with his librarian, or the wife-swapping in Swindon market-place, or Lady O'Looney's epitaph, or the rhubarb in Waterworks Road, or... – None of it really matters, except to those of us who like to indulge in small talk.

Sources

NOTE: Frequently cited sources are abbreviated as follows: *WAM* = *Wiltshire Archaeological and Natural History Magazine*; W.Cuttings = Wiltshire Cuttings, in Wiltshire Archaeological and Natural History Society Library, Devizes; *WNQ* = *Wiltshire Notes & Queries*; WRO = Wiltshire Record Office. Books are cited in full on their first occurrence only; thereafter the author's surname and the date of publication only are cited.

INTO PRINT. Prefaces and other Mishaps: Duke, E., 1837, *Prolusiones historicae, or essays illustrative of the Halle of John Halle...*; *WAM*, 28, p.265; W.Cuttings, 3, p.9. A Librarian's Treachery: Bodman, J., 1814, *A concise history of Trowbridge...* (see also *WA&NHS Bi-Annual Bulletin*, 17, pp.11-12). All a Matter of Confidence: Bodman, 1814; Daniell, W., 1850, *Warminster Common...*; Morris, W., 1885, *Swindon fifty years ago...*; *WAM*, 28, pp.5-12. A Cynic: Davis, J., 1754, *Origines Divisianae, or the antiquities of the Devizes....* A Two-Edged Sword: Duke, 1837; Slow, E., 1899, *Humourous west countrie tales*. Envoi: Duke, 1837.

SUPERSTITIONS. A Donkey to the Rescue: Morris, 1885, pp.502-3; The Medicine Chest: *WAM*, 14, pp.325-6. Who needs a Doctor?: *WNQ*, 1, pp.167, 315, 317; *WNQ*, 2, p.242. Garden Warfare: *WNQ*, 4, pp.280-1. Rooted to the Spot: W.Cuttings, 3, p.6. Wilkinson's Questionnaire: WAS Library, Devizes. Oram's Grave: *WNQ*, 3, pp.275-6.

CLERGY. Broughton Gifford: WRO 501/1-2 (typed transcript by W.A. Webb in WAS Library, Devizes); *WAM*, 5, pp.267-341; WAM, 6, pp.11-72. A Temperate Vicar...: WRO 1505/32; WRO 1505/90; *Marlborough Times*, 6.9.1879, p.8. ...And an Intemperate Curate: Hunt, H., 1820, *Memoirs of Henry Hunt...*, vol.1, pp.189-92.

LIFE'S RICH TAPESTRY. Great Native Stamen: W.Cuttings, 3, p.36; *WNQ*, 3, pp.377-8; *WAM*, 17, 306-26; W.Cuttings, 3, p.18. Death's Rich Tapestry: Ravenshaw, T.F., 1878, *Antiente epitaphes* (see also *Notes and Queries*, 6th series, 2, pp.284-5; and W.Cuttings, 3, p.94); Bouverie, B.P., 1890, *A few facts concerning the parish of Pewsey...*, p.32; *WAM*, 28, pp.169-70. More Ham, less Calf: W.Cuttings, 3, p.103. Dabchicks, Gudgeons and Dogs: Gandy, I, 1975, *The heart of a village*, pp.16-17; Richardson, E., 1934, *Wiltshire folk*, pp.48-9, 102; *WNQ*, 2, pp.83-4; *WNQ*, 1, 129-30.

CRIME... The Darker Side of Cherhill: Blackford, J.H., 1941, *The manor and village of Cherhill*, pp.242-4; *WAM*, 24, pp.262-3. Mine Host: W.Cuttings, 3, p.3 (from *Wiltshire Gazette*, 13.1.1842). To Bournemouth for Tea: *WNQ*, 5, p.324. More Problems on the Road: W.Cuttings, 3, pp.24, 14; *WNQ*, 4, p.278. Rising Again: Richardson, E., 1919, *The story of Purton...*, pp.50-2. A Poet who lost his Head: *WAM*, 29, pp.3-10.

...AND PUNISHMENT. A Gruesome Business: Britton, J., 1850, *The autobiography of John*

Britton, vol.1, pp.36-7. <u>More Hanging About</u>: WNQ, 3, pp.333-4. <u>Incident at Watkins'</u> <u>Corner</u>: Richardson, 1934, pp.55-7. A Final Twist: Large, F., 1931, *A Swindon retrospect*, pp.55-6. <u>Fiendish Devices</u>: WAM, 1, pp.68-91. <u>Coming round for more</u>: *WAM*, 7, pp.1-44; WNQ, 1, pp.220-1. <u>A Barbarous Villain</u>: *WNQ*, 2, p.224. <u>Salisbury Water Torture</u>: W.Cuttings, 3, p.23. <u>A Courtroom Drama</u>: Jefferies, R., 1873, *Reporting, editing and authorship...*; various local newspapers, March-July, 1881.

NEWSPRINT. <u>Unexpected Arrivals</u>: Jefferies, 1873; *Swindon Advertiser*, 17.5.1869, p.2 (see also Silto, J., 1981, *A Swindon history, 1840-1901*, p.67, where it is misquoted); Buchanan, C.D., 1958, *Mixed blessing: the motor in Britain*, p.126; W.Cuttings, 1, p.29. <u>Fillers</u>: *Wiltshire Times*, 27.8.1881, p.8; *Trowbridge Chronicle*, 7.6.1879; W.Cuttings, 1, p.27. <u>A Whiff of the Orient</u>: *Trowbridge Chronicle*, 17.5.1879, p.6. <u>The Rustic Polymath</u>: WNQ, 1, pp.469-70. <u>The Man in the Moon</u>: *Trowbridge Chronicle*, various issues in 1883. <u>More Trivia</u>: *Wiltshire Times*, various issues, summer 1881.

FAIRS. <u>Selling a Wife</u>: Jefferies, 1873; Morris, 1885, pp.500-2. <u>Salisbury Fair</u>: W.Cuttings, 1, p.277. <u>Curiouser and Curiouser</u>: W.Cuttings, 3, pp.13, 12. <u>Up to no Good</u>: Price, F, 1774, *A description of that admirable structure the cathedral church of Salisbury...*, p.26.

DIALECT. 'Leabourin Volk': Chandler, J., 1982, *Figgetty pooden: the dialect verse of Edward Slow*; Slow, E., c.1903, *Humourous west countrie tales...*, p.37 (not to be confused with Slow, 1899, which has a similar title). <u>Edward Slow's Novel</u>: Slow, E., 1913, *Jan Ridley's new wife...*, pp.131-3. <u>A Parish on Wheels</u>: Swinstead, J.H., 1897, *A parish on wheels*, pp.212-16.

LOST CAUSES. <u>The Art of Flying</u>: *WAM*, 1. pp 351-2. <u>The Wiltshire Coalfields</u>: Hunnisett, R.F., 1981, *Wiltshire coroners' bills 1752-1796*, p.61 (Wiltshire Record Society, vol.36); *WAM*, 2, pp.159-61. <u>A Cracked Existence, or... Swindon is Flat</u>: *Swindon Advertiser*, 31.1.1891; *Wilts and Gloucestershire Standard*, 31.1.1891 (see also R. Schadewald, in *Smithsonian*, 4.1978).

Index

NOTE: This is a selective index of persons, places and subjects, and omits many minor references

BRADFORD VOICES
A Study of Bradford on Avon in the Twentieth Century by Margaret Dobson
This book is a remarkable achievement and a fitting tribute to a century of life in Bradford on Avon.
256 pages; Illustrated; ISBN 0 948578 89 0; Price £9.95

BRADFORD on AVON'S SCHOOLS
The story of education in a small Wiltshire town by Keith Berry
The author is a former headteacher of John of Gaunt School in Trowbridge and resident of Bradford on Avon. His acclaimed book on his former school was published in 1994 with a new edition appearing in 1996. Here he turns his attention to the development of education in Bradford on Avon, and in so doing offers the reader a fascinating insight into a hitherto neglected aspect of the town's history.
240 pages; Illustrated; ISBN 0 948578 96 3; Price £8.95

BRADFORD ON AVON: PAST AND PRESENT by Harold Fassnidge
This updated edition remains the standard history of the town.
192 pages; Illustrated; ISBN 0 948578 62 9; Price £7.95

WHERE WILTSHIRE MEETS SOMERSET
20 Best Walks in the Country around Bath, Bradford on Avon, Trowbridge, Westbury, Warminster and Frome by Roger Jones
A completely revised and redesigned edition of a book which has been going strong since 1982.
128 pages; Illustrated; ISBN 0 948578 94 7; Price £5.95

THE LIMPLEY STOKE VALLEY by Margaret Wilson
In our West Country Landscapes series, this is the only book currently in print on the Limpley Stoke Valley.
160 pages; Illustrated; ISBN 0 948578; Price £7.95

TOURING GUIDE TO WILTSHIRE VILLAGES by Margaret Wilson
144 pages; Illustrated; ISBN 0 948578 29 7; Price £5.50

Books by Richard Jefferies:
ROUND ABOUT A GREAT ESTATE
120 pages; Illustrated; ISBN 0 948578 10 6; Price £5.50

THE OLD HOUSE AT COATE
176 pages; Illustrated; ISBN 0 948578; Price £2.95

EX LIBRIS PRESS has over 60 titles in print on the West Country, Country Life and the Channel Islands. Available through your local bookshop or direct from the publisher on receipt of net price.
EX LIBRIS PRESS, 1 The Shambles, Bradford on Avon, Wiltshire, BA15 1JS
Tel/Fax 01225 863595   Email Roger@ex-libris.jpcinet.co.uk

WILTSHIRE BUS LINE is the public transport enquiry line operated by Wiltshire County Council's Passenger Transport Unit, offering comprehensive information about bus, rail, and coach services throughout Wiltshire and Swindon at local call rates. Phone 0345 090 899. The Unit produces a free county transport map and guide each year, together with timetable leaflets for most services. It also operates the Wiltshire Day Rover ticket, allowing one day's unlimited travel on most bus services throughout the county. Details are available from Libraries, Tourist Information Centres, and the Unit (County Hall, Trowbridge BA14 8JD).

WILTSHIRE LIFE, in which many of the pieces in this book first appeared, is the monthly county magazine, and was refounded by Mark Allen in 1995. It is published at Dinton, near Salisbury, and is available from newsagents throughout Wiltshire and Swindon, or by subscription. For details phone Wiltshire Life Subscriptions Department, Freephone 0800 137201.